SHE SOARS

SHE SOARS

TRAILBLAZING FEMALE PILOTS IN FLORIDA

BRIDGES DELPONTE

PINEAPPLE PRESS
Palm Beach, Florida

Pineapple Press
An imprint of Globe Pequot, the trade division of
The Rowman & Littlefield Publishing Group, Inc.
4501 Forbes Blvd., Ste. 200
Lanham, MD 20706
www.rowman.com

Distributed by NATIONAL BOOK NETWORK

British Library Cataloguing in Publication Information available

Library of Congress Cataloging-in-Publication Data
Names: DelPonte, Bridges, 1958- author.
Title: She soars : trailblazing female pilots in Florida / Bridges
  DelPonte.
Description: Palm Beach, Florida : Pineapple Press, 2024. | Includes
  bibliographical references and index.
Identifiers: LCCN 2024007347 (print) | LCCN 2024007348 (ebook) | ISBN
  9781683343707 (paperback ; alk. paper) | ISBN 9781683343714 (electronic)
Subjects: LCSH: Air pilots—United States—Biography. | Women air
  pilots—United States—Biography. | Aeronautics—Florida—History.
Classification: LCC TL549 .D45 2024 (print) | LCC TL549 (ebook) | DDC
  629.13092—dc23/eng/20240403
LC record available at https://lccn.loc.gov/2024007347
LC ebook record available at https://lccn.loc.gov/2024007348

To my remarkable nephew, Rob

—pilot, sailor, rock climber, scuba diver, outdoorsman, and global citizen—

with love and admiration for his adventurous spirit

CONTENTS

CONTENTS

INTRODUCTION

EVERY YEAR, FLORIDA ATTRACTS NEARLY ONE HUNDRED FORTY MILLION visitors to a state approaching a population of twenty-two million people. What makes Florida so special to visitors and residents alike? Beautiful beaches. Warm weather. Exciting theme parks. Great fishing. Diverse nature trails. Unique flora and fauna. But few people may mention or may even be aware of Florida's distinct place in aviation history.

With its mild winters and hard-packed beaches, Florida became an early proving ground for aviation pioneers, especially female pilots who went on to chalk up impressive nonstop flying, altitude, speed, aerobatic, military, and space records. The first female pilot to undertake a night flight, to complete a nonstop flight from New York to Miami, to break the sound barrier, to win the US National Aerobatics Championship, and to command the space shuttle are all part of Florida's aviation history.

From daredevil pilots barnstorming across the state during the early 1900s to ferrying seventy-seven different types of aircraft during World War II to commanding military, commercial airline, and NASA flights, Florida sustains its prominent role in female aviation history. Some female pilots, such as Dessie Smith Prescott, Jacqueline Cochran, and Betty Skelton Frankman, were Florida natives who made aviation history with flying exploits in the Sunshine State and elsewhere. In other instances, female pilots born outside Florida, such as Ruth Law, Patrice Clarke Washington, Linda Pauwels, and Eileen Collins, claimed their indelible place in aviation history flying high in the Florida skies. Even famed African American aviator Bessie Coleman shaped a major, albeit tragic, chapter in Florida aviation history. All of these groundbreaking women pilots displayed tremendous courage, skill, and determination in the face of daunting social, legal, and economic barriers that aimed to exclude them from the profession or to undermine their impressive flying abilities.

In this anthology, the selected stories of female pilots will be grouped by time period to help show the evolving role of women pilots from flying rickety fabric-and-wire airplanes to controlling technologically sophisticated aircraft. Each chapter explores a little known or long-forgotten Florida tale of a pioneering female pilot in an engaging, informative way. Some stories will delight and inspire as spirited women buck the traditional conventions of their day to chart their own courses, triumphing as pilots in the face of incredible odds. Other tales will speak of brave women whose flying days ended in terrible misfortune, reminding us about both the exhilaration and inherent dangers of taking flight.

Hopefully, by the end of this book, you will add "trailblazing female pilots" to your list of what makes Florida special.

Bridges DelPonte

SHE SOARS

"*The surest way to make me do a thing is to tell me I can't do it.*"

—Ruth Bancroft Law
(May 21, 1887–December 1, 1970)

CHAPTER 1

RUTH LAW

Loops de Loops and Dips of Death on Daytona Beach

AT FIRST GLANCE, SHE APPEARED TO BE AN ENTICING NOVELTY. "WOMAN to Give Flights at Clarendon" declared the front-page headline of the *Daytona Daily News* on January 7, 1913. The newspaper announced that Miss Ruth Bancroft Law, a woman pilot, had arrived with her Wright plane to offer her services. The newspaper gloated that Miss Law had granted it the exclusive privilege of selecting her first passenger for her inaugural flight of the winter season.

Might a petite, young woman piloting a flying machine on her own be a danger to herself and her passengers on these flights? Law seemed an oddity with her knit cap pulled down over her hair, her bulky woolen coat and jodhpurs, and those knee-high leather boots. Even the great Orville Wright had refused to train her, believing that women didn't possess the mechanical ability or mental stamina necessary to handle the stresses of flying his new invention. Besides, Law had recently witnessed the tragic accident of renowned aviator Harriet Quimby, the first American woman to earn a pilot's license and the first woman to cross the English Channel, who plunged to her death from her monoplane at a Harvard–Boston air meet in July 1912.

Yet despite his initial concerns, Orville sold a Wright Model B biplane to Law for seventy-five hundred dollars under an installment plan. The Lynn, Massachusetts, native then promptly returned to her home state, taking lessons for several weeks with the Burgess Company and Curtiss Flying School in Marblehead. Ruth talked pilot Phil Page into teaching her and learned critical maintenance skills from a mechanic at the school. She advanced at a brisk pace, shocking flight instructor Arch Freeman by reaching the altitude of seventy-eight hundred feet, higher than he ever experienced.

By August 1912, she undertook her first solo flight at Atwood Park in Saugus. She accumulated further flight time debuting her flying skills at exhibitions and brief hops with passengers in exchange for newspaper coupons or for a small fee on Staten Island. Reporters trailed her and wrote stories about this only female flier on the East Coast. On November 18, 1912, at age twenty-five, she passed her flying tests at Baldwin's Flying Field in Oakwood on Staten Island. Ruth became the sixth woman in the United States to earn her pilot's license from the Aero Club of America, a private social club that promoted aviation in its early years.

Two months later, she made her way to Florida with her husband and manager, Charles Oliver. Oliver had entered into a contract with the Hotel Clarendon for Law to fly hotel guests during the January to April 1913 winter season. Over the previous two winters, first city officials, then the Hotel Clarendon, contracted with male pilots for short flights, hoping to drum up business with northern visitors curious about these newfangled flying machines. Pilots W. Starling Burgess in the 1911 season and her former instructor, Phil Page, in the 1912 season became popular locally in this new sport and attracted tourists from across the country. With takeoffs and landings on Daytona Beach in front of the hotel, area residents and tourists gathered with amazement to watch these magical machines glide above the flat shoreline.

Ultimately, Col. C. M. Bingham won the opportunity to join Law as her first passenger to great local fanfare. On January 13, 1913, more than five thousand people gathered on Daytona Beach to watch her inaugural flight with the colonel, becoming the first female pilot to fly in Florida's skies. Col. Bingham told reporters that he "thoroughly enjoyed the sensation of being carried through the air far above the heads of the big crowd on the beach." That same day, Law made a second flight showing off her solo piloting skills in her Wright biplane. In less than six months, Ruth had gone from aviation aficionado to licensed pilot paid by contract to carry passengers—likely the first licensed woman pilot to do so in the country.

Although having just arrived, Law delighted in generating enthusiasm for her services. At that time, rich tourists with automobiles often challenged each other to races on the hard-packed sands of Daytona Beach—well before the creation of a formal speedway. The *Daytona Daily News* reported that A. E. Donnelly in a Mercer speedster threw down the gauntlet to Charles Lockwood and his National auto for a car race on the beach. Ruth immediately jumped into the fray, declaring that she would race the winner of that competition in her biplane on the beach. The paper never reported whether the beach auto race took place, but Law became known as a fierce competitor who did not back down from a challenge. She and her manager-husband continued to make bold pronouncements about her flying prowess over her three winter seasons at Daytona Beach from 1913 to 1915.

Just ten years after the Wrights flew at Kitty Hawk, airplanes remained quite primitive and dangerous. Despite the public's natural uneasiness about flying, Ruth rapidly became a major draw for seasonal tourists flocking to Daytona Beach hoping to catch a glimpse of her and her amazing flying machine. Her flights typically cost about fifteen dollars (more than four hundred fifty dollars in 2023), which meant most of her clients were wealthy vacationers escaping cold northern climes. The *Daytona Daily News'* gossipy society column, News of the Hotels, reported regularly on which elite guests from Hotel Clarendon, the Prince George, or other upscale lodgings bravely accepted the challenge of flying as a passenger with Law.

From millionaire entrepreneurs to military men to high-society ladies, the paper covered Law's flights, nipping pithy quotes from her clientele about the fun and safety of flying with her. W. H. Peters, a visiting lawyer and Wisconsin assemblyman, told reporters that he completely

Law offers rides in a Wright Model B biplane on Daytona Beach in 1914.
(*Courtesy of the State Archives of Florida, Florida Memory*)

enjoyed his trip in the air and felt "as safe in the machine with Miss Law as he would feel sitting in an office chair." Dietrick Lamade, the wealthy head of Grit Publishing Company, declared that soaring in the air with Miss Law felt like being "whisked to the top of the Woolworth Building in an express elevator and looking out upon the island of Manhattan."

Articles promoting her flights often highlighted her perfect safety record to placate concerns about the risks of flight and simmering doubts about a woman pilot's ability to fly. During her career, Law chafed against questions about her piloting skills based on her gender. Despite his brother Orville's uncertainties, Wilbur Wright later conceded that Law proved herself as "one of the safest as well as one of the nerviest air pilots, either male or female, that he had ever met."

Yet Law wasn't satisfied with short tourist hops. By December 1914, Ruth began offering flight instruction for pilots seeking full licensure for three hundred dollars (about nine thousand dollars in 2023). Her newspaper advertisements boasted that licensed pilots could earn twenty-five thousand dollars per season in exhibition flying—approximately seven hundred and fifty thousand dollars in 2023. She became the first female pilot to offer formal flying instruction at her Wright School of Aviation from a hangar next to the Nautilus Casino in Seabreeze (a community later merged into Daytona and Daytona Beach). She also began to consult with Glen Curtiss, the founder of Curtiss Aeroplane Company, to discuss plane designs for a nonstop flight from San Francisco to New York.

Law also started experimenting with more dangerous exhibition flights at Daytona Beach and other East Coast events at county fairs and flying exhibitions during the summer months. In 1913, she became the first American female pilot to fly at night, doing so for twenty minutes at Staten Island, repeating that spine-tingling moonlight flight at a summer 1914 air show in Newport, Rhode Island. That same year, the Daytona Beach community watched in astonishment as Law practiced the "Dip of Death" for a planned Christmas Day show. Few aviators had survived the "Dip of Death," in which a pilot reaches a high altitude and then speeds the plane toward the ground, pulling up at the last moment to land the plane safely. Bad weather prevented that effort. But on January 2, 1915, she undertook another rare evening flight with only the moonlight to guide her over Daytona Beach, thrilling a large crowd on the beach—the first female pilot to fly at night in Florida.

Law further augmented her income with promotional flights, dropping golf balls out of her plane to market local golf courses and providing flights for baseball players on the Brooklyn Superbas (later Brooklyn Dodgers), including famed player Casey Stengel. The team manager, William Robinson, even excused players during a game to allow them an opportunity to fly with Law. Ruth invited Charles H. Ebbets, the president of the Superbas, to join her on a flight and drop the first baseball from her plane for the 1915 opening-day game of spring training. For that publicity stunt, Law reportedly planned to drop a baseball from her plane into Robinson's waiting glove since he was considered an ace at catching high flies.

In a disputed bit of baseball lore, some reports indicated that Law never received a baseball for the stunt, so she launched a red ruby grapefruit. Others claimed that Robinson missed two baseball tosses and Law threw out a grapefruit from her lunch as a final attempt. Others assert that prankster Casey Stengel intentionally arranged to substitute a grapefruit for a baseball with Law or the team's trainer, a passenger on the flight. Allegedly, the grapefruit exploded on impact, knocking over Robinson and soaking his uniform in red juice. Players claimed he screamed out about being wounded upon seeing red stains on his uniform or blinded due to the spray of citrus juice into his eyes. Others contend that this mishap served as the origin of the name "The Grapefruit League" for baseball teams participating in spring training in Florida. Regardless of the truth of these competing stories, Law flew into baseball legend with this tale.

Despite these silly stunts, Law continued to hone her piloting skills and push the limits of her airplane while at Daytona Beach and

Law pilots her Curtiss "Model D" Pusher plane in 1915. (*Photo by Lt. H. M. Benner, US Air Force*)

Seabreeze. In 1915, she sold her Wright plane and purchased a Curtiss Model D Pusher with its custom Wright-style controls to enhance her exhibition flying. In December 1915, she spontaneously executed her first "loop de loop" at Daytona Beach. To her husband's horror, she then immediately repeated that difficult maneuver a second time before landing. Law became only the second American woman to perform this aerobatic trick after her friendly Arkansas rival Katherine Stinson did so earlier that same year. After her first loop de loop at Daytona Beach, Law began setting records for continuous loop de loops, breaking her own record of sixteen in a row by completing seventeen loop de loops in a row at a subsequent New Orleans air show.

With her Curtiss pusher, she wowed Daytona Beach audiences at a January 1916 exhibition and continued to be an in-demand performer at air shows across the country. She also pursued altitude records for female pilots, reaching eleven thousand two hundred feet, and twice came in second to male pilots in altitude and bomb-dropping contests. As her stunts became riskier, including performing the infamous "Dip of Death," Law's husband became more worried about her safety. She claimed that he lost a pound of weight each time she flew.

A strong competitive streak and love of danger seemed to course through her veins and her family tree. Despite growing up in a conservative New England family, Ruth and her brother, Rodman, spent their childhood egging each other on to numerous hazardous pranks, much to their parents' chagrin. As an adult, Rodman became a fearless stuntman, first making a name for himself climbing tall structures with his bare hands, earning him the moniker "The Human Fly." He gained further notoriety with other madcap exploits, such as scaling and parachuting off the Statue of Liberty and the Brooklyn Bridge. His Lady Liberty jump became the first time he ever used a parachute. His assistant broke down into a fit of tears as he stepped over the railing and plummeted 345 feet, pulling open his small chute and landing safely—perhaps making him the first base jumper in history. He narrowly survived his Brooklyn Bridge jump when his chute barely released in time to avoid a deadly fall into the East River.

The public could not get enough of his fearless escapades and he quickly became a media favorite, featured in newspapers and newsreels. Hollywood soon sought him out for stunt work in the burgeoning movie industry. At one of Ruth's exhibition shows, Ryno Films captured Rodman jumping out of her plane in a parachute and promptly injuring his neck. His overall success with risk-taking feats secured him the Hollywood nickname "The Unkillable Actor."

Their father, Frederick Law, worried about his children's daredevil ways. He initially expressed doubts about Rodman risking his life for Hollywood. Yet he voiced pride in Ruth's mission, demonstrating that "a woman can do things and I believe she has benefited aviation by shaming some of the men who lacked the nerve to help develop the airplane." Over time, Mr. Law even recognized that his son's fearlessness proved that one could parachute safely from an airplane.

Yearning for new challenges, Law began to plan a cross-country solo trip. She lobbied aviation expert Glen Curtiss for a customized plane with a larger fuel tank for her planned flight. But echoing Orville Wright's previous concerns, Curtiss doubted that she could handle a heavyweight plane. Undeterred, Ruth made several modifications to her older Curtiss pusher and slept in a tent on the roof of the Hotel Morrison in Chicago to prepare for the flight's frigid air temperatures. With her own funds, she plotted out her nonstop flight.

On November 19, 1916, Law's greatest aerial triumph came when she smashed the American nonstop flight record from Chicago to Hornell, New York, flying 590 miles nonstop in five hours, forty-five minutes, beating Victor Calstrom's nonstop record of 452 miles nonstop. She also set the female pilot's world record for continuous flight. Her feat of skill and nerve in freezing November winds and temperatures in her outdated Curtiss pusher only added to the acclaim for her achievement.

She eventually sputtered into New York City with her gas tank almost empty. Law became the toast of American aviation and an instant celebrity. Peppering her with questions, a reporter asked, "You have made the longest flight a woman ever made, haven't you?" Ruth retorted, "I have made the longest flight an American ever made." A reminder that she had bested both US male and female pilot records for her nonstop flight.

Newspapers across the nation declared her the "Queen of the Air." Numerous awards and tributes were heaped upon her, including being the guest of honor at a reception with President and Mrs. Woodrow Wilson in attendance. Schoolchildren flooded her with letters, many both shocked and pleased that a woman had beaten a man's record. One little girl wrote, "[y]ou have made me feel that I may be proud to be a girl." Suffragettes rallied around her groundbreaking flight as proof of women's equality in their fight for the right to vote.

Promoters from face creams and perfumes to raincoats and petticoats courted Law in hopes of benefiting from the endorsement of this newly minted superstar. Yet Ruth showed no interest in becoming a product pitch woman. She asserted that "[n]ine-tenths of the people who make these offers do not want any real service I could give them. They are merely after the use of my name. I don't want any such business. I don't mind taking money for flying or aiding flying, but that is the only business in which I intend to engage."

Law remained laser-focused on her next aviation accomplishment, either a solo cross-country trip from San Francisco to New York or a solo transatlantic flight—more than a decade before Charles Lindbergh's record-breaking flight. The media keenly followed her efforts to strategize and seek out a plane that could handle these groundbreaking trips. Articles reported on her review of different aircraft and her efforts to collaborate with Curtiss on a specially tailored plane. Yet busy with building planes for the war effort, Curtiss never developed the custom plane for her. She also inspected military aircraft and other designs in France, even offering her piloting services to the French government to help battle the Kaiser in World War I.

When the United States entered the war in 1917, Law wrote bellicose editorials and advocated for women aviators to be permitted to join the fight. She lobbied Congress and President Wilson in the

White House, wearing an Army officer's uniform by special permission of the War Department, the first woman to receive such a privilege. At home and abroad, her efforts to serve as a military pilot were soundly rejected. In the end, Ruth wore her Army uniform on civilian flights across the country to promote Liberty Bonds and to encourage enlistment. As World War I raged on, Law's opportunity to undertake a solo cross-country or transatlantic flight slipped away.

Greatly disappointed, Law returned to exhibition flying, earning as much as nine thousand dollars per week (more than two hundred and thirty thousand dollars in 2023 dollars). She also continued to break altitude records for female pilots, setting a record of fourteen thousand seven hundred feet in 1917. She later formed her own flying troupe, Ruth Law's Flying Circus, chasing cars on racetracks, wing-walking as a pilot performed loop de loops, and performing car-to-plane transfers on rope ladders. Her troupe made stops across the country, continuing to capture news coverage with aerial stunts. Ruth also toured Japan, China, and the Philippines, drawing massive crowds and providing the first airmail delivery to the Philippine Islands.

After ten years of a nearly perfect safety record, Madeline Davis, a young wing-walker from Fort Pierce, Florida, died when she slipped from a ladder while rehearsing a transfer from a speeding car, driven by Law, to a plane flying above. After this incident, her anxiety-ridden husband, worried that Ruth's luck might run out, put an end to her career by publishing news of her retirement from flying without consulting her. To keep the peace at home and in the face of calls for more regulation of air shows to prevent such accidents, she acceded and quit flying.

After a decade of a quiet life of gardening in California, Ruth suffered a nervous breakdown. She believed the loss of the intense thrill of flying led to her illness. Despite her challenges, she would later attend a 1948 ceremony on the donation of the Wrights' Kitty Hawk plane to the Smithsonian Institution, showing support for their achievement despite Orville's initial doubts about her flying abilities. In her lifetime, she flew a Wright biplane and watched astronauts landing on the moon, dying at the age of eighty-three in San Francisco in 1970.

After her initial three seasons, Ruth never again flew above the sands of Daytona Beach, where she honed her early flying skills and astounded crowds with her acrobatic flying. The *Daytona Beach Daily News* published a fitting farewell to her, writing that "[t]he people of this vicinity have missed the gentle purring of Ruth Law's engines among the clouds. The winter hardly seems complete without her."

"I will never forget the first time I ever went up. I was afraid to come down!"

—DESSIE SMITH PRESCOTT
(AUGUST 4, 1906–APRIL 19, 2002)

CHAPTER 2

DESSIE SMITH PRESCOTT
A Florida-Born Pioneer in the Sky and the Great Outdoors

ISLAND GROVE, ALACHUA COUNTY, 1906. POPULATION SEVENTY-FIVE or one hundred, depending upon whom you ask. Dessie Smith faced many hardships early on in life. At only two and a half years old, Dessie's father died after being beaten with a fence post, mistaken for a sheriff. Her mother moved her family into a log cabin with Dessie's grandmother, who struggled to support them on her husband's veteran's pension from the Spanish-American War. Too poor to care for her, Dessie's mother sent her to live with her uncle and aunt in Sparr, a nearby rural community, where locals survived by hunting, fishing, picking oranges, and living off the sandy scrublands of central Florida.

In one of her earliest memories, four-year-old Dessie retrieved quails her uncle shot for dinner from palmetto thickets. As a child, she spent many hours wandering the woods and wading through the riverways of central Florida. Her strict aunt wanted her to wear dresses and shoes, but Dessie preferred overalls and bare feet. She stubbornly walked barefoot for more than two miles to a one-room schoolhouse. Not much for studying, she often got into fistfights with older boys at recess and reached only the eighth grade at county schools. Her mother died in the 1918 flu epidemic, leaving Dessie orphaned at age twelve. With such hard-scrabble beginnings, it may have been hard to predict that this little girl would make history in Florida, not once, but twice, and eventually land in the Florida Women's Hall of Fame.

From her teens into her early twenties, Smith bounced around different careers and locations, first waitressing and bussing tables in Baltimore, where her older brother and his family lived. At age sixteen, she met and married the first of six husbands, divorcing him a year later. Dessie contended that "Kissin' wears out. Fishin' don't." Saving up her money, she visited Florida for a month in the winter to hunt, fish, and explore the outdoors. With a .22 rifle slung over her shoulder and a Bowie knife tucked into her belt, she killed and skinned her prey or fileted bass and other fish she caught for dinner.

After her first divorce, she moved on to Atlantic City to wait tables again and then became a beautician. But Smith dreamed of returning to Florida, squirreling away money to buy acreage bordering her uncle's land and starting to build a log cabin at age nineteen. She later scouted prospective buyers for real estate brokers in Orlando during the Florida land boom in 1926. Dessie married again, but it didn't last. As the boom turned to bust, Smith luckily withdrew five thousand dollars in savings just before a local bank collapsed. She bought a Chevrolet and slapped a sticker on it that read, "Don't laugh, big boy. This is paid for," driving to Philadelphia where her oldest brother moved for work. Dessie sold cars, an unusual job for a woman at that time.

Planes buzzing out of nearby Rydell Field in Camden, New Jersey, sparked her first interest in flight. Smith spent part of her remaining savings to take pilot lessons, the only woman in a class with twelve male students. Dessie learned fast and soon soloed in a Curtiss JN-4 biplane, called a "Jenny." After the end of World War I, retired Jennys became publicly available for purchase, and many barnstorming troupes bought them for their air exhibitions. No fan of frilly dresses, Dessie liked wearing pants and boots to climb in and out of those planes, which had no doors and routinely splashed castor oil fuel on pilots.

Known for being a fearless outdoorswoman, Dessie admitted that "it took a lot of nerve" to fly. On her first solo, she grew anxious about landing the plane and was forced to do so when it nearly ran out of fuel. At that time, the Aeronautics Branch of the Department of Commerce, an early predecessor of the Federal Aviation Administration, commenced issuing pilot's licenses in an effort to standardize and professionalize the

After World War I, barnstormers, like Smith, flew retired "Jennys" in air shows. (*Photo by Air Service, US Army*)

industry under the Air Commerce Act of 1926. Dessie claimed to be the third woman in the country to receive a pilot's license from the federal government, declaring that Amelia Earhart was "not even heard of" yet. With her government-issued license, Dessie became the first female pilot from the state of Florida.

In the late 1920s, Dessie barnstormed in the Northeast and then returned to her Florida roots to fly. Dessie recalled receiving letters admonishing her for taking up flying. Some upbraided her as blasphemous for daring to fly like God and the angels or warned that she must be in league with the devil to fly a plane. Undeterred, she shared two planes with various groups of pilots who traveled to fairs in small towns with plenty of open fields or flat beaches where planes could take off and land. Dessie remembered one troupe she joined was named "Wild Hogs." Dessie tried out some stunt work, but she mostly flew customers excited about the opportunity to swoop in the air. In her band, one pilot would sell tickets to the passengers, originally charging two dollars per passenger to generate buzz, and then hiking up prices to five dollars per person. Another pilot would crank the airplane motor while a third piloted the plane in an open-air cockpit with the passenger seated in the rear.

Dessie piloted some customers at Daytona Beach but mostly accommodated patrons from Davis Island near Tampa. The island stood largely undeveloped, except for a makeshift maintenance shed and hangar. A sandy strip served as a runway for flights, later developing into the Peter O. Knight Airport. With the cost of fuel, flights lasted no more than fifteen minutes, often traveling over Tampa Bay to Gadsden Point before crossing above Tampa, and up along the Hillsborough River. With little regulation of flights, pilots took passengers up to altitudes above three thousand feet. Many people were petrified during their first, and sometimes last, flight.

As the Depression loomed, Smith enjoyed flying, but it did not fully pay the bills. She continued to scrape up money from other work and leased out a small apartment building in Tampa's Hyde Park neighborhood. Over time, her concerns about flying intensified as the planes became more battered and proper maintenance depended largely on the limited technical knowledge and sobriety of local mechanics. After about eighteen months, Dessie stopped flying due to safety issues. She sought out steady work in Tampa's Tax Department as the Depression gripped the country.

During the Depression, she regularly visited her log cabin and married a local doctor who enjoyed her preferred activities of hunting in the backwoods and fishing riverways from a small motorboat. They often spent time at her cabin in Sparr on weekends. At one point, Smith was bitten by a bobcat and a friend urged her to seek medical treatment in case of rabies. With her tongue-in-cheek humor, she replied, "Not yet. There are a few people I need to bite first."

Dessie and her husband later became acquainted with a New York couple, Charles and Marjorie Kinnan Rawlings. In 1928, these writers sought a refuge from big-city life in rural Cross Creek, not far from Dessie's Island Grove hometown. They hoped to explore the rich tapestry of life in a rural community, but the inexperienced couple struggled to maintain a rundown grove. Friends of the Rawlings asked Smith to help them make their way in this unfamiliar territory.

Dessie's frank talk and backwoods acumen impressed Marjorie, who became quick friends with her. Smith showed Marjorie how to shoot, fish, and trap animals as well as develop the grove into a more productive farm. Although ten years younger than Marjorie, Dessie referred to her as "young un" due to Rawlings's inexperience in the ways of backwoods living.

Prone to depression and unhappy in her marriage, Rawlings looked forward to outings with Dessie to overcome her difficulties, including evening fox hunts on horseback. The women talked about their lives, and Smith liked to share backcountry traditions with Marjorie over a bottle of moonshine. Throughout the years, the women would also enjoy hunting and fishing adventures in the Everglades, Alaska, and Cuba.

Rawlings's first book, *Under the South Moon*, a novel about life in Florida's backcountry, became a successful debut novel for her in 1933, creating further tension in her strained marriage. In March of that year, Dessie convinced Rawlings that she needed time on the river to settle her nerves and decide how to move forward in her life. Lacking accurate charts, Dessie helmed a motorboat along a treacherous route on the St. John's River. Camping under the stars, hunting and fishing for food, and observing the rhythms of nature for ten days served as a healthy tonic for Rawlings. She wrote about Dessie and their experiences on the river in a 1933 article, "Hyacinth Drift," for *Scribner's Magazine*, and then later revised the story for inclusion in her noted memoir on the Florida backwoods, *Cross Creek*, published in 1942. Her time in Cross Creek proved pivotal in the evolution of her writings about rural Florida, including her Pulitzer Prize–winning novel, *The Yearling*, in 1938. Without Smith's help, Rawlings's experiment in the backwoods grove could have been a failure both financially and creatively for her.

In 1942, Smith enlisted in the Women's Army Auxiliary Corps, later termed Women's Army Corps (WACs), training first in Daytona and then heading off to officer training school in Iowa. She became a first lieutenant and hoped to become a member of a women's antiaircraft battalion with her crack shooting skills. Similar to Ruth Law before her, military officials abandoned that idea over concerns about women being in combat positions. In later years, Marjorie wrote about a Cross Creek visit from Dessie during World War II with "a tough bunch of pistol-packing Mamas" serving in the WACs.

Dessie's past piloting experience played a useful role in her assignment to the Central Flying Training Command in Texas. She recruited and gave military intelligence tests to both men and women for the Army's Air Corps.. At bombardier training bases, male cadets were trained to fly in formation in remote parts of Texas and Oklahoma. As a pilot, Smith recognized that this "desert" duty was necessary to avoid injuries to local communities when planes on training flights bumped each other and hurtled to the ground. Being a Floridian, she remembered concerns raised about the dangers of B-26 bomber training at MacDill Army Air Force Base in Tampa. Risky training flights alarmed local residents and the sardonic phrase "one a day in Tampa Bay" referred to constant bomber crashes into the harbor. In these more desolate bases, she organized vocational skills courses in carpentry, electricity, and plumbing to keep the men busy, instead of standing idle and drinking beer in their time off.

After serving for three years, Dessie was discharged from the Army at the end of the war. In 1945, she bought land in Inglis, Florida, on the Withlacoochee River and built small cottages, and then a lodge on the property. With her knowledge of Florida's backcountry, Smith offered fishing and hunting excursions on the river. After years of informal guiding, Dessie became the first female licensed fishing and hunting guide in Florida. She led trips to hunt quail, antelope, deer, turkey, and wild hogs, claiming to have thirty-six dogs for various kind of prey. She ran a lodge for fifteen years and entertained a wide range of guests, including baseball great Babe Ruth.

On her return from military duty, Dessie's relationship with Marjorie suffered its ups and downs, in part, due to Marjorie's bouts with depression and heavy drinking, according to Smith. They last met for dinner in Gainesville in 1951, and Dessie noticed that her friend appeared to be in ill health, having lost weight. After Rawlings's death in 1953 at age fifty-seven in St. Augustine, Smith continued to speak fondly of their times together. Having played a major role in Rawlings's personal and literary life, Dessie became an esteemed member of the Marjorie Kinnan Rawlings Society in Florida. She loved to chat up journalists and researchers in interviews, offered lively talks for historical and literary groups, and participated in the making of a documentary film about her memorable St. John's River trip with Rawlings. In 1986, Rawlings was inducted into the Florida Women's Hall of Fame for her literary contributions. Little did Dessie suspect at that time that she would be joining her friend on that honor roll.

Dessie Smith Prescott was inducted into the Florida Women's Hall of Fame in 1999. (*Courtesy of the Florida Commission on the Status of Women*)

Dessie married her sixth and final husband, William "Howard" Prescott Jr., in 1960. She remarked, "[i]f you consider all of my husbands, my full name would be Dessie Smith Shuhart Campbell Vinson Burgess James Prescott. I'm not bragging, only stating a fact." Yet Prescott would be the only husband Smith did not divorce. Like many of her other husbands, Howard shared her love of the outdoors as they resided in both Florida and his home state of Ohio. They traveled extensively in Canada and Africa for fishing and hunting trips and also operated a hunting lodge in the Adirondacks.

In 1977, they bought and ran the Wahoo Ranch on Lake Rousseau in Crystal River, Florida. The Citrus County ranch offered many opportunities to fish and hunt. It would be Dessie's last home. At age ninety-three, Dessie attended her 1999 induction into the Florida Woman's Hall of Fame for her flying, hunting, and fishing achievements. The state further memorialized her love of Florida's natural world by dedicating the Dessie Smith Prescott Memorial Inglis Dam Recreation Area on Lake Rousseau to her.

Throughout her life, Dessie charted her own path as an authentic pioneer of a bygone era in Florida. Smith lived at Wahoo Ranch until her death at age ninety-five. Her dedicated caregiver of eighteen years, Candace Booth, said that "Dessie always wondered what was around the next bend in the river. On April 19, 2002, she took her final trip and now she knows."

"You've never lived until you have flown. The air is the only place free from prejudice."

—Elizabeth "Bessie" Coleman
(January 26, 1892–April 30, 1926)

CHAPTER 3

ELIZABETH "BESSIE" COLEMAN
Brave Bessie's Inspiring Career Ends Tragically in Florida

THOSE LAST FEW MONTHS IN ORLANDO WERE SOME OF THE HAPPIEST times in her life. Bessie enjoyed a close personal relationship with Reverend H. K. Hill, pastor of the Mount Zion Missionary Baptist Institutional Church, and his wife, Viola Tillinghast Hill, a noted social justice activist.

The couple invited Bessie to stay with them at their airy parsonage on a quiet leafy street in Orlando's Callahan neighborhood while she gave talks and performed at air shows in central Florida. During this peaceful period with the Hills, Bessie reconnected with her religious faith and proclaimed herself to be a born-again Christian. Weary from touring, Coleman looked forward to retiring soon from stunt flying and fulfilling her dream of starting a flight school for African American pilots. At age thirty-four, Coleman had journeyed a long way from her challenging childhood in rural Texas.

The tenth of thirteen children, Elizabeth "Bessie" Coleman was born in a dirt-floor cabin without electricity or running water in Atlanta, Texas. Her father, George, a day laborer of African American and Cherokee or Choctaw heritage, tried to persuade Bessie's mother, Susan, an African American, to leave Texas and move to Native American lands in Oklahoma. He hoped to avoid Texas's oppressive Jim

Crow segregation laws and protect his family from ever-present threats of lynchings and other racial violence. But Susan wanted to stay put in their cramped home that George built in Waxahachie, Texas. As a single parent, Susan struggled financially as a housekeeper and cook for a local White family while Bessie shouldered most of the household chores after her parents split up. Her younger sisters did not remember Bessie having much time to play.

Despite family hardships, Susan wanted her children to be educated, renting books from a traveling book dealer. In a one-room schoolhouse four miles from their home, Bessie showed a superior talent at math, completing all eight grades. She grew active in the Baptist Church, where her mother expected weekly attendance at Sunday services. Coleman chafed at being dragooned into working the annual cotton harvest. Yet she used her math skills to stand watch at the cotton weigh scales to make certain that pickers were paid properly for their loads.

Bessie didn't want to follow in her mother's footsteps as a maid or cook. She "wanted to find a bigger life . . . to amount to something." When she turned age eighteen, her chances of living a bigger life seemed possible when she enrolled in college at the Langston Colored Agricultural and Normal School in Oklahoma (now Langston University). Yet her hopes of obtaining a degree were dashed after one semester when she lacked the resources for tuition. Coleman returned to Waxahachie to a life she wanted to escape through education.

In 1915, she accepted her older brother Walter's invitation to join his family in Chicago, where he worked as a Pullman Porter and her brother John, a World War I veteran, also resided. At age twenty-three, Bessie became part of the First Great Migration of African Americans from southern to northern states. After completing beauty school, Bessie became known as the best and fastest manicurist at local barbershops. At the White Sox Barbershop, she sat in a window so passersby could admire the pretty, petite manicurist with her effervescent smile tending to elite members of the Black community. Bessie enjoyed wandering through the streets of the vibrant neighborhood, called "The Stroll," housing prominent Black-owned businesses, restaurants, theaters, bars, and nightclubs open to all races.

Coleman soon became acquainted with the city's major movers and shakers, including Robert Abbott, the successful publisher of the *Chicago Defender*, a leading newspaper serving largely the fast-growing Black community, and Jessie Binga, a real estate mogul and founder of the Binga State Bank, one of the few Black-owned financial institutions in Chicago. One day at the shop, her brother John regaled customers with tales of his World War I service in France. He teased Bessie that French women were so much more advanced than any woman in Chicago, even piloting planes, something his sister would never be able to do. "That's it. You just called it for me. I'm gonna be a pilot," replied Bessie. They all laughed at her, but Coleman was serious and determined to live that bigger life. For four years, she continued to save money as a manicurist and chili parlor manager to pursue pilot training.

Bessie applied to flight schools in the United States and was rejected as both a woman and an African American. "I refuse to take 'no' for an answer," she famously said, adding that "every 'no' takes me closer to a 'yes.'" France became her best option for pilot training. With Abbott's encouragement and sponsorship, she took French lessons at night for a year to complete her applications.

In 1920, the well-regarded Caudron Brothers Aviation School accepted her and she left Chicago for Le Crotoy, France, with financial help from Abbott and Binga. Flying a French Nieuport Type 82, she excelled in their program, completing her instruction in seven months for a typically ten-month training. At the school, she witnessed a fellow student die in a training accident. Bessie stated, "[i]t was a terrible shock to my nerves, but I never lost them; I kept going."

On June 15, 1921, Coleman became the first African American and the first Native American of any gender to earn an international pilot's license from the Fédération Aéronautique Internationale, the only organization in the world to offer a global license at that time. She was the only woman of any nationality to earn that license during that six-month cohort of sixty-two candidates. Bessie stayed in Paris for two more months to receive further flight instruction.

Upon her return to the United States in September 1921, both Black and White reporters in New York mobbed Coleman, trumpeting her groundbreaking achievement, including the *New York Times*. A special guest of honor at the popular all-Black Broadway musical *Shuffle Along*, Bessie received a ceremonial silver cup from famed actress and singer, Ethel Waters, and a standing ovation from a diverse audience. Despite the media attention and accolades, she quickly realized that to make a living as a pilot required her to become a barnstormer performing death-defying aerial stunts.

In February 1922, she went back to Europe, where she took additional training in France, the Netherlands, and Germany. Bessie reached out to famed Dutch airplane designer, Anthony H. G. Fokker, who invited her to visit his aircraft plant and to try out some of his planes. Coleman became acquainted with other European aviators and went to Germany for ten weeks of additional flight instruction. She secured a Pathé News newsreel of her buzzing the Kaiser's palace, which she later showed at her aviation talks at local churches, theaters, and schools.

Upon her return, Bessie began to fashion her public image, wearing tailored Canadian-style military uniforms with a captain's hat, shiny leather boots, and a white silk shirt. She shaved six years off her age, claiming to be twenty-four rather than thirty. She spoke boldly about ordering Fokker planes for her aviation school and produced letters from European flying aces that attested to her successful fifty flights in a German Benz plane with two 220-horsepower engines and her skill in handling a heavy Dornier seaplane. Like Ruth Law before her, not all of her bold claims panned out, but they generated great publicity. Coleman made savvy use of a press hungry for exciting news about her aviation adventures. In interviews and lectures, she enthusiastically promoted aviation careers and the creation of a flying school for African American pilots. Coleman said, "[i]f I can create the minimum of my plans and desires, there shall be no regrets."

Her mentor Abbott's newspaper, the *Chicago Defender*, arranged her first air show in New York, proclaiming Coleman "the world's greatest woman flyer" and the newspaper, "the world's greatest weekly." On September 3, 1922, Coleman became the first Black woman to fly a plane in the country as a band struck up the national anthem at Glenn Curtiss Field in Long Island. Although no stunt flying was permitted at that

Coleman often showed newsreels of her flying exploits at her aviation talks. (*From the New York Public Library Digital Collections*)

airfield, Bessie's flight proved that a Black woman could fly a plane solo without incident.

In October, she followed up her New York debut with stunt flying exhibitions at the Negro Tri-State Fair in Memphis and the Checkerboard Aerodrome in Chicago. Bessie's mother, sisters, nieces, and a nephew, Arthur, who inspired by his aunt, later became a pilot, were in attendance at the Chicago show along with nearly two thousand spectators. Coleman thrilled the crowds with figure eights and daring death dips, giving rides to courageous passengers after her dazzling performance. Using borrowed planes, other successful air shows followed with Black-owned businesses or organizations as Bessie's enthusiastic sponsors. Coleman often honored segregated Black military units in her programs. Nicknamed "Brave Bessie" or "Queen Bessie," she rapidly became a popular stunt pilot entertainer.

Yet she faced rocky business relationships as she clashed with different agents and sponsors over her performances. Shortly after her Chicago success, Coleman walked off a film set, *Shadow and Sunshine*, that she felt portrayed Blacks in a negative way. The producers of the African

In her pilot's outfit, Coleman poses at a Chicago studio in 1925. (*From the New York Public Library Digital Collections*)

American Seminole Film Producing Company labeled Bessie as difficult and eccentric, hurting her reputation in the entertainment industry and causing friction with her old mentor, Abbott. Others criticized her for doing only stunt work and for not trying to break long-distance air records. The attacks on Coleman highlighted a mix of racial animosity and sexism prevalent during her career.

Fiercely independent, Bessie looked to buy a plane to chart her own course forward. She headed to California in search of a stunt plane and fresh opportunities. With many surplus World War I airplanes on the market, Bessie could afford only an outdated Curtiss Jenny, costing about three hundred dollars, in January 1923. She also became an endorser for Coastal Tire and Rubber Company in Oakland and planned to drop leaflets about the company from her plane—a popular marketing stunt at the time. A month later, she readied for an air show to celebrate the opening of Palomar Park in Los Angeles with ten thousand patrons in attendance.

Taking off from Santa Monica, Bessie suffered a terrible accident when her plane's engine stalled and crashed from three hundred feet above. She lost consciousness, breaking her leg and several ribs. From her hospital bed, Coleman declared in a telegram, "[A]s soon as I can walk, I'm going to fly!" She remained hospitalized for nearly three months, a stark reminder of the high risks of early aviation. In fact, five pilots died in similar crashes in Los Angeles the few weeks before Coleman's accident. Bessie was lucky to be alive.

Convalescing back in Chicago, she spent time in her South Side apartment socializing with friends and family. Despite rekindling her family ties, she itched to fly again. On September 9, 1923, she returned to barnstorming at an Ohio air show flying a Curtiss JN-4 biplane with an OX-5 engine. She found another manager who booked air shows for her at the Checkerboard Aerodrome. Without a plane or sponsors, Bessie recognized that her aviation career was losing steam. She headed back home to Texas to kickstart her livelihood with a series of aviation lectures and air shows. Her Chicago manager quit over fears about risks to her personal safety and threats of racial violence against a groundbreaking African American female pilot in the South. Yet Bessie knew that she risked her life every time she went up in a plane.

Undaunted, Coleman established Houston as her base for her southern barnstorming tour. She scheduled her first air shows in Houston to coincide with Juneteenth, a celebration of the last freed slaves in Texas after the Civil War, now a federal holiday. She astonished crowds numbering nearly fifteen thousand with nose dives, loop de loops, barrel rolls, and figure eights. Her thrilling Houston debut led to a string of wildly successful shows in San Antonio, Galveston, Wharton, and her Waxahachie hometown, a moment of community pride and personal triumph. She even collaborated with other aerialists to undertake risky parachute jumps and wing-walking, substituting herself in those dangerous roles, when needed. That summer, she also starred in air shows in other small Texas communities. Despite harsh segregation laws, Coleman refused to participate in Texas air shows unless Blacks and Whites were admitted through the same front entrance. Bessie's Texas summer tour became a sensation without any canceled performances and earned rave reviews.

To replace her destroyed plane, Bessie contracted to purchase a second Jenny biplane in installments from a Texas company. She continued to augment her stunt flying income with speaking engagements, showing newsreels of her flying exploits. Coleman encouraged community members to become pilots and diligently promoted her plans to create the first flight school for African Americans. In January 1926, she began a southern speaking tour, offering lectures in Savannah and Augusta, Georgia, with subsequent talks in Tampa, St. Petersburg, and Orlando. She also performed at charity air shows in Orlando and Palm Beach. Coleman saved her money but still needed sponsorship to help pay off and ship her plane from Love Field in Dallas.

The Negro Welfare League invited Bessie to be the star of an air exhibition for its annual Field Day festivities on May 1 in Jacksonville, Florida. Crowds in excess of ten thousand were expected to watch her stunt flying and parachute jump from two thousand feet. At that time, Jacksonville, a bustling silent-film capital, housed about thirty independent studios in operation, including Norman Studios. Richard Norman, a White producer of silent films for Black audiences, offered positive depictions of African Americans in contrast to movies filled with negative racial stereotypes, common in that era. Bessie's continuing popularity in the United States and Europe inspired Norman to write "The Sky Demon," an aviation adventure episode for a planned movie serial.

D. Ireland Thomas, the *Chicago Defender* critic and theater manager in Tampa and Charleston, South Carolina, reached out to Norman about making a biographical movie about Coleman, *Yesterday, Today and Tomorrow*. Thomas noted that "she desires to have a production made of her self . . . with a story built around her and her plane . . . I think it would be a winner." Norman wrote back two weeks later about featuring Bessie in a film. He envisioned a five- or six-reel movie with Bessie in the leading role as a popular draw for Black audiences. Bessie also personally corresponded with Norman about her successes in Chicago and other cities and her position as one of the biggest Black celebrities alive aside from popular jazz singers. She wanted to team with Norman and thought a film about her life and flying feats would "go big" in movie theaters. Perhaps this second shot at movie stardom would bring her plane and flight school within her reach?

Anxiously awaiting the completion of her plane purchase, Bessie remained in Orlando with the Hills, whom she called "Mother" and "Daddy." After one of her church talks, she invited parishioners to take rides on a borrowed plane at a local Orlando airfield; an exciting first for most of her passengers. For more steady income, Mrs. Hill suggested that Bessie operate a local beauty shop to finalize installments on her plane and to help establish a flight school.

While living in Orlando, the chamber of commerce invited Coleman to participate in an air exhibition, parachuting from a plane for an annual flower show. She balked when the sponsors advised her that only Whites would be invited to her Orlando performance. Coleman protested and the chamber changed its course, agreeing to allow all to attend, and she parachuted to the crowd's delight. Orlando hosted other air shows and began to convert a nearby racetrack into an airfield.

Edwin Beeman, a wealthy Orlando heir of the Beeman Chewing Gum Company, was captivated by aviation. He met Bessie and became enthralled with her tales of her flying exploits. He paid the final installment on her plane, stored at Love Field, and the costs to deliver it to Jacksonville's Paxon Field. Before leaving for Jacksonville, Bessie confided to the Hills that she planned to settle down in Orlando, stepping away from stunt flying and opening her flight school. She confirmed those wishes in a letter they received after her death.

On April 27, she boarded a train for Jacksonville, and John Thomas Betsch, a young publicity chairman for the Negro Welfare League and aviation enthusiast, met her at the train station. In deeply segregated Jacksonville, Betsch managed to garner publicity for Bessie's show in a White-owned newspaper as well as Black community publications and set up several talks for her in the city.

That same day, William D. Wills, a twenty-four-year-old White mechanic and pilot with Curtiss Southwestern Airplane and Motor Company, began the more than twenty-hour flight from Dallas to Jacksonville. Coleman's surplus Jenny suffered engine trouble during the long flight, requiring Wills to make two unplanned stops in Mississippi. When Wills arrived on April 28, local pilots expressed surprise that he made it to Paxon Field considering the poor condition of the plane's aging engine.

The next morning, Bessie went out to breakfast with friends and ran into her old mentor, Abbott, at a Jacksonville restaurant. They embraced and she introduced him as "the man who gave me my chance." When Abbott learned about Wills piloting the plane during her planned parachute jump, he warned Bessie that he had a bad feeling about Wills and advised her to find a more experienced pilot for the show. Coleman waved off his concerns.

Later that day, Coleman spoke to local schoolchildren at Stanton High School, Darnell Cookman Middle/High School, and Davis Street Elementary School, the three segregated Black public schools in Jacksonville. She impressed them with her sharp-looking pilot's uniform and her inspiring stories about Blacks becoming pilots. That evening, she spoke to a packed crowd at the famous Strand Theater (now the campus of the LaVilla School of the Arts).

Early on Friday morning, Betsch drove Coleman and Wills to Paxon Field to scout locations for Coleman's parachute jump. As Wills prepared the plane, Bessie knelt on the ground and whispered in prayer. Betsch watched as Wills took off and circled the field, climbing from 2,000 to 3,500 feet. Not wearing her parachute, Bessie unbuckled her safety belt in the open-air cockpit in order to look over the sides of the plane to scout good landing spots. With Wills at the controls, the Jenny suddenly accelerated from 80 to 110 mph, stalling then falling into a tailspin and flipping upside down. Bessie tumbled out of the plane and died instantly upon impact with the ground.

Wills never regained control of the plane, clipping the top of a pine tree and crashing in farmlands about a thousand feet away from Coleman's body. Betsch and the police rushed to the plane's crash site but were unable to lift the plane off Wills. Distressed at the double tragedy, Betsch nervously lit up a cigarette, accidentally causing gas fumes to explode and consuming the plane in a raging fire. Ultimately, experts determined that a loose wrench, jamming the plane's controls, caused the horrendous accident. That incident would not have happened in newer planes, which provided protective shields.

In shock, Jacksonville's Black community grieved the terrible loss as Bessie lay in state at the Lawton L. Pratt Funeral Home. Mourners filed past her closed casket, starting at sunset until well after midnight. On Sunday afternoon, nearly two thousand mourners filled the Bethel Baptist Institutional Church while another three thousand honored her on the street, outside of the packed memorial service. Three ministers praised the fallen pilot and a soloist sang Bessie's favorite hymn, "I've Done My Work." A second service was held that evening at St. Phillip Episcopal Church before her casket was taken by train to Orlando.

On Monday morning, the distraught Hills met the train and took Bessie's casket to their flower-filled church. Reverend Hill eulogized Coleman, remembering her kindness and faith. Black ministers from throughout the Orlando community spoke, honoring Bessie's achievements, while a church choir led mourners in singing hymns. After the service, Mrs. Hill escorted Bessie's casket to an Orlando train bound for Chicago. News accounts stated that more than five hundred African Americans hummed "My Country 'Tis of Thee" as her casket was lifted onto the train.

By Wednesday morning, several thousand mourners waited at the Chicago train station, where the African American Eighth Infantry Regiment of the Illinois National Guard escorted her casket to the

South Side's Kersey, Morrell, and McGowan Funeral Home. About ten thousand mourners paid their last respects to Bessie on Wednesday and Thursday at the funeral home.

On Friday morning, uniformed pallbearers of the Eight Regiment carried Coleman's flag-draped casket to the Pilgrim Baptist Church. Bessie's grieving mother, brother John, and three younger sisters sat in the front pew while 1,500 mourners attended the church service with more than 3,500 people standing outside. Ida Wells Barnett, a prominent social justice advocate, led off the service in which Viola Hill delivered a passionate eulogy about Bessie's accomplishments and refusal to perform where African Americans were barred from attendance. Pastor Junius C. Austin spoke about Bessie being "one hundred years ahead of the Race she loved so well" and chastised community members who failed to support her efforts to break barriers. Bessie was buried in Chicago's Lincoln Cemetery, Illinois, and Florida friends sponsored a memorial gravestone a year later, featuring a photo medallion of Bessie in full pilot's uniform standing beside a plane.

While the African American community mourned the loss of the aviation pioneer, many White-owned newspapers made scant mention of her death. Even the *New York Times* only corrected its failure to report on her death in its Overlooked column in 2019, providing a worthy obituary nearly ninety-three years after her death. Although her achievements did not receive full acknowledgment during her lifetime, Bessie's legacy grew and continues to strengthen through the many people of different races and genders that she inspired to fly, especially in African American and Native American communities.

In 1929, William J. Powell, a successful Black owner of service stations, became a pilot and founded the Bessie Coleman Aero Club, to promote aviation in the African American community and to keep Bessie's legacy alive. In the 1930s, Black pilots with the Challenger Pilots' Association in the Chicago area started annual flyovers and dropped flowers over Bessie's gravesite. In the 1980s, other Black pilot organizations revived this memorial flyover. Bessie's groundbreaking efforts inspired Black pilots who later joined the famed Tuskegee Airmen in the 1940s. In 1977, African American female student pilots created the Bessie Coleman Aviators Club. In 1992, Dr. Mae Jemison, the first African American woman in space, carried a photo of Bessie Coleman with her on the space shuttle *Endeavor*.

Over time, Bessie and her achievements have become more broadly recognized and honored through numerous museum exhibits, books, news articles, documentaries, plaques, memorial flyovers, school buildings, governmental resolutions, and street names in the United States and abroad, including a section of Orlando's West Washington Street where she lived with the Hills, renamed Bessie Coleman Street in 2014. The US Postal Service honored Coleman with a stamp in its Black Heritage series in April 1995 while the US Mint featured her on a special quarter in its American Women Quarters Series in 2023. In August 2022, an all-female Black flight and ground crew for American Airlines honored the one-hundredth anniversary of Bessie Coleman becoming a pilot, the first time in the airline's then ninety-six-year history.

Halls of fame in aviation have also come to recognize Coleman's groundbreaking achievements. Bessie was inducted into the Texas Aviation Hall of Fame in 2000, National Women's Hall of Fame in 2001, National Aviation Hall of Fame in 2006, and International Air and Space Hall of Fame in 2014. Although she never had the opportunity to start her flight school, the Aviation Youth Empowerment Foundation offers Bessie Coleman Aerospace Legacy Scholarships to a diverse group of socially and economically disadvantaged students pursuing STEM college degrees.

Based on her pioneering flying accomplishments and continuing legacy, Bessie Coleman lived a bigger life that amounted to something, something truly inspiring in aviation history.

"After that flight, there was no living without flying. I haven't come down to Earth yet."

—Ruth Rowland Nichols
(February 23, 1901–September 25, 1960)

CHAPTER 4

RUTH ROWLAND NICHOLS
Co-Piloting the First Nonstop Flight from New York to Miami

AN UNUSUAL PRESENT IN HONOR OF RUTH'S GRADUATION FROM AN exclusive finishing school started it all. Her father, Erickson Nichols, owner of a successful New York investment firm, gifted her with a ten-dollar flight over Atlantic City. Eddie Stinson, a World War I flying ace, sat at the controls of a Jenny biplane on a summer day in 1919. Terrified of heights, Ruth summoned up her courage, hoping to please her adventuresome father, whose favorite motto was "Try anything once."

Jittery as the plane took off, Ruth soon found herself laughing with giddy delight, no longer frightened of soaring high above the beach. "What had I been afraid of?" she wrote. "A minute ago, I had been an earthbound caterpillar. Now, I was an airborne butterfly . . . free as the air itself. I wasn't afraid of *anything* any more." That taste of freedom in the air soon became a lifelong obsession for Ruth Rowland Nichols.

Much to the chagrin of her conservative mother, Edith Corlies Nichols, Ruth chafed at the suffocating social strictures of her wealthy upbringing in her family's stylish Manhattan brownstone or at their country home in Rye, New York. Her parents, members of Manhattan's social elite, objected to Ruth's desire to attend Wellesley College as a premed student. They preferred their eldest daughter attend parties and debutante balls, filling up her dance card with the names of eligible men. Her maternal aunt, Angel, a more liberal Quaker, supported Ruth's ambitions. "If thee wants to go to college, thee go," she said in traditional Quaker speech.

Enrolling in 1919, Nichols reveled in her newfound freedom at Wellesley, taking classes and excelling at a wide range of sports. Yet in her sophomore year, her parents pressured her to take a leave from Wellesley. She placated them by spending a year earning a certificate in domestic science for cooking, millinery, and dressmaking from the Commonwealth School in New York. Her mother also demanded that Ruth make her society debut during the 1922 winter social season in Miami where her family wintered. Edith carefully organized dances, theater trips, and Junior League activities in hopes of finding a wealthy husband for her daughter.

Instead, Nichols became enamored with pontoon planes taking off and landing in calm waters off Miami's coast, often safer than landing at primitive airfields. She wangled an introduction from her brother to Capt. Harry Wright Rogers, a famed World War I US Navy pilot and popular stunt barnstormer, who ran a flight school in Miami. Rogers took Ruth on a seaplane ride and even allowed her to briefly operate the controls, another pivotal life moment. Nichols said that once taking hold of the plane's yoke, she "was sold forever . . . feeling the power of my own hands managing this fierce and wonderful machine." While her parents hoped for marriage proposals, Nichols secretly took flying lessons from Rogers at $60 per hour (equivalent to nearly $1,000 per hour in 2023).

Known for his bad temper and gruff manner, Rogers did not treat his privileged customer with kid gloves. He constantly cursed and called her names, and sometimes he gave her a "clout to the head" when she failed to meet his exacting standards. His demanding approach reflected his overarching concerns about pilot safety, especially since aviation tragedies occurred often in those rudimentary planes.

In 1923, Ruth made her first solo flight in a seaplane in Miami, the first American woman to do so. After returning to Wellesley, Nichols continued to train with Rogers, who bounced between homes in Queens and Miami. In 1924, she obtained her college degree as well as earning her international pilot's license, a first for a woman in New York State. Subsequently, Nichols became the first American woman to earn a seaplane pilot's license and the second American woman to earn a transport license, which permitted her to fly any licensed type of aircraft.

During a yearlong world cruise and tour, she flew extensively in Europe, including a flight from Paris to Vienna. When she got back in 1926, her family steered Ruth toward a career in banking, instead of flying, in hopes of her meeting a future husband in finance. Nichols continued to fly borrowed planes from time to time, making trips in short hops from Los Angeles to Salt Lake City and from Miami to Rye. In her mundane banking job, she felt stifled and suffered bouts of depression, finding it difficult to reconcile "an adventurer's heart and a Quaker spirit."

A surprise telephone call on New Year's Eve 1927 from her former instructor, Rogers, changed her life. He established Rogers Air Line to develop regular passenger air service between New York and Miami. To gin up business, Rogers knew that the rarity of a female pilot would draw much-needed publicity to his fledgling business. He proposed that she co-pilot a nonstop flight from New York to Miami with Maj. M. K. Lee. Rogers framed his participation on the flight as a customer on a business trip to promote airplanes as a fast, practical form of transportation. Ruth jumped at the opportunity to fly the route but hid the upcoming trip from her parents.

Before departing, Ruth telephoned her father to let him know she planned to stay in town rather than return to Rye that evening. The next morning, on January 4, 1928, Ruth took off from Naval Air Station Rockaway in Rogers's Fairchild FC-2 pontoon monoplane. The trio brought sandwiches, tea, and coffee with a makeshift bed in the rear fuselage for napping. Ruth piloted the plane for five hours and then two shorter segments while Lee slept. Nichols logged about 450 miles of the 1,200-mile flight. Despite the bitter cold in New York, the flight remained largely uneventful, only experiencing turbulence near the Georgia–Florida line.

Twelve hours later, Lee touched down in darkness on Biscayne Bay, guided by bonfires lit near Rogers's air terminal. With no advance publicity for the flight, reporters eagerly waited in the Royal Palm Hotel for a press conference to learn about the first nonstop flight from New York to Miami. While reporters pestered Ruth with personal questions about her love life, she steered their attention back to flying. When asked about the daunting trip, Nichols replied that she was not the "least bit tired" from the flight. She told reporters, "Choose any other method of transportation when I could fly? I should say not. It is the only real way to go an appreciable distance." Her declarations were prophetic about the future of aviation. Throughout her life, she diligently promoted air travel as not only a sport but also an important business venture and safe mode of travel.

Newspaper wires lit up across the country about the historic flight with a woman co-pilot. The press nicknamed her "The Flying Debutante," which annoyed Nichols, who wanted to be known for her flying skills, not her blue blood roots. Ruth's father only learned of her aviation feat from a front-page story in the *New York Times*. Accolades, letters, and telegrams flooded in, with Ruth prizing her Aunty Angel's telegram, which simply read, "More power to thee, child."

Capitalizing on her nonstop flight's publicity, Fairchild Airplane and Engine Company briefly hired Nichols as their northeast sales manager. Ruth then became one of the founders of Aviation Country Clubs, Inc., a corporation promoting a network of private aviation clubs for elites to make short hops across different states. The first three clubs were developed on Long Island and Westchester in New York and in New Jersey. From 1928 to 1930, Nichols flew a Curtiss Fledgling biplane twelve thousand miles in a forty-six-state tour to market the air clubs. She also became one of the founders and first female editor of the aviation club's magazine, *Sportsman Pilot*. Upon completing her tour, Nichols became the first woman to pilot and land an airplane in all of the lower forty-eight states.

During this time, women pilots found themselves blocked from participating in lucrative air races with men. In 1929, twenty women, including Nichols, aviation pioneer Louise Thaden, and Amelia Earhart, participated in the Women's Air Derby, the first all-female transcontinental air race from Santa Monica, California, to Cleveland, Ohio. Dubbed the "Powder Puff Derby," Nichols flew a Rearwin biplane with a Ken-Royce motor, but she did not complete the race after two unplanned landings and a runway accident. Thaden took first place and Earhart finished third.

Nichols poses with a Curtiss Fledgling plane in her cross-country promotional tour for private aviation clubs. (*Photo by National Photo Company, Library of Congress, LC-DIG-npcc-17217*)

In the wake of the air derby, Nichols helped co-found The Ninety-Nines, the first women's aviation organization named for the number of its charter members, which still actively supports female pilots today. The group elected Earhart as its first president and Thaden as its secretary, and Nichols became lifelong friends with her fellow aviation stars. Earhart, who lived not far from Nichols's Rye family estate, nicknamed Ruth, "Rufus." The affable rivals stayed at one another's homes and raced planes together.

In 1930, Nichols served as a test pilot for new types of planes, including a new Chamberlain cabin monoplane being evaluated by the US Navy. Ruth also set her sights on achieving more aviation records. Yet she needed a fast, powerful plane to push the limits of existing marks. Despite her wealthy family ties, she lacked the funds to buy, fuel, and maintain a heavy plane. Undeterred, Nichols made speeches to groups about the promise of aviation and relentlessly sought out financial backers. With the Depression on the horizon, few businesses wanted to invest in costly aviation ventures.

Eventually, Ruth made a personal pitch to Ohio manufacturing and broadcasting magnate Powel Crosley Jr., who wanted to marry promoting his businesses with his interest in aviation. In fall 1930, Crosley loaned Ruth his prized red Lockheed Vega, *The New Cincinnati*, a high-wing monoplane with fixed landing gear, modern instrumentation, and a formidable single engine. In her initial flight from Ohio to New York, a dense fog bank in western Pennsylvania forced her to crash-land his plane, badly damaging the propeller. Nichols wondered if Crosley would clip her wings after the accident. But the sensational publicity over her crash splashed the Crosley name across the country, much to his delight.

Despite the poor start, Ruth soon scored major aviation records in Crosley's plane. In December 1930, she set a new women's transcontinental flight record of 16 hours, 15½ minutes from New York to Burbank, nearly 9 hours shorter than the previous record. A week later on her return flight eastward, Nichols bested Charles Lindbergh's transcontinental record, finishing the flight in 13 hours, 21 minutes, setting a new women's speed record.

Nichols demonstrated a new Chamberlain cabin monoplane for US Navy officials in 1930. (*Photo by Harris and Ewing, Library of Congress, LC-DIG-hec-35819*)

In March 1931, Nichols bundled up in heavy mittens, long underwear, and sweaters under a hooded leather flight suit and fur-lined boots, setting a women's world altitude record of 28,743 feet. With temperatures about fifty degrees below zero, gale-force winds blew her from New York to Long Island as she soared nearly six miles up. Lacking a pressurized cabin, she breathed air through a tubed-mask attached to an oxygen tank under her seat. "I almost froze my tongue during my flight," she told a radio show host. The next month, she broke the women's air speed record, flying at 210.704 mph in Detroit, 30 mph faster than Earhart's previous speed record. Her records were scrawled on the plane's nose next to the Crosley brand.

With this streak of record-breaking flights, Nichols quietly planned her biggest challenge yet—flying solo across the Atlantic in spring 1931. She wanted to show that women were just as capable as men in aviation. Despite her achievements, she found it challenging to raise enough money to prepare and retrofit Crosley's plane with a 650-horsepower engine for a cruising speed of 200 mph. She even took out a personal loan of $4,500 to help finance the trip. If a successful flight, she anticipated reaping about $215,000 in endorsement, book, movie, magazine, and lecture deals to pay off her investors. The plane was repainted white with golden wings and rechristened *Akita*—meaning to search or explore in the indigenous Dakota language. Yet some fellow Ninety-Niners worried about the dangers of the trip and tried to talk her out of it.

After months of mechanical problems and weather delays, Ruth's mother handed a bouquet of flowers to Nichols before she climbed into the cockpit on June 22, 1931. In light of her Quaker roots, she jotted down various Bible passages in notes she brought on board. Nichols flew without incident up the coast from New York to Saint John, New Brunswick, Canada.

Shockingly, she discovered the Canadian airstrip was a narrow bowl meant for light aircraft, not an expansive airfield required to land Crosley's heavy plane. Running out of daylight, Nichols tried to set the plane down. With a setting sun blinding her vision, she overshot the runway. Nichols tried to pull up for another pass, but the propeller caught the ground. Rocks shattered the plane's underbelly and split the cockpit from the fuselage, jolting *Akita* to a violent stop in thick brush. Ruth broke five vertebrae, dislocated her knee, and suffered other injuries. Crawling out of the wreck, Nichols drily stated, "Wire for another plane." She spent the next two months in a hospital, the lower half of her body in a plaster cast.

Nichols made history by being the first woman to attempt a transatlantic flight. But the crash ended her hopes for big money deals to pay back her investors and fund future flights. Still physically recovering and more than $20,000 in debt, Nichols strapped herself into a steel corset to pilot *Akita* once more in October 1931. As Nichols once said, "where ever the air trail leads, I will follow with bells on." Ruth flew from Oakland, California, to Louisville, Kentucky, breaking a women's nonstop distance record flying 1,977.6 miles. The next day, *Akita* became engulfed in flames on the tarmac due to a faulty engine valve with Nichols surviving by diving out of the cockpit window. She became the only woman to simultaneously hold speed, altitude, and distance records for women, and the International League of Aviators named her the "U.S. Woman Champion of the Air for 1931."

While Nichols further recuperated, Earhart became the second woman to attempt a transatlantic flight. Learning from Nichols's flight, another pilot ferried Earhart to Newfoundland before commencing her flight. She touched down in Ireland on May 21, 1932, and flew into history. Although greatly disappointed, Nichols remained gracious in defeat. Ruth cabled Earhart declaring, "a splendid job. My greatest admiration for your planning and skill in carrying out the hop." Nichols proclaimed Earhart's flight as the most important achievement since Lindbergh's historic trip, proving the abilities of female pilots and the overall safety of air travel.

Hoping to recapture her former glory, Nichols planned to embark on another solo transatlantic flight, heading all the way to Paris to surpass Earhart's distance. Shortly thereafter, Nichols had an accident when the landing gear on the *Akita* failed at takeoff for a flight distributing President Herbert Hoover's campaign literature. With this third accident in less than a year, investors refused to gamble on her second transatlantic attempt. Ruth endured another personal blow, the death of Harry Rogers in April 1932, after his plane crashed in Queens due to engine failure.

Although outshined by Earhart, Nichols continued to break barriers. She became the first female commercial pilot to fly passengers for New York and New England Airways, a private flight service from 1932 to 1933. When that airline went bankrupt, she continued to lecture about air travel at various schools and colleges. In 1935, she drummed up support for Newark's Chamberlin Flying Service, which owned two Curtiss Condors, each a nine-ton twenty-passenger plane with 600-horsepower engines and a ninety-foot wingspan. Nichols flew passengers from Troy, New York, to Teterboro, New Jersey, with plans for charter services to Florida, her old pilot stomping grounds.

On October 21, 1935, Nichols co-piloted a flight with Capt. Harry Hublitz carrying two bridal parties planning a double-wedding ceremony over New York City. With Hublitz at the controls, one of the plane's motors failed during takeoff and Hublitz struggled to return the plane to the airport. The plane dipped and creased nearby trees, plunging to the ground and bursting into flames. At the crash site, Nichols and Hublitz were unconscious and severely injured. Luckily, the passengers suffered only minor injuries, including Ruth's brother, Army Air Corps Lt. E. Snowden Nichols, the best man of one of the grooms. The passengers credited Hublitz and Nichols with great heroism for remaining in the cockpit, rather than bailing or moving back, in an effort to land the plane safely.

Unfortunately, Hublitz died in the hospital a few hours later while Ruth barely clung to life. She suffered fractures to her right wrist and ankle, a broken nose, severe burns, internal injuries, and other cuts and bruises. Various news outlets proclaimed her near death as the public closely followed her hospitalization. Nichols underwent three separate operations and plastic surgery to mend her broken, burned body. Walking initially with a cane, she recuperated for more than a year in her family's Rye home.

Many people might have given up on flying after such a terrible accident and grueling recovery, but not Ruth. In her autobiography, *Wings for Life*, she wrote, "[t]o the public I suppose I have often seemed to be the original 'flying fool.' . . . I have piloted a plane in a plaster cast and a steel corset, too impatient to wait for bones to knit from the last crash

. . . family and friends have urged me to keep my feet on the ground. The only people who haven't tried to change me are flyers. They comprehend."

In 1936, the Quakers' American Friends Service Committee reached out to Nichols about a planned around-the-world air tour to foster world peace as war clouds hung over Europe. Once well enough, Nichols crisscrossed the country in a fundraising effort for the Emergency Peace Campaign from 1936 to 1937, excited about the upcoming prospect of flying across the globe to promote peace among nations. In July 1937, Nichols and the world were stunned when Earhart went missing on her attempt to circumnavigate the globe, and the planned global tour never materialized.

After the national campaign, Nichols applied to every airline seeking a position as a pilot. Despite her vast experience and many aviation records, all of them turned her down because she was a woman. She returned to the lecture circuit and began offering flight instruction and freelance writing on aviation topics.

As World War II gripped Europe, Nichols organized Relief Wings, a civilian ambulatory service, and later part of the Civil Air Patrol. As executive director, then lieutenant colonel, she operated a small group of employees along with more than two hundred volunteers to provide domestic and international humanitarian flights. She developed mobilization and training protocols for flight doctors and nurses, aircraft owners, and amateur radio operators. She managed and fundraised for the organization, collaborating with domestic and foreign relief services from 1940 to 1945.

After the war, UNICEF asked Nichols to fly a global air tour to evaluate the impact of war on children. This project brought together her piloting skills and her humanitarian concerns and would "finally unite an adventurer's heart with a Quaker spirit," Nichols remarked. She flew west from Hartford, Connecticut, to California and then on to Japan, Thailand, India, Greece, and Italy. The UNICEF report found that nearly sixty million children lacked adequate housing, food, and health care in the wake of World War II.

In Rome, Transocean Airlines offered Ruth a flight to London, accompanying Italian war refugees. She agreed to serve as a reserve pilot

47

and flight attendant, if needed, on the flight. The pilot missed Ireland's Shannon Airport and ran out of fuel, bellying the plane into Galway Harbor. The frigid North Sea waters engulfed the plane and passengers barely escaped through the plane's torn-away tail. Local sea trawlers rescued Nichols and the other passengers after a long and fearful night in an overcrowded life raft. Nine people perished in the crash. She telegraphed her mother, simply stating, "I am feeling fine. Back home soon. Ruth."

Upon her return, Nichols searched for work, but she got nowhere in the aviation industry that she championed for decades. She settled for a public relations job with a White Plains hospital. Feeling alone and missing flying, she often reached out to her old friend Louise Thaden. They wrote each other and Nichols enjoyed visiting Thaden and her family. Thaden noticed Ruth was struggling and reminded her that she had accomplished so much in her life.

Indeed, for during her lifetime, she held 37 different aviation records and flew 140 different types of aircraft, including dirigible, glider, autogyro, fixed wing, seaplane, transport, and finally a supersonic jet. In July 1958, she scored one more aviation record, co-piloting a TF-102A Delta Dagger and setting two new women's world records; 51,000 feet for altitude and 1,000 mph for speed, at age fifty-seven. "It takes special kinds of pilots to break frontiers and in spite of the loss of everything, you can't clip the wings of their hearts," Nichols said.

In 1959, she persuaded military officials at Wright-Patterson Air Force Base to allow her to participate in early-stage space testing on a woman's ability to handle high g-forces, to respond to weightlessness, and to tolerate total isolation and sensory deprivation. She managed to pass all three tests and publicly advocated for women to be allowed into the space program. Some women were already being tested for potential space exploration in New Mexico under privately funded Project WISE (Women in Space Earliest). But higher-level government officials refused to allow Nichols to participate in any further testing, claiming an astronaut age limit of thirty-five. Thirteen women successfully completed the identical testing of the male astronauts in the Mercury program, later known as "the Mercury 13." Subsequently, Project WISE was also abruptly canceled as authorities put up discriminatory roadblocks to women in space. American women would have to wait for more than two decades for the first female astronaut, Sally Ride, in 1983, and more than three decades for Col. Eileen Collins to become the first female space shuttle pilot in 1995.

Some of her friends contended that this official dismissal of Ruth's flying abilities and denigration of her lifelong promotion of aviation left her more despairing. "Truly, you must have wings for life, as there is no living without flight," she wrote. Racked with pain from her many crash injuries and battling depression, Ruth overdosed on barbiturates in September 1960 in her New York apartment.

Posthumously, Nichols was inducted into the National Aviation Hall of Fame (1992), Women in Aviation International's Pioneer Hall of Fame (2009), and SP's Aviation, Hall of Fame (2021). Although she felt that the aviation industry had forgotten her, Ruth Rowland Nichols should be proudly remembered for her numerous aviation records, her advocacy for female pilots, and her promotion of the safety and convenience of air travel—something many take for granted today.

"I might have been born in a hovel, but I determined to travel with the wind and the stars."

—Jacqueline Cochran
(May 11, 1906–August 9, 1980)

CHAPTER 5

Jacqueline Cochran

From Panhandle Poverty to International Aviation Fame

SHE CLAIMED NOT TO KNOW HER ACTUAL BIRTHDATE. OR WHERE exactly she was born, the identities of her biological parents, and even what her real name was. She contended that her early beginnings reflected the deprivations of a Dickens novel with daily hunger, flour-sack clothing, wooden pallets for beds, and deplorable child labor conditions. But by the end of her life, her chosen name remained on the lips of presidents, first ladies, prime ministers, generals, CEOs, and celebrities—Jacqueline "Jackie" Cochran.

Born into poverty on Florida's Panhandle, Jackie contended that her foster parents, Ira and Molly Pittman, made up her birth date and gave her the name Bessie. Others contradicted her claims, asserting that the Pittmans were her biological parents that she shunned over time. During her youth, the family of seven roamed between different sawmill company towns in Alabama and Florida, including Muscogee and Bagdad, east of Pensacola, and then to the Bibb City cotton mill in Columbus, Georgia. With their nomadic lifestyle, Jackie completed only two years of formal schooling.

At age eight, she pushed a heavy cart of bobbins for weavers in twelve-hour shifts, starting at six o'clock in the evening. Jackie walked barefoot on concrete floors in a hot, dusty cotton mill, earning a meager six cents per hour. A quick learner and motivated employee, she soon

Born into poverty, Cochran became a record-setting pilot, groundbreaking military leader, and successful businesswoman. (*Courtesy of the State Archives of Florida, Florida Memory*)

was promoted at age nine to supervise other mill children for five dollars a week. She also made extra pennies babysitting for mill families, saving enough money to buy her first pair of shoes. When she turned ten, Jackie worked in beauty salons in both Georgia and Alabama, shampooing hair, giving perms, and mixing chemicals for hairdressers for several years.

In one of her family visits to Florida, she met her first husband, Robert Cochran, a traveling salesman, in 1920. Pregnant at age fourteen, she hastily married Cochran and gave birth to her son, Robert Junior, three months later in DeFuniak Springs, Florida, in 1921. When her son turned one year old, she left her husband behind and her son under her foster parents' care to return to salon work in Montgomery, Alabama. A prodigious saver, she bought a Ford Model T and loved wearing fashionable clothing. While in Montgomery, she also trained for three years as a nurse at St. Margaret's Hospital, never taking the final licensing exam out of fear of not passing it due to her limited writing abilities.

Tragically, her son, playing with matches, died in an accidental yard fire at her foster parents' home on May 19, 1925. Jackie returned to Florida to mourn his death. With her prior nurses' training, she undertook unlicensed nursing duties in nearby Bonifay. Always restless for the next challenge, she headed back to Mobile beauty salons and then became a co-owner of a Pensacola hair salon in 1928.

With her Pensacola home base, Jackie continued to bounce around the beauty industry for several years, working for salons in Mobile and Biloxi, Mississippi. Driving her Model T, she also sold dress patterns as a traveling saleswoman and then sought additional beauty training in Philadelphia. Jackie found she possessed better skills than her instructors, and the school offered her a teaching job. After nine months training beauty students, she decided to return to Pensacola for three months, continuing the roving lifestyle of her youth.

On impulse at the age of twenty-three, Jackie sold her Model T, packed up her belongings, and bought a one-way ticket to New York City in 1929. She wrote that despite the nation's financial crash, "it was a year of great growth for me." To potential salon employers, she now introduced herself as Jacqueline Cochran. Jackie later claimed she randomly chose the name out of the phone book, omitting her marriage to Robert Cochran, which ended in divorce in 1927. Over time, Jackie continued to mix fact and fiction in creating her carefully honed image.

Determined and energetic, Jackie persuaded the manager at Antoine de Paris, a prominent Saks Fifth Avenue salon, to hire her as a hair stylist. Attractive and vivacious, she rubbed elbows with the city's rich and influential as a sought-after hair stylist and took on part-time supervisory roles at other high-end salons. She began wintering at Antoine's Miami location to accommodate her clientele and enjoyed a vibrant social life among the city's rich elites.

At a 1932 society dinner, she was seated next to Floyd Odlum, a lawyer turned financier who made millions during the Depression buying, reorganizing, and liquidating distressed companies. Floyd was unhappily married and living separately from his wife. Jackie was unaware of his reputation and wealth and was pleasantly surprised to learn about his humble roots on a family farm. She liked that he listened to and respected her goal of developing a cosmetics company. He suggested that Jackie obtain a pilot's license to travel more quickly to sell her products.

Upon returning to New York City, Jackie decided to spend half of her six weeks of saved vacation to take flying lessons and earn her pilot's license. Odlum doubted her ambitious timeline and bet her the price of flying lessons that she couldn't accomplish her goal. True to her steadfast nature, she accepted his challenge and asserted that she would obtain her license in three weeks and use her remaining vacation time to relax.

Making good on her promise, Jackie sought out flight instruction at Roosevelt Field on Long Island from Husky Llewyn in July 1932. He seemed skeptical about this young, petite blonde handling the airplane's controls and offered her a half-hour flight to test her commitment. Jackie experienced sheer delight as Husky took off and then circled the airport in a Fleet biplane trainer. She easily comprehended his explanation of how the stick and pedals operated the plane. When it came time to land, Llewyn told Jackie to take over the controls as he talked her through a flawless landing.

Husky advised her that it would take twenty hours of instruction and passing a written exam to earn a pilot's license. Jackie told him she only set aside three weeks for lessons. He warned that optimistically it would take at least two to three months to earn a pilot's license. Undeterred, Jackie plunked down a nonrefundable $495 for lessons. "When I paid for my first lesson, a beauty operator ceased to exist and an aviator was born," Cochran said.

Llewyn found his new student to be one of the brightest natural fliers he ever trained. Jackie felt immediately in sync with the plane, forming an instant union with the flying machine. By her eighth day of instruction, she soloed and calmly glided into a perfect landing after the engine failed. Lacking confidence in her writing skills, she persuaded a flight examiner to give her an oral licensing exam, which she passed. On August 17, 1932, Jackie earned her pilot's license after less than three weeks of instruction, happily collecting on her bet from Odlum.

With Odlum's support, Jackie quit the salon and took additional lessons at the Ryan School of Aeronautics in San Diego, but she struggled with class readings and lectures. Air Officer Ted Marshall offered her practical flight training at Long Beach if she secured a plane. Learning "the Navy way," Marshall focused on practical lessons and Cochran logged more than sixty-five flight hours in an aged Travel Air trainer. She paid for individualized ground classes and math tutoring. With a year of intensive training, Cochran earned her limited commercial pilot's license and then her transport pilot's license in 1933, only sixteen months after first stepping into a cockpit.

Exploring the California desert in her plane, she fell in love with Coachella Valley and bought twenty acres in Indio, California, for a future home with Odlum. He later bought another nine hundred acres abutting her property. In 1935, they constructed an estate on the property and entertained many luminaries of the day, including friends Amelia Earhart, Walt Disney, and President Dwight Eisenhower.

Taking Odlum on a winter flight from New York to Florida, Jackie faced bad weather and barely made it safely to their destination. She navigated using landmarks but resolved to learn blind flying before taking passengers out again. After five hundred hours training with airmail pilot Wesley Smith, she mastered blind flying techniques, including "flying the beam." Under this method, she relied on Morse Code tones between radio beacons to guide her course, rather than landmarks. Cochran also learned to trust her compass, air speed indicator, and artificial horizon, instead of looking out the window, critical while flying in inclement weather.

Accomplishing blind flying, Jackie became driven to compete in air races, where victorious aviators became instant celebrities. Cochran did not want to be known as a successful female pilot, she wanted to be heralded as the world's greatest pilot, period. Yet most prestigious races were limited to male pilots, including the Bendix Transcontinental Race, which encouraged aircraft designers to develop faster, more reliable airplanes. Cochran used her influential social contacts to pressure the organizers of the Bendix race from Burbank to Cleveland to open the race to female pilots in 1934. Unfortunately, Jackie's Northrop Gamma plane suffered engine trouble so she was unable to participate, but she opened the door for other women to compete.

Odlum then used his substantial financial resources to compel organizers of the MacRobertson International Race from London to Melbourne to allow women participants in 1934. Cochran would co-pilot a plane with Wesley Smith. The flying team dealt with numerous mechanical issues when evaluating potential racing planes before securing a Granville R-6H QED for the mcct. Unexpectedly, their race quickly ended in Bucharest, Romania, when Cochran crash-landed the plane after serious mechanical problems.

In 1935, Cochran made a second attempt at the Bendix Trophy in another Northrop Gamma with an experimental 400-horsepower engine and a controllable pitch propeller. Despite concerns about excessive engine vibrations, Jackie flew as far as Kingman, Arizona, before an over-heated engine and leaky gas valve forced her to bow out of the race. Her dear friend Amelia Earhart would become the first woman to complete in the Bendix race, finishing fifth.

On May 11, 1936, Odlum and Cochran wed in a private ceremony in Kingman with only two witnesses present before making another run at the Bendix Trophy. In August, Jackie pulled out two weeks before the race when the engines of her Northrop Gamma burst into flames twice over Indianapolis. Much to Jackie's chagrin, Louise Thaden and co-pilot Blanche Noyes became the first women to win the Bendix race in that year's New York to Los Angles route. Jackie's early race efforts frustrated her, yet she persisted in her plans.

With Amelia's disappearance in July 1937, Cochran felt the pain of loss and a sense of responsibility that her close friend "placed the torch in the hands of others to carry on to the next goal, and from there on and forever." With a wealthy husband and impressive piloting skills, Cochran sought out better planes and finally began smashing more aviation records. That year, Jackie broke two international speed records before making her fourth attempt at the Bendix Trophy as the only female com-petitor. This time, she flew a green and white Beechcraft D-17W Stag-gerwing, finishing third overall with a $5,500 award and an additional $2,500 prize for being the first and only female finisher.

Still dissatisfied, Cochran began working with aircraft visionary Alexander de Seversky. She became the first woman to fly Seversky's P-35 pursuit plane, a powerful military aircraft he hoped to sell to the US military. Flying different versions of the P-35, Cochran rapidly broke speed records. On December 3, 1937, she set the air speed record from New York to Miami and completed the trip in 4 hours, 12 minutes, and

27.2 seconds—faster than any man or woman at that time—beating Howard Hughes's previous northbound record. On December 9, 1937, she achieved a national women's speed record of 252.875 mph and broke her own record on December 13, achieving 255.942 mph, setting both marks in Miami.

In 1938, Jackie finally succeeded in winning the Bendix Trophy in a modified Seversky P-35 plane with extra gas tanks and a 1,200-horsepower engine. The only woman in a field of ten pilots, she flew 2,042 miles to Cleveland in 8 hours, 10 minutes, with an average speed of 249.774 mph. After a brief photo stop with her husband before a cheering crowd of two thousand spectators, Jackie flew on to Bendix Field, New Jersey, for an additional prize. Pushing herself, Cochran then made a final stop at Floyd Bennett Field, New York, setting a new women's west-to-east transcontinental speed record of 10 hours, 7 minutes, 10 seconds. With news of her victory splashed across newspaper front pages, the media crowned Cochran as the new queen of the air, and she became an international celebrity. As Jackie would later remark, she'd gone from "sawdust to stardust" and the public loved her "rags to riches" story.

While striving to succeed in a male-dominated aviation field, Cochran also pursued her cosmetics business with Odlum's financial support. He helped her lease a Fifth Avenue office and laboratory space and staff for Jacqueline Cochran Cosmetics in 1935. She played up her aviation fame by marketing her cosmetics, skin creams, perfumes, and dyes under a "Wings to Beauty" brand. She acquired accounts with major department stores and recruited women to independently sell her products. Taking advantage of media fascination with female pilots, she often powdered her nose before getting into the cockpit, touched up her lipstick when exiting her plane, and shared her travel fashion and beauty tips with lifestyle reporters. With her glamorous image and business savvy, her cosmetic company's revenues skyrocketed in the wake of her Bendix Trophy win.

Cochran continued to set national and international speed, distance, and altitude records. In August 1939, she became the first woman to make a blind landing using only instruments at a Pittsburgh airport. She received the Harmon Trophy as the female aviator of the year in 1938 from First

Lady Eleanor Roosevelt and then again in 1939. Cochran would go on to win the award four more times in the female pilot's category and once in the overall national category with her last victory coming in 1961. "I used to tell people that I would stop racing once I won the Bendix. But I couldn't. I guess racing was in my blood from the beginning," said Jackie.

As war loomed in Europe, Cochran proposed training a civilian force of female pilots to ferry planes domestically, freeing up male pilots for combat missions in a September 27, 1939, letter to Mrs. Roosevelt. British, French, German, and Russian forces were turning to women pilots to fly courier, ambulatory, and transport planes as World War II raged. The First Lady shared Jackie's letter with the president and War Department officials. Despite Cochran's urging to be prepared and Mrs. Roosevelt's support, her plan failed to gain any traction. The public initially favored staying out of the war, and military strategists doubted any future shortage of male pilots.

In March 1941, Cochran sat at a luncheon for the Collier Trophy, being the first female committee member to judge the past year's aviation achievements. She met Gen. Henry "Hap" Arnold and Clayton Knight, who sought pilots to deliver aircraft to England under Britain's civilian Air Transport Auxiliary (ATA). Arnold asked Cochran about delivering a US bomber across the Atlantic from Canada as a popular show of support for the British. Reaching out to the Canadian ATA, the organization questioned any woman's ability to fly bombers.

Using her high-level contacts once more, Jackie received permission to undergo extensive bomber flight training with sixty takeoffs and landings in Canada. When assigned to fly a Lockheed Hudson bomber from Montreal to Prestwick, Scotland, male pilots threatened to strike, outraged about Cochran invading their turf. To quell concerns, Jackie was allowed to fly the bomber with a male pilot handling takeoffs and landings. On June 17, 1941, Jackie flew the bomber across the Atlantic, another first for female pilots.

She remained for more than two months in England, gathering information for Arnold about the ATA's utilization of female pilots. Returning stateside, Cochran explained her findings to President Roosevelt and the First Lady over lunch. Intrigued by her report, they connected her with leading War Department officials who were reviewing a competing proposal from experienced pilot Nancy Love. Love already worked administratively in the military's Air Transport Command and her plan focused on recruiting an elite group of pilots for a ferrying program. The military officials also listened to Cochran's more ambitious proposal to train a large number of females pilots. In the end, the War Department was unwilling to support either program. But Arnold promised Cochran that if he won government approval, she would be a top contender to run it.

Never one to give up easily, Cochran decided to recruit female pilots to aid the ATA, holding initial interviews at her cosmetics company office in New York City. Twenty-five female pilots with at least three hundred flight hours were chosen for further medical testing and flight training in Canada. In March 1942, Cochran took her recruits to England, immediately ruffling feathers by showing up in a glamorous mink coat and Rolls Royce at a time when British citizens suffered severe food, clothing, and fuel shortages.

Yet under Cochran's leadership, her recruits flew more than 121 different types of planes, including British Supermarine Spitfires and Hawker Hurricanes, becoming some of the first American women to fly combat aircraft. The success of the initial group under Cochran's supervision resulted in another cohort joining them in June 1942. By September 1942, the ATA had flown 30,000,000 miles and delivered 100,000 aircraft with only one American fatality, which was due to propeller failure.

On September 1, 1942, First Lady Eleanor Roosevelt wrote in her newspaper column, My Day, about her support for giving women a more active role in the war effort. She noted that "[w]e are in a war and we need to fight it with . . . every weapon possible. Women pilots . . . are a weapon waiting to be used." Within days, Gen. Harold George received approval to establish the Women's Auxiliary Ferrying Squadron (WAFS). No fan of Cochran's flashy and assertive style, George proposed Love to lead WAFS in Jackie's absence. Love already worked with military ferrying units and had shown herself to be professional and collaborative in her interactions while some viewed Jackie as having a personality "like sandpaper."

Hearing rumors about Love's pending appointment, Jackie immediately took a military flight from England back to Washington. She became enraged at a photo of Love being sworn in by George with the *New York Times* September 11, 1942, headline reading: "SHE WILL DIRECT THE WOMEN PILOTS." Upon arrival, Cochran demanded that Arnold fulfill his promise to appoint her after years of lobbying for female pilots and her efforts with the ATA. To avoid further controversy, Arnold struck an uneasy compromise with Cochran recruiting and training pilot recruits under the Women's Flying Training Detachment (WFTD) and Love supervising ferrying operations for experienced pilots under WAFS.

Nearly 25,000 women applied to WFTD, and Cochran whittled their numbers down to 28 in the November 1942 inaugural class. Recruits traveled on their own dime, assembling daily at Howard Hughes Field in Houston, Texas. Although the women were considered civilians, Cochran established a strict training regimen with hours of flight training, fitness routines, and classroom studies. Once training was complete, the recruits graduated into Love's WAFS.

As training cohorts swelled, WFTD relocated to Avenger Field in Sweetwater, Texas, with trainees living in military-style barracks, answering daily roll calls, and wearing flight uniforms. Jackie's code of conduct was very strict, with recruits required to obtain permission to leave the grounds, and the base became known as "Cochran's Convent." Eventually, maintaining two different female pilot groups became complicated, and they were merged into the Women's Airforce Service Pilots (WASPs).

By July 1943, Jackie maneuvered herself into the role of director of women pilots, with Love now reporting to her on ferrying operations. The WASPs increased to more than 1,074 female pilots serving at one-hundred-plus military bases, including Eglin Army Air Base (Niceville), Buckingham Army Air Field (Fort Myers), Marianna Army Air Base (Marianna), and Tyndall Army Air Base (Panama City) in Florida. Of that number, two Asian Americans, one Native American, and two Hispanic Americans participated in the WASPs. Pioneering African American pilots, Janet Waterford Bragg, Willa Brown, and Mildred Hemmons Carter, sought to become WASPs but were rejected due to stringent military segregation rules and harsh Jim Crow laws forbidding racial integration in Florida and other southern states.

The WASPs logged 60,000,000 air miles and ferried nearly 50 percent of all of the country's fighter planes. They delivered 12,650 aircrafts of seventy-seven different types, oftentimes flying damaged or aged planes. These female pilots instructed and evaluated male pilot recruits, towed targets for live-round gunnery practice, undertook cargo and weather flights, provided tracking flights for radar operator training, and flew searchlight tracking missions. Thirty-eight WASPs lost their lives in the program with their families having to pay to repatriate their remains for burial.

As the war wound down, the WASPs sought an opportunity to earn military status and benefits. Despite vigorous lobbying efforts by Arnold, Cochran, and Love, Congress rejected a bill to militarize the WASPs and they were disbanded on December 20, 1944. In 1945, Arnold presented Jackie with the US Distinguished Service Medal at the Pentagon for her WASPs leadership. She received a commission as a lieutenant colonel in the Air Force Reserve in 1948.

WASPs lobbied for three more decades before finally receiving veteran's status in 1977. In 2010, two hundred WASPs, most aged in their eighties and nineties, received Congressional Gold Medals, the highest congressional civilian honor, for their wartime service.

After the WASPs disbanded, Jackie acted as an international correspondent for Odlum's *Liberty Magazine* and became only one of two women to witness the Japanese surrender on the USS *Missouri*. She met Chairman Mao Tse-Tung and dined with Madame Chiang Kai-shek in China. Cochran then attended the Nuremberg Trials and had an audience with the Pope in Rome. She also interviewed the Shah of Iran and Spain's Gen. Francisco Franco. That poor child from Florida's Panhandle could never have imagined being in the thick of such consequential events with major historical figures.

Yet Jackie was not done making history. During the 1950s and early 1960s, she continued to garner more national and international speed, altitude, and distance records. Friends with Chuck Yeager since 1947, she trained with him on a borrowed Canadair F-86 Sabre jet. On May 18, 1953, she took off from Rogers Dry Lake, California, and became the first woman to break the sound barrier, hitting Mach 1 with two sonic booms. When flight trackers didn't hear the booms, she climbed back in

Cochran trained on an F-86 Sabre with then-Maj. Chuck Yeager to break the sound barrier. (*Photo courtesy of Air Force Test Center History Office*)

the jet that afternoon and repeated her feat, at age forty-seven. With her friend Yeager's further aid, she became the first woman to surpass Mach 2 in a USAF Lockheed F-104G Starfighter in June 1964, setting three new speed records.

By the end of the 1960s, a heart condition grounded Jackie's jet career. At that point, she had earned more speed, altitude, and distance aviation records than any pilot in the world. Unable to fly a jet, she earned her helicopter license at age sixty-one. Over time, Cochran received honorary wings from Chinese, French, Spanish, Thai, and Turkish air forces and became enshrined in numerous Halls of Fame, including the National Aviation Hall of Fame (1971), the Florida Women's Hall of Fame (1992), the Motorsports Hall of Fame of America (1993), and the Florida Aviation Hall of Fame (2003).

Despite her renowned status, Cochran's later opinions on women in aviation confounded many. She actively lobbied against women as astronauts, even after paying for independent testing in 1960 that showed females could handle flight conditions. Citing concerns about maintaining equal standards and winning the space race, she argued that time and money would be wasted training women who inevitably would leave for marriage and children. Later, Cochran similarly opposed women as commercial airline pilots and as cadets in military academies. Her remarks illustrated that she had grown out of step with American women's changing societal roles. Others suggested that Jackie's opposition may have reflected her unwillingness to witness other females surpassing her aviation achievements.

In 1970, Jackie and Floyd retired full-time to their Indio ranch, where Odlum died in 1976. Upon his death, Jackie and Yeager found her wedding gift to Floyd, an envelope sealed with wax from a private investigator who researched the actual circumstances of Cochran's birth and youth. Without reviewing the report's contents, she wanted Odlum to know the truth about her before they wed. Floyd never opened it during their forty years of marriage. Not wishing to read the report, Jackie let Yeager burn the unopened letter, keeping her early life shrouded in mystery. A complex woman, Cochran passed away on August 9, 1980, completing her incredible life's journey from "sawdust to stardust."

"If you are to fly with me, you must believe in yourself."
—Betty Skelton Frankman Erde
(June 28, 1926–August 31, 2011)

CHAPTER 6

Betty Skelton

Florida's First Lady of Aerobatics Speeds into the Record Books

Her dad, David, told her not to tell anyone, including her mother, Myrtle. Betty climbed into the cockpit and slipped off her shoes, preferring to fly barefoot. She soloed for the first time at age twelve, not quite legal in Florida. She managed to keep their secret from her mother for about a week. Yet it is unlikely that Myrtle was surprised since Betty had been fascinated by airplanes from an early age.

From her back steps, Betty loved watching yellow Navy N3N biplanes buzz overhead during military training runs out of Naval Air Station Pensacola. Her young parents noticed aviation magazines and airplane brochures filling up their mailbox. Turns out that Betty, age eight, wrote to various aircraft companies telling them her father wanted to buy a plane and asking them to send information right away. Betty happily pored over every pamphlet and book she could find about airplanes.

The Skeltons supported their only child's interest, taking her to watch planes at the municipal airport and allowing her to hop plane rides with local pilots. Bemused by this young redhead's enthusiasm for planes, US Navy Ensign Kenneth Wright offered to teach the entire Skelton family how to fly when Betty turned age ten. On her sixteenth birthday, Betty made her first legal solo flight in Wright's 40-horsepower Taylorcraft plane and soon thereafter earned her private pilot's license.

By age seventeen, she logged enough hours to apply to the Women's Airforce Service Pilots (WASPs) during World War II. The WASPs turned her down for being too young; recruits had to be at least eighteen and one-half years old. Unfortunately, the WASPs disbanded four months before she reached the required age. "I wanted very much to fly in the Navy, but all they would do is laugh when I asked," said Skelton. Later, Betty joined the Civil Air Patrol (CAP) and rose to the rank of major.

Her family moved to Tampa and established a fixed-operation base at the Peter O. Knight Airport. Right before graduating high school, Betty took a job as a clerk for Eastern Airlines on the graveyard shift from midnight to eight a.m. During the day, she rented and flew planes, earning her commercial pilot's license at age eighteen and her single-engine land and sea, multi-engine, and flight instructor ratings before turning age twenty. Skelton stacked up these aviation credentials before she even obtained her driver's license.

Itching for a new challenge, Betty leaped at an invitation to fly in a local Jaycees air show in 1945, except she did not know any stunts. Tampa-based 1930s aerobatics pilot Clem Whittenbeck offered to teach her loops and air rolls. Two weeks later, she flew a borrowed Fairchild PT-19 and displayed these basic maneuvers in the show. Betty's flying impressed a spectator who operated a nearby airport, and he asked her how much she charged to fly in an upcoming exhibition. "And that's when I became a professional aerobatic pilot. It was quite by accident," Skelton said.

Betty bought her first plane, a 1929 Great Lakes 2T1A biplane, with a finicky Kinner engine. "My first aerobatic plane was a real crate ... sluggish and not nearly as responsive as a true aerobatic plane should be," she contended. Only standing five foot three and weighing less than one hundred pounds, Betty added cushions to her seats to reach the controls and two safety belts with towels under the restraints to reduce bruising. Practicing her moves, the pressure from both positive and negative g-forces caused bruising, black eyes, and splotchy skin until she built up her resistance.

Betty dealt with a number of accidents in her older plane, including a news report about enduring a bad bump to her head in a crash in a wooded area near Cross City, Florida. Over time, Skelton prevented serious injury by practicing maneuvers hundreds of times, first at high altitudes and then at continuously lower altitudes. She applied her own 10 percent safety rule, adding an extra 10 percent of altitude, speed, or both in her aerobatic flying to avoid accidents.

Her first major professional air meet occurred at the Southeastern Air Exposition in Jacksonville in June 1946. At this event, Betty flew along with the Navy Flight Exhibition Team's first public air demonstration, showing the agility and precision of post-war naval aircraft. At a subsequent Omaha, Nebraska, air show, the Navy team introduced themselves as "The Blue Angels" for the first time. Betty would fly in shows with the Navy team throughout the Midwest and Southeast, earning the nickname, "The Sweetheart of the Blue Angels." In 1947, she was named "Miss Florida Aviation" for her aerobatic abilities.

Over time, Betty showed not only a flying prowess, but a flair for marketing air shows along with her good friends Bill Brennand and Steve Wittman, 1940s air show legends. She drummed up interest by persuading local mayors to announce a special "Aviation Day" to welcome the pilots and asking area businesses to sponsor newspaper ads or post flyers promoting the show. Soon the whole town descended on a nearby airfield, paying for seats and parking, without the pilots having to dish out any money.

Skelton became a sought-after performer on the traveling air show circuit, including air meets and benefit shows in Miami, Bradenton-Sarasota, Pensacola, Venice, and Punta Gorda, Florida. Her schedule became packed and quite stressful with back-to-back air competitions and often several events in one day. Her career boomed when she won her first Feminine Aerobatics Championship in her Great Lakes plane in January 1948 at the sixteenth annual All-American Air Maneuvers in Miami.

At that competition, she spied a Pitts Special S-1C, only the second one of its kind, with the first one owned by the plane's inventive designer, Curtis Pitts. The handcrafted single-seat biplane, with its open cockpit, weighed only 544 pounds, and Betty admitted that it was love at first sight. She asked the plane's original owner if she could fly it, but he refused her despite her aerobatics experience. At that time, Skelton noted that "[e]veryone who lets a girl use their mechanized equipment just lives in great fear until you return it all in one piece." But she continued to pester the owner, who sold it to her in August 1948.

She painted it a bright red-and-white color and named it *Little Stinker* after it gave her trouble on her first Tampa landing. With its painted cartoon skunk behind the cockpit, Betty wowed audiences at air shows, bringing along her chihuahua, Little Tinker, as her mascot with his custom-made parachute and favorite toy airplane. Skelton would go on to win two more Feminine Aerobatics Championships, becoming the first woman to win three years in a row from 1948 to 1950 and making Pitts's planes an esteemed brand for aerobatic planes. Betty famously remarked, "I didn't just sit in that little airplane; I wore it. If I sneezed, it sneezed with me."

Before 1972, male and female aerobatics competitions were held separately. Yet both genders were evaluated on the same flight movements, such as the triple roll snap, outside loop, and hammerhead. For a triple roll snap, a pilot makes three horizontal 360-degree rolls in a row while maintaining altitude. An outside loop starts with a plane twisting into an inverted position and then making a full loop with the plane returning to an inverted position. A hammerhead requires a pilot to fly a quarter loop speeding upwards vertically and then whipping the plane 180 degrees straight down before pulling up at the last moment with a half loop. Betty had progressed a long way from her basic loops and rolls at the Jaycees show.

Skelton bristled when the press referred to her piloting skills as stunt flying. Betty contended that she "spent a great deal of time trying to convince people that it was not simply diving to thrill a crowd and to make a lot of noise and put out a lot of smoke; it was an effort that took many, many, many thousands of hours to perfect, and it in its own self was an art, and you had to look at it that way." She earned praise as the first female pilot to successfully complete an inverted ribbon cut, flying her plane upside down and slicing a ribbon strung between two poles only ten feet off the ground.

With national championships under her belt, Betty was invited to participate in the International Air Pageant in London and the Royal Air Force Air Show in Belfast, Ireland. She traveled to the United Kingdom on the *Queen Mary* with *Little Stinker* stored in the ship's hold. Her aerobatics and inverted ribbon cut thrilled overseas crowds, appearing in a 1949 British Pathé newsreel. She then became the first person to fly the smallest airplane across the Irish Sea. Betty was later awarded honorary US Navy Wings and Royal Air Force Wings.

Betty also made waves outside of aerobatics, competing in air races and setting both speed and altitude marks. She came in first in a free-for-all race at the 1947 first All-Woman Air Show in Tampa and second in a race from Key West to Havana, Cuba, in the 1948 All-Woman Air Show. She also raced in the national 1949 Cleveland Air Show and finished third against male pilots at the 1950 Miami Air Maneuvers. In a P-51 Mustang, Skelton unofficially beat Jackie Cochran's world speed record, hitting 426 mph in 1949. But an engine explosion caused her to land at a different spot than her takeoff, preventing an official mark.

Before a crowd of ten thousand spectators, Skelton then set a national altitude mark of 25,760 feet for light aircraft in a Piper PA-11 Cub Special at the seventeenth annual Miami All-American Air Maneuvers in 1949. Betty would later break that altitude record in 1951, achieving 29,050 feet in a Piper PA-18 Super Cub at MacDill Air Force Base. Taking nearly two hours to accomplish that mark, temperatures dropped to fifty-four degrees below zero and ice glazed over the plane's windshield. Barefoot Betty exclaimed, "my feet darn near froze to death."

Yet the constant stress and hectic schedule of the aviation circuit took its toll on Skelton. She felt burned out from nonstop air shows with little reliable income. Her nomadic lifestyle also damaged personal relationships as Betty admitted returning several engagement rings during those years. Not only lost relationships, but tragic losses of life constantly lurked in the shadows. Acknowledging the dangerous risks, Skelton stated, "At times it felt like a waiting game, wondering who would be next. Learning to fear death without actually being afraid was something you had to do to make it through." She suffered only minor injuries in her aerobatics career, with her most serious injuries resulting from a 1949 car crash in Tampa, nearly losing her eyesight and confined to bed for weeks.

With opportunities in commercial airlines and military service closed to her because of her gender, Betty struggled to cobble together a more financially stable aviation career. She served as a demonstration pilot for Beech aircraft and a test pilot for various helicopters, dirigibles, and gliders. She also wrote aviation columns for *Air Trails* and *Flying* magazines and other newspapers. In October 1951, Betty officially retired from the aerobatics circuit, sold *Little Stinker*, and worked for her family's air services operation in Tampa before moving to Raleigh, North Carolina, to fly charter flights.

That move unexpectedly opened up her next major career development. In a 1953 charter flight, she piloted several race car drivers and Bill France Sr., the founder and president of a young National Association for Stock Car Auto Racing (NASCAR). Impressed with her daredevil flying background, he invited her to participate in Daytona's Speed Week and secured her a sponsor in 1954. She became the first woman to drive a pace car and then promptly set a Stock Car Flying Mile Record of 105.88 mph in a Dodge "Red Ram" V-8 in the sands of Daytona Beach. With France's support, Dodge hired her as the auto industry's first female test driver.

Utilizing her prior marketing experience at air shows, Betty created numerous exciting events for Dodge. At Florida's Cypress Gardens, she zoomed a jump boat, *Little Miss Dodge*, up a ramp and over a 1955 Custom Royal Lancer convertible, becoming the first US female boat jumper. She broke her own record at Daytona Beach in 1956 in a Dodge Fire Arrow, whizzing past tide pool hazards at 156.99 mph the following year. In her new love affair with cars, she was the first woman to drive an Indy race car, earning her AAA race car driver's license. Yet Skelton was blocked from racing at the Indianapolis Speedway since female racers were banned from the oval, a combination of superstition and sexism.

In 1956, Campbell-Ewald, a Detroit marketing agency, hired her to promote General Motors in TV and print advertising and she created various marketing events, including twenty-four-hour endurance runs. GM chose Betty as its first female test driver and first female technical narrator at auto shows and demonstrations. A fashionista, she became the glamorous face of the Corvette brand in her custom-made gold model during the 1950s and 1960s. A speed demon at heart, Skelton racked up a series of impressive speed records driving Corvettes.

She established four women's land speed records, including a new record of 145.044 mph in a Corvette at Daytona Beach, just 3 mph shy of the men's land speed record in 1956. She went on to set transcontinental speed records in the United States and South America. As she amassed more records and accolades, she became known as "The First Lady of Firsts" for her combined list of auto and aviation achievements.

In 1959, aviation knocked on her door once more. An editor at *Look* magazine asked her to participate in the same tests as the Mercury 7

Skelton was nicknamed the "First Lady of Firsts" for her aviation and auto achievements. (*Courtesy of the State Archives of Florida, Florida Memory*)

male astronauts were undergoing as the United States entered the space race. Betty spent nearly five months undergoing a battery of tests at Cape Canaveral in Florida, the Naval Acceleration Laboratory in Johnsville, Pennsylvania, and the Brooks Aerospace Medicine School in San Antonio, Texas. Too petite for existing training suits, she wore a set of oversized men's pajamas for a series of tests. The astronauts respected her flying credentials, nicknaming her "Mercury 7½" when she successfully completed the testing phase.

Others hoped Betty's success would lead to women being included in the initial astronaut training program. But Skelton recognized it would be many years before women would be admitted into the program since they lacked the opportunity to earn jet pilot credentials. Similar to Jackie Cochran, she rejected different standards for women and worried about the costs and impact of female inclusion on the goal of reaching the moon within a decade. But Skelton later admitted that becoming an astronaut was something she "really wanted to do, and would have given my life to do at that time."

Her last major land speed record came in 1965. Art Arfons, a land speed champion and dragster designer, offered his open-cockpit Green

Monster Cyclops with its J-47 jet engine to Skelton at Bonneville Salt Flats in Utah. Wearing goggles and only six inches off the hard surface, Skelton set two women's land speed records, averaging 276 mph across the flats and hitting a maximum speed of 316 mph in a one-way dash, the first woman to exceed 300 mph in a jet car.

Now a vice president at Campbell-Ewald, Betty directed marketing activities for Corvette and helped establish *Corvette News* (later known as *Corvette Quarterly*). She locked horns with her main competitor at Ford's advertising agency, Donald Frankman, a Navy veteran. They subsequently married on New Year's Eve 1965 and moved out to Hollywood, where Frankman served as a director, producer, and writer for popular TV shows, such as *Bonanza*, *My Three Sons*, and *Route 66*. Betty and Don would also work together on a sports film, *Challenge*, about Art Arfons's efforts to break land speed records in his Cyclops. Their documentary won a Silver Award of Excellence at the New York International Film Festival in 1965.

In 1971, Betty and her husband would return to her home state. "Nothing in the world like Florida. You can go away and stay awhile, but you have to come back," Betty observed. The Frankmans sold real estate and Betty flew Taylorcraft and Lake Buccaneer seaplanes docked at their Winter Haven home. She maintained her pilot's license, logging more than ten thousand miles, and enjoyed driving fast cars, boats, and motorcycles with her husband. Betty reflected that "my heart and my will and my desires are mixed up with challenge. I love any kind of challenge. . . . Anything that's challenging, usually with mechanized equipment, I find most interesting."

Frankman passed away in 2001, and Skelton wed another Navy veteran, Dr. Alan Erde, in 2005, moving to The Villages in central Florida. Into her eighties, Betty enjoyed tooling around in her bright red Corvette, one of ten she owned during her lifetime. She passed away from cancer at age eighty-five.

Since 1988, the International Aerobatic Club awards the Betty Skelton First Lady of Aerobatics Trophy to that year's top performing female in the US National Aerobatic Championships. Florida's Patty Wagstaff became its first recipient and later the first woman to win the national aerobatic championships against both male and female pilots in 1991. The First Lady of Firsts reached out to Wagstaff about her groundbreaking victory. Congratulating Patty, Skelton humorously wrote, "Receiving my first Medicare card a few months ago was not much of a thrill. I wanted to burn it immediately and go out and buy a Pitts!"

Betty hadn't forgotten about her favorite Pitts plane. In 1967, Betty and her husband bought back *Little Stinker* and loaned it to the Florida Sports Hall of Fame in Cypress Gardens in 1976. In 1985, Skelton donated it to the Smithsonian's National Air and Space Museum (NASM). Fully restored to its original red-and-white color scheme in 2001, *Little Stinker* hangs from the ceiling at NASM's Steven F. Udvar-Hazy Center, which displays other notable aircraft, including space shuttle *Discovery* and a Concorde.

Currently, Skelton is inducted into ten Hall of Fames, including Florida Sports Hall of Fame (1977), International Aerobatic Club Hall of Fame (1988), Florida Women's Hall of Fame (1993), National Aviation Hall of Fame (2005), and Motorsports Hall of Fame of America (2008). During her lifetime, Betty Skelton established more combined records in the aviation and automotive fields than any other person. That Pensacola girl who dreamed of airplanes is still flying high in the record books of aviation and automotive history.

Skelton's Pitts Special S-1C plane is on display at the National Air and Space Museum. (*Photo by Sanjay Acharya/CC BY-SA 4.0*)

"Since when did men get the idea that flying was a strictly masculine operation anyway?"

—GLADYS "PENNY" THOMPSON

(OCTOBER 17, 1917–SEPTEMBER 22, 1975)

CHAPTER 7

GLADYS "PENNY" THOMPSON
Her "Flying Car" Stunt Boosts Women's Air Shows and Florida Aviation

GLADYS GOT VERY ANGRY AT THE ORGANIZERS OF MIAMI'S 1947 All-American Air Maneuvers. During World War II, the air show was suspended, but women competed in the 1946 show and had flown in the meet since the 1930s. Her childhood idol, Amelia Earhart, personally promoted the air show in 1932 and boosted Miami as an aviation hub at local speaking engagements. Last year, Gladys lobbied diligently to change the name of the Miami Municipal Airport in Opa-Locka to Amelia Earhart Field to honor the fallen aviator. Yet suddenly, the men wanted to oust female pilots from one of the premier aviation events of the year by intentionally failing to organize any events for them.

Born Gladys Rhodes, she loved watching planes fly above her family's farm in Sylvania, Georgia. Her father died young and her mother raised five children, two girls and three boys, on her own. Gladys skipped Girl Scout meetings to watch planes and talk to pilots at a nearby airport. She dreamed one day of becoming a pilot, like Earhart, earning her private pilot's license in 1936. The young pilot saved her money to make a deposit on her first Piper Cub, rather than a car.

Rhodes decided to move to Miami to be in the thick of the burgeoning aviation field. In 1940, she met and married her first husband, Roy Pennington, also a pilot, garnering her lifelong moniker "Penny." She became active in the local aviation scene and founded and edited

Southeastern Airport News, starting in 1945. A respected aviation trade paper, pilots from around the country read her latest reports on private aviation issues and national developments in the aviation industry. Her peers elected her vice chair of the Florida chapter of The Ninety-Nines, an international organization of female pilots, in 1946.

As a Ninety-Nines' state vice chair and editor of *Southeastern Airport News*, this rebuke in her own backyard by organizers of Miami's 1947 All-American Air Maneuvers truly stung. Recently, she had been instrumental in drafting and distributing the Florida Pilots Association's petition to prevent exorbitant fees from being charged to private pilots and charter services at Miami-area airports. In addition, Miami papers bragged that local female and male aviators won all of the big prizes at an Orlando air meet in May 1946 before a crowd of four thousand spectators. Penny snagged the first Bertram Trophy, besting other Florida female aviators with her precision flying in spot landings and bomb droppings in her 65-horsepower Cub. This abrupt change further denigrated the vital role of women pilots, especially those who served their country in the Women's Airforce Services Pilots (WASPs) and Civil Air Patrol (CAP) during World War II.

During World War II, Pennington flew for Florida's Civil Air Patrol, watching for Nazi submarines in the Gulf of Mexico. (*Courtesy of Bob East, Miami Herald/CC BY-SA 4.0*)

In the war, Pennington flew with Florida's Civil Air Patrol hunting Nazi submarines that might attack merchant ships in the Gulf of Mexico. Her new Aeronca Chief 65-horsepower plane, a single-engine, light aircraft with two side-by-side seats, burned to ashes at Miami's Richmond Naval Air Station disaster just as the war ended.

Penny had recently returned from the plane's first cross-country flight with Roy when a major hurricane approached Miami. The Navy

Penny's Aeronca Chief plane was destroyed in a fire at Miami's Richmond Naval Air Station during a massive 1945 hurricane. (*Courtesy of the State Archives of Florida, Florida Memory*)

base's massive wooden hangars were thought to be hurricane-proof. Military and civilian aircraft, including Pennington's plane, were corralled into the structures in the wake of the September 1945 storm. The powerful storm blew 170 mph winds with gusts of 196 mph, badly damaging the hangars. Sparks in a dirigible hangar touched off a colossal blaze, destroying twenty-five blimps and 368 military and civilian aircraft, including Penny's plane.

Having served as an officer in CAP, Pennington had no plans to take orders from a bunch of show organizers. Penny decided that women must convene their own air show to fight back, and no men would be allowed to compete. "Just let any man dare to break into it," Pennington declared publicly. She acted quickly to organize the first All-Woman Air Show in the World at Peter O. Knight Airport in Tampa on March 15 and 16, 1947. Serving as chair of the show, Pennington hoped to display the excellence of female piloting skills and convince women about the safety and convenience of air travel. Tampa officials welcomed the event, pleased about the opportunity to promote the city as an important aviation center.

Invitations were sent to more than two thousand Ninety-Niners, including Jackie Cochran and other prominent female pilots. Transcontinental races from Palm Springs, California, to Tampa were planned for different classes of aircraft with one race for stock commercial aircraft of less than 250 horsepower and another free-for-all race with any airplane and horsepower. Many viewed this 1947 annual All Woman Transcontinental Air Race (later formalized as AWTAR) as a revival of the 1929 Women's Air Derby, nicknamed "The Powder Puff Derby." That air race featured such famed pilots at Earhart, Louise Thaden, Florence "Pancho" Barnes, and Ruth Elder, and it led to the subsequent formation of The Ninety-Nines.

Admission to the all-female show would be free to the public with grandstand seating costing one dollar. Donation envelopes were distributed at the Davis Island Bridge to solicit contributions for the Amelia Earhart Scholarship Fund to offer advanced flight training to female pilots. Amelia's mother, Amy Otis Earhart, planned to fly from Boston to give out ten different trophies at the event, including the Bertram Trophy

Penny had won in 1946. Her own *Southeastern Airport News* sponsored a trophy for one of the event races. As the show organizer, Pennington included a Ninety-Niners' "Aviation's Man of Distinction" award for a male pilot to be honored at the Aviation Ball, highlighting the women's collegiality with their fellow pilots compared to the poor sportsmanship of some of their male aviation peers.

With a penchant for marketing along with her trade paper contacts, Penny drummed up support from sponsors for the event, enticing aviation companies to show off their latest planes at this one-of-a-kind air show and local businesses to show their support for Tampa aviation. She also provided broad media access to Florida newspapers, splashing lots of photos of female pilots in action. A number of radio interviews with Penny and other female pilots trumpeted this first-of-its-kind event. She further grabbed media attention flying a plane painted with the words "Follow Me" along with the name, place, and dates of the air show in an across-the-state tour with the event's secretary, Karo Bayley. Pennington also reached out to a wide range of aviation clubs and enthusiasts to support the program.

Pennington's leadership served as a catalyst to other female pilots who set up all-women air derbies and air marking parties across the country to coincide with Tampa's air show. The Tampa newspapers excitedly reported about fliers and spectators coming in from different states across the nation and from The Bahamas. The papers noted that famed aviator, Blanche Noyes, had flown in from Cleveland for the air show. Noyes served as Louise Thaden's co-pilot in winning the 1936 Bendix Trophy, the first time women were allowed to compete against men in that air race. Her presence only further emphasized that women pilots could compete on an equal footing with men.

Although rain delayed the opening events, more than thirteen thousand spectators thrilled to the flying feats of female pilots at Peter O. Knight Airport. The two-day air show included various air races for different classes of aircraft with one race reserved for women pilots who served in the WASPs and British Air Transport Auxiliary to honor their wartime efforts. The crowds applauded aerobatic flying by Tampa's Betty Skelton and by Alverna Babbs, who flew after having lost both legs, as well as novelty acts, such as aerobatics in a 1910 pusher plane, parachute jumping, and an aerial comedy act. Attendees hitched free rides with female pilots on the latest aircraft. Carolyn West and Beatrice Medes won the meet's first 2,242-mile transcontinental race in an Ercoupe plane. The show received a national publicity boost when Margie Hurlburt flew her Navy Corsair to a new women's international speed record of 337.635 mph over a three-kilometer course, breaking Jackie Cochran's 1937 speed record.

Unfortunately, illness prevented Mrs. Earhart from attending the show, but a commemorative watch was given to her representative at the Aviation Ball for presentation in Massachusetts. Beverley "Bevo" Howard, a South Carolina aerobatics champion, received the Man of Distinction award. A copy of Winifred Wood's newly published book, *We Were WASPs*, was auctioned off for two hundred dollars. In total, the air show and ball contributed $4,638 to the Earhart scholarship fund, nearly $65,000 in current dollars. Penny's gamble on the first all-woman air show became a smashing success.

In a published "Letter to the Editor" in *Tampa Bay Times*, Pennington graciously thanked supporters and volunteers for community-wide support of this new event. She noted the excellent safety record of the female pilots with no accidents or injuries at the meet. Penny added that the show achieved its purpose, displaying "the competency and sportsmanship of women pilots to the general public in the hope that the average woman would become interested in flying and accept the airplane into the family's activities as she has the automobile." She stated that "the participation of women in aviation can play a major part in advancing the industry . . . and that exhibitions such as this will do an inestimable amount of good."

Pennington's peers elected her chairman of Florida's Ninety-Nines, where she would continue to guide and support the organization as event secretary of the second annual All-Woman Air Show in Miami on June 4 and 5, 1948. The program expanded its activities, including the annual Ninety-Nines convention and a post-event all-women cohort speeding their planes from Key West to Havana, Cuba. Famed pilot Jackie Cochran donated a $1,500 prize and "The Jacqueline Cochran Transcontinental Trophy Race" for the AWTAR from Santa Monica, California, to Amelia Earhart Field, part of the Naval Air Station Miami.

While only two teams participated in the first AWTAR, seven teams signed up for the second race, including Lakeland-born singer, movie star, and pilot Frances Langford. Even more female pilots organized air derbies in other parts of the country, including Dallas, Detroit, New York City, St. Louis, and Wichita. Capt. R. N. Hunter, who aided in the renaming of the Earhart airfield, pledged Navy logistical assistance to the show organizers along with help from the Women Accepted for Volunteer Emergency Service (WAVES) Naval Reserves. Recovered from her prior illness, Mrs. Earhart participated as the guest of honor, stating that the all-female air shows were "a lovely memorial to my beloved daughter, who would herself choose this way of being remembered."

Ignoring the exclusion of women from the 1947 All-American Air Show, some Miami news reports focused on male pilots being barred from any of the races, even as a passenger, belittling the idea of an all-woman air show. One article in the *Miami Herald* stated that "if the lady birds want to take along a girl companion with or without her knitting, that's all right. But the only role open to the men is that of spectator—and from the ground, at that."

Penny applied for ten thousand dollars to help sponsor the convention and show in Miami, which city officials roundly rejected as "ridiculously excessive" and twice as much spent previously on the men's All-American Air Maneuvers. No city funds were allocated to market the all-woman air show in 1948. Pennington continued her efforts to seek sponsorships from businesses, collaborate with other aviation and community organizations, and generate events to increase publicity for the upcoming shows, including a Ninety-Nines' swim in Miami.

Penny's most outlandish publicity stunt came in conjunction with the third All-Woman Air Show at West Palm Beach in 1949. That year, Cochran again sponsored AWTAR from San Diego to Miami while Rib-N-Rite supported a $2,000 prize for a second race from Montreal to Miami. In the Montreal–Miami race, Pennington and co-pilot, Ellen Gilmour, a veteran flier who later owned Skylark Helicopters, flew in a borrowed Roadable Ercoupe. At that time, many aircraft designers wanted to develop combined vehicles that could operate in the air and on the road. James Wismer Holland patented his version of the flying car and was photographed driving it on the streets of his Valdosta, Georgia, community. To capture media attention, the city of Miami sponsored the flight with "Miss Miami" painted on the side of Holland's flying car to promote city tourism and the all-female air show.

Under the race rules, planes were not allowed to fly after sunset. But the rules fell silent on driving after dark. The women planned to fly from Montreal to Craig Field in Jacksonville and then drive the vehicle down US Route 1 in the evening to beat their fellow contestants. In Jacksonville, they folded the wings up and started to drive to Miami at approximately 30 to 35 mph. However, a dead car battery forced them to stop at Daytona overnight before flying to Miami. Although the flying car did not win the air race, it won lots of free publicity for the 1949 women's air show and women in aviation, including a blurb in the *New York Times*. As Gilmour later reminisced about the flying car stunt, "[i]t was a great idea, to publicize women in aviation. Penny was the brains, I was the brawn."

After the third annual show, Pennington remained active in aviation circles and continued editing and writing about aviation issues. Divorced in 1951, Penny met her second husband, *Miami Herald* columnist Larry Thompson, when he interviewed her for a story about Florida's female pilots. They married in 1953 and had three children together, including a set of twins. The couple became local celebrities, with Penny being a regular feature of his humorous column, Life with Larry, referring to her solely as his "good wife."

Larry's lighthearted stories portrayed their growing family's daily activities from the birth of their twins and their quirky menagerie of pets to their funny misadventures on cross-country road trips and camping outings. They both championed the preservation of green spaces, visiting forty-eight states and nearly every national park on their family vacations. She also created the first Miami Twins Easter Parade in 1955, bringing together more than two hundred sets of twins, which turned into an annual event on Biscayne Boulevard for many years. Penny also organized the Miami–Dade County Mothers of Twins Club, a supportive club for women who had twins or other multiple-birth pregnancies. Ultimately, Penny gave up flying to spend more time with her family and on community projects as well as working as a proof-reader for the *Miami Herald*.

After twenty years of marriage filled with laughter and love, Larry died in 1973 from emphysema due to cigarette smoking. Penny raised $30,000 from his column's fans for a Larry Thompson "Green Thumb" Memorial, planting nine thousand flowering trees and shrubs along I-95 in South Florida. In 1975, Penny passed away after battling adult leukemia at the age of fifty-seven.

Little did Penny know that AWTAR would outlive her, continuing until 1977, thirty years since its inception at the first All-Woman Air Show of the World. Her leadership in promoting women in aviation and all-female air races was critical for women fliers who followed in her footsteps. Thompson was inducted into the Florida Aviation/Aerospace Historical Society's Hall of Fame in 2020 and the Florida Aviation Hall of Fame in 2022.

After her death, Miami–Dade County Parks, Recreation and Open Spaces Department dedicated the 270-acre Larry and Penny Thompson Memorial Park in 1977. Coincidentally, this Miami woodland park sits adjacent to the grounds of the former Richmond Naval Air Station, where Penny's Aeronca plane burned in 1945. With its seven-acre freshwater lake, miles of hiking paths and bike trails, and 240 campsites, the park stands as a living memorial to this nature lover and groundbreaking female pilot.

"I've grown up with flying. It's practically second nature to me. . . . Flying's in my blood."

—Capt. Judith Neuffer Bruner
(June 13, 1948–December 13, 2022)

CHAPTER 8

CAPT. JUDITH NEUFFER BRUNER (RET. NAVY)

A "Hurricane Hunter" Flies into the Eye of the Storm

WHEN SHE SWEPT THE FLOOR AT OHIO'S ORVILLE AIRPORT, ELEVEN-year-old Judy never dreamed of a career as a pilot. Her dad, Raymond Neuffer, had been a civilian pilot before serving as a World War II pilot, flying P-47 and P-48 fighter planes over Burma (now Myanmar). Judy grew up around airports as her father either worked at or managed local airfields in Ohio and started teaching her to fly when she was age fifteen. When Judy soloed in a Piper Cub at age sixteen, she considered flying as primarily a sports hobby, rather than a vocation, since few career opportunities existed for female pilots. Besides, Judy set her sights even higher in the sky, hoping for a career in astronomy at NASA searching for signs of life in the galaxies. Judy and her father often explored the evening sky with an amateur telescope in their backyard, gazing at constellations and searching for planets.

At Ohio State University (OSU), she initially majored in astronomy but was disappointed to learn that she would need a PhD to be able to progress in that field. Concerned about the costs and time of that academic path, Judy looked for an alternative approach to reach her goals. She decided to major in computer science, a key discipline for space exploration. Putting herself through college, Neuffer worried in her junior year about having enough money to pay for her final year's tuition at OSU.

By chance, an Army recruiter visited her dorm to talk to students about opportunities to enlist to help defray college expenses. Judy became interested and checked out other military branches, deciding to enlist in the Navy at the end of her junior year. That summer, she headed off to basic training in Newport, Rhode Island. In 1970, Neuffer completed her computer science studies and noted, "I graduated in the morning receiving my bachelor's degree, and was commissioned as an Ensign in the afternoon."

She returned to Newport to complete Officer Candidate School before being assigned to Naval Base San Diego. For nearly two years, Neuffer contended that she "led a rather obscure life as a computer programmer at a Navy base." But her humdrum routine took a sudden turn in 1972. Due to social and legal pushes for equal opportunity for women, the Navy opened up more billets for females, including noncombat pilot roles. Neuffer jumped at the opportunity and became the first of eight female applicants for naval flight training. Judy declared that "I was in the right place at the right time. When I enlisted, I had no idea that the Navy was going to open up flight training to women. When they did, the course of my life and career changed."

On January 10, 1973, Lt. (j.g.) Neuffer made history as the first woman selected for flight instruction in the Navy. During the highly publicized ceremony, Secretary of the Navy John Warner asserted that this test program would help determine the future expansion of opportunities for women in the Navy. In response to reporters' questions, Judy stated her interest in serving as an astronaut someday, still hoping to find her way to NASA.

Neuffer's initial cohort of female candidates were dubbed "The First Six." Along with Neuffer, Barbara Allen, Rosemary Conatser, Jane Skiles, Joellen Drag, and Ann Marie Scott became the first Navy flight cadets. If they completed their eighteen-month training program, they would become the only female pilots in all of the military service branches.

The women went through a three-week initial orientation that focused on aerodynamics, engine mechanics, survival training, swimming skills, and physical conditioning at Naval Air Station (NAS) Pensacola. The group then moved on to basic flight training at Saufley Field Naval Air Station, five miles outside of Pensacola, Florida. Like their male counterparts, they would fly T-34B Mentors and single-engine prop trainers, be dunked in the waters of Pensacola Bay, and be left in remote Panhandle scrublands for survival training.

On May 10, 1973, Neuffer became the first woman to fly solo in a Navy aircraft when she flew a T-34B Mentor. However, the female cadets would not be allowed to train for aircraft carrier takeoffs and landings due to combat exclusions. Judy was disappointed that the women would not be permitted to prove their piloting skills in carrier training. "Hitting

Lt. j.g. Neuffer undertakes her pre-flight checks in the cockpit of a WP-3A Orion in 1974. (*Photo by US Navy*)

the boat is something that sets the Navy aviator apart from other flyers. I really regret that I missed this experience," said Neuffer.

The women then went on to advanced flight training in Corpus Christi, Texas. The rigorous training regimen provided the female cadets with the chance to fly a wide range of naval aircraft. On February 22, 1974, Barbara Allen became the first Women Naval Aviator (WNA #1) to earn her Wings of Gold. Neuffer soon followed as the second Women Naval Aviator (WNA #2) that same month and went on to become the first woman to serve as a Navy P-3 pilot. The successes of "The First Six" slowly pried open the doors of opportunity for future female cadets in naval aviation.

Yet with strict combat limitations in place until 1993, Navy officials cautioned the women that their flying opportunities would be largely limited to flying transport planes or helicopters in noncombat situations. Unlike her peers, Neuffer took a gamble and applied to fly weather reconnaissance. While the other five female pilots landed in transport, Neuffer became the first woman to join Weather Squadron #4, the two-hundred-man "Hurricane Hunters" at NAS Jacksonville, in June 1974.

Since 1944, the Navy undertook weather reconnaissance as an early warning system for approaching hazardous climate conditions. That role evolved into the Hurricane Hunters, who worked with the National Hurricane Center (NHC) in Miami during the annual June to November hurricane season since 1952. When a tropical storm reached hurricane status in the Atlantic or Caribbean, NHC contacted the Hurricane Hunters to penetrate the storm every three hours to take temperature and pressure measurements. This data aided NHC in determining wind speed and direction to help forewarn residents along the east coast of the United States and residents of the Caribbean and Mexico about upcoming storms. This early detection approach supported NHC's creation of weather advisories for the public to make essential preparations in advance of a hurricane.

Neuffer's first introduction to her new squadron involved a smoke-filled poker game. Cmdr. Richard Sirch and top officers chomped on cigars with their feet up on a table covered with betting money. Judy felt surprised and wondered how she might fit in with this group. However, she soon realized that the faked poker game was a practical joke and not how the squadron normally operated. The team took her under their wing as she continued to develop her weather surveillance flying skills.

The Hurricane Hunters mainly flew four-engine turboprop P-3 Orions, used for maritime and anti-submarine surveillance. Having previously trained on that plane, Neuffer quickly learned from Cmdr. Sirch about maneuvering the aircraft in stormy weather situations. Sirch, a Vietnam War veteran, advised her that flying into hurricanes was the most perilous flying a Navy pilot could perform outside of combat. He warned about the dangers from "the possibility of mechanical failure, heavy turbulence, severe up and down drafts, and high, gusting winds which range up to 200 miles over hour near the eye of the storm. It's a very rough ride." She further honed her skills on twelve-hour reconnaissance flights.

Hurricane Hunters flew WP-3A Orion weather reconnaissance aircraft out of NAS Jacksonville in the 1970s. (*Courtesy of Naval History and Heritage Command Photo Archives/National Archives [#USN 1147578]*)

Judy's opportunity to apply her skills came quickly when Hurricane Carmen, the storm featured in the movie *Forrest Gump*, barreled toward South Florida over Labor Day weekend in 1974. With wind gusts reaching 175 mph, the storm became the most powerful hurricane in five years in the wake of deadly Hurricane Camille. In 1969, Hurricane Camille devastated the coasts of Louisiana and Mississippi with high winds and flooding that resulted in the deaths of 258 people. The Hurricane Hunters were dispatched, and their readings suggested that the storm would miss Florida. But NHC grew concerned that the hurricane could regain strength over the Gulf of Mexico and cause destruction on Mexico's Yucatan Peninsula. The Mexican Army began to mobilize support systems, and their residents evacuated to higher ground.

On Sunday, September 1, 1974, Sirch briefed the team on an upcoming flight in which Neuffer would participate in piercing the eye of the hurricane. At the time, Neuffer stated, "I didn't know what to expect, but I think I can honestly say I didn't feel fear. I have lots of confidence in the aircraft and in the crew. They know their job and they know it well."

During the flight, Judy remained focused at the P-3's controls, keeping her eyes on her instruments, as a thick wall of white clouds completely obscured her view. At 7:49 p.m., Neuffer penetrated the eye of the storm in heavy turbulence with winds pounding the plane at 150 mph. She successfully flew through the eye of the storm and a fiery red sunset greeted her on the other side. Judy became the first female Navy aviator to pierce the eye of a hurricane. When she completed her task, her fellow pilots did not erupt into raucous cheers but rather offered a simple handshake or "thumbs up" for what had become a routine activity for them.

Yet Neuffer's achievement was not commonplace to the general public, still largely unaccustomed to seeing women serving as pilots in the military or for commercial airlines. When Neuffer stepped out of the cockpit in her Navy uniform, she remarked that "[p]eople stop, their mouths fall open, and I feel them staring as I climb down the steps." On the ground, the media rushed to cover this groundbreaking milestone for female aviators and her actions became a national story. Not one to toot her own horn, Neuffer made it clear that she was merely doing her job as a Navy flier, part of an experienced weather surveillance team. Sirch told reporters that Neuffer "did a super job." Thankfully, Hurricane Carmen missed key population centers in Mexico and made landfall in remote jungle areas without causing major damage.

After the initial flurry of attention, Judy would continue with the Hurricane Hunters on their routine flights and participate in an eight-day oceanographic mission in the Caribbean, England, and Canada. Yet changing military priorities, funding cuts, and technological advances brought storm clouds over the Navy's storied Hurricane Hunters. Sophisticated satellites and computer modelling were starting to provide reliable data on upcoming storms and other weather conditions. The field that Judy had majored in at OSU rapidly reduced the need for human pilots to undertake risky weather surveillance.

In February 1975, the Jacksonville squadron learned that the era of the Navy's Hurricane Hunters would come to an end. The Hurricane Hunter tradition would continue with the Air Force Reserve handling weather reconnaissance and National Oceanic and Atmospheric Administration (NOAA) undertaking meteorological research. The Navy's Hurricane Hunters disbanded on April 15, 1975. Sirch was sorely disappointed over this news, stating that "[i]t breaks my heart that the squadron is being broken up. They were a special breed of people."

With the closure of the Hurricane Hunters' unit, Neuffer was reassigned to an oceanographic research squadron at the Patuxent River Naval Air Station in Maryland. In that role, she flew twelve- to thirteen-hour data-gathering flights across the globe several times, landing on every continent except Antarctica. Yet she still ruminated about her youthful dream of working for NASA. After ten years of active duty, Judy transferred to the Navy Reserve to pursue a career with NASA in 1981.

After leaving active duty, Neuffer (now Bruner) returned to her computer science roots as a senior systems analyst on the Hubble Space Telescope as a contractor for Unisys Corporation. She developed and tested the software code for the ground systems that commanded Hubble's mission in space. By 1989, Judy fulfilled her childhood goal when she formally joined NASA's Goddard Space Flight Center in Greenbelt, Maryland.

For two years, she served as a ground system implementation manager addressing Earth Observing System (EOS) satellites that make observations of the planet's atmosphere, oceans, rain forests, and mountain ranges. Subsequently, she served in a number of key roles at Goddard, including project manager for the Solar and Heliospheric Observatory (SOHO), studying the Sun and the solar winds. She later was appointed director of the Spacecraft Control Center Branch, creating and implementing all satellite control centers, and then director of the Safety and Mission Assurance Directorate, developing and overseeing safety and quality assurance policies and procedures.

While at Goddard and in the reserve, she earned a master of science degree in engineering management from George Washington University. She actively advocated for and mentored women and veterans at NASA as she continued to score further aviation firsts with the Navy. Bruner became the first female naval aviator promoted to captain and the first female P-3 aircraft commander. She would continue for eighteen years in the Navy Reserve, including a tour at the Pentagon, before retiring in 1998. After twenty-eight years of military service, Bruner earned numerous naval awards, including four Naval Meritorious Service Medals and the Navy Commendation Medal.

In her time at NASA, she received several civilian awards, including the Exceptional Service Medal, the Exceptional Achievement Medal, the Outstanding Leadership Medal, and the Outstanding Management Award before her retirement in 2016. Reflecting on her esteemed career, Bruner noted that "NASA and the Navy are two parts of me, intertwined. I can't separate them. My experience in each has defined who I am, how I approach things and how I conduct my life."

On November 5, 2014, the National Aeronautic Association awarded Bruner its 2014 Kathryn Wright Award, given annually to a woman for her long-term contributions to aviation and space flight. The selection committee noted Bruner's "over 40 years of distinguished and historic contributions as one of the first female Naval aviators, a pioneering research pilot and a senior NASA technical leader." In 2017, Bruner was also present when Women's Aviation International inducted "The First Six" into its Hall of Fame.

Her life of service to the Navy and NASA remains a testament to her willingness to recognize opportunities and to change her course to meet these challenges. She leaves behind a remarkable record of firsts in Navy aviation that broadened opportunities for all women in the armed services, especially those who dreamed of flying. On December 13, 2022, Bruner passed away peacefully in Annapolis, Maryland, joining her husband of twenty-six years, Clarence, who predeceased her. In line with her decades of Navy service, Judith Neuffer Bruner is buried in Arlington National Cemetery.

Bruner's lasting advice to others: "Be open to new opportunities, and always take advantage of each one. You never know where it will lead!"

"I hate to speak about goals. But doesn't everybody want to fly a jet?"

—Capt. Beverley Bass
(March 27, 1952–)

CHAPTER 9

Capt. Beverley Bass

Call Her Captain in the Cockpit . . . and on Broadway

In one of her first attempts to fly, Beverley bruised her knees jumping off her family's washing machine. Her mother wasn't surprised since Beverley giggled and stretched her hands skyward in her baby stroller whenever planes passed overhead. As a youngster, she loved hopping into her aunt Ginger's Volkswagen Beetle to visit the local airport to watch National Airlines' Boeing 727 jets land in Fort Myers. It became a game to see how far away she could spot their landing lights on their final approaches. When Beverley saw a handmade sign for plane rides costing a penny a pound, she began to scrounge for quarters to pay the fare. She got a bit annoyed when her beloved aunt told her she was too young to fly.

When she turned age sixteen, Beverley lobbied her parents, Bob and Marge Bass, for flying lessons. They turned down her request, hoping to keep her focused on the family's twenty-acre ranch operation. Generations of the Bass family pioneered ranching in southwest Florida and Beverley followed in their footsteps, riding and hunting in the Everglades. She participated in barrel riding and showing quarter horses for ten years, but she kept dreaming about flying.

At Texas Christian University (TCU), she majored in Spanish and interior design and excelled in her studies. Yet soaring in the sky still called to her. In 1971, on school break after her freshman year, she took her first flying lesson in a Cessna 150 with instructor Ed Wilson, co-founder of Fort Myers Airways, at nearby Page Field. "Just walking out on the ramp and going up the stairs and the smell of the airplane was wonderful, and taking off and seeing everything so tiny. So, I took my first lesson and I got home, and I announced I was going to fly for the rest of my life," said Beverley.

Back at TCU, Beverley continued to take flying lessons at Meacham Field in Fort Worth. She remained diligent in her college courses, recognizing that airlines hired only pilots with college degrees. By her senior year, she organized her classes for morning sessions and spent time logging hours as a flight instructor from three to nine o'clock every weekday. She was only one of two female flight instructors in what persisted as largely a male-dominated industry. "I am an only child, and my parents raised me to believe if I worked hard, I could do anything. I didn't know there were girl jobs and boy jobs," noted Bass.

She continued to train and earned her private pilot's license, then her commercial pilot, multi-engine, and instrument ratings. She scrambled for any opportunity to fly while she worked on attaining her airline transport license. In 1973, Emily Howell Warner became the first female pilot for Frontier Airlines; nearly forty years after Helen Richey briefly served as a commercial pilot for Capital Airlines in 1934. Richey was forced out of her job after ten months when male pilots would not let her join the union and then threatened to strike if Capital allowed non-union pilots. After Warner, Bonnie Tiburzi then became the first female pilot for American Airlines. Times were changing, and Bass realized her dream of becoming a pilot for a major commercial carrier might become a reality.

After graduation, she became the chief pilot for Meacham Field's charter department. A Fort Worth mortician needing a corpse transported to Arkansas became her first professional piloting job. For about two years, she transported bodies on stretchers in a single-engine 1953 Beechcraft Bonanza across Texas and surrounding states, earning five dollars an hour. The plane was so small that she needed to step over white-sheeted corpses to get into the cockpit. Despite the conditions, Beverley reveled in being "responsible for everything in that plane, and it felt so empowering. I loved every minute."

Bass wisely perceived this unglamorous, low-paying job as an effective way to log flight hours and a stepping-stone to expanded opportunities in her field. She also flew corporate executives on chartered flights in a twin-engine Cessna 411 and Piper Aztecs to different areas in the country. Beverley learned that some wives did not like the idea of a young, pretty blonde pilot with piercing blue eyes flying their husbands' trips. Yet she persisted in her efforts to reach the next level.

By 1976, Beverley had flown several thousand hours, earning an airline transport license and her ticket to better opportunities. She moved to Dallas and flew cargo planes five nights a week out of Love Field through "Thunderstorm Alley" between Texas, Oklahoma, and Kansas. Bass sent in an application to her top choice, American Airlines (American), and continued to hone her skills on twin-engine Piper Aztecs and Navajos and Beechcraft Barons. Cargo planes lack the safety standards of passenger planes and were often poorly maintained with no radar for night flying. On her cargo flights, Bass racked up more flight time and dealt with unpredictable, dangerous weather conditions while hauling canceled bank checks, various airplane parts, and Fotomat film for processing.

Beverley felt a bit discouraged when major carriers started hiring her East and West Coast peers. She worried that Texas's more conservative streak might limit her piloting opportunities. Her spirits were lifted when American contacted her regarding her application. But she knew that many candidates washed out during the rigorous process of medical examinations, simulator tests, and pilot interviews.

With her various piloting jobs, Bass easily met the minimum of one thousand hours of flight time. Yet many applicants knew to be apprehensive about the stringent medical testing, lasting about two days. Applicants were required to have perfect uncorrected vision, to pass hearing and lung-capacity examinations, and to undergo heart EKGs and brain EEGs. Further psychological testing considered a pilot's mental fitness for the role. Fortunately, Beverley passed all of these medical tests. With her extensive flying time, she performed well in a flight simulator. At the end of the process, a board of five captains quizzed her on a variety of topics, including American's stock price to the different types of propellers on various aircraft she flew.

Exhausted, she returned to her parents' home to rest and wait for the results of American's hiring gauntlet. At the age of twenty-four, Bass was hired as American's third female pilot on October 24, 1976. "It was one of the top five best days of my life, but I almost had trouble believing it was true," said Beverley.

After completing a six-week training program at the airlines' flight academy in Arlington, Texas, Bass relocated to New York City and served as a flight engineer on a Boeing 727, the same jet she loved to watch land at Page Field as a child. By 1979, Beverley was promoted to first officer and American's first female co-pilot. She flew some of American's earliest jet flights into Southwest Florida International Airport (RSW) in Fort Myers, including a trip her proud parents enjoyed as passengers.

In January 1978, the Zonta Club in Washington, D.C., invited one female pilot from each US airline to participate in an event honoring Amelia Earhart. Beverley represented American and was happy to meet other female airline pilots, including Stephanie Wallach, who flew for Braniff International Airways. In February, Bass and Wallach sent letters to female pilots at major carriers to invite them to a Las Vegas convention in May 1978 sponsored by Continental Airlines. Twenty-one female airline pilots attended the inaugural event and formed the International Society Affiliation of Women Airline Pilots, known as ISA+21, to reflect the number of its charter members. Bass and Wallach spearheaded the effort to provide social connection, which led to discussions about workplace conditions and encouraging more women to become airline pilots.

One day shy of her tenth anniversary year at American, Bass continued to inspire her peers by earning her four stripes as the airlines' first female and youngest captain in November 1986. That same month, Beverley's heart thumped with excitement as she piloted a Boeing 727 over St. Petersburg on her approach to RSW. Passengers on the Dallas-based flight and friends and family at the terminal applauded and hooted their approval when the new captain arrived. Even her first flight instructor, Ed Wilson, came to welcome Beverley. "I think she's done great—this makes her at least the most famous student I've ever had," he exclaimed.

Beverley Bass became the first female captain for American Airlines in 1986. (*Courtesy of Beverley Bass*)

On December 30, 1986, Bass again made aviation history by commanding the first all-female flight crew for American. In the cockpit, Capt. Bass, co-pilot Terry Claridge, and flight engineer Tracy Prior pinned red roses to their lapels while four female flight attendants staffed the passenger cabin. The women organized the flight on their own, swapping spots with their peers to create an all-female crew. More than one hundred and fifty passengers and well-wishers cheered for the crew when it arrived at Dallas–Fort Worth International Airport on a foggy morning. Much to Beverley's surprise, the history-making flight gained laudatory national and international media coverage.

Bass was not done making aviation history yet. In 1998, she became the first female pilot to train on and fly American's jumbo jet, a new Boeing 777. For ten years, Bass flew the "Triple Seven" on domestic and international flights, and the airline selected her as its first female flight instructor on that wide-body jet. In her thirty-two years with American, she flew a variety of aircraft, including B-727, MD 80, DC 10, B757, B767, and B-777.

But one flight on September 11, 2001, unexpectedly turned into a life-changing experience for Beverley, making a profound impact on her. Captaining a Triple Seven from Paris to Dallas, Bass received a radio report that an aircraft collided into a World Trade Center tower. Originally, Bass thought it might be an airplane accident until the second tower was struck and the shocking realization of terrorist attacks sank in. Over the North Atlantic, Bass was informed that US airspace was closed and ordered to land her plane at Gander International Airport in Newfoundland.

As captain, she held the difficult task of deciding how to inform the 156 passengers and 15 crew about their flight diversion without causing panic. Beverley did not want to lie, undermining her authority and trust. In a measured announcement, she stated, "Ladies and gentlemen, this is Capt. Bass. There's been a crisis in the United States. All of the airspace is closed, and we will be landing our airplane in Gander, Newfoundland. I will get back to you with more information when we get on the ground."

Reluctantly, Bass dumped fuel to make the landing within safety standards, hoping to retain enough for a return flight. On the ground, her plane became the thirty-sixth out of thirty-eight jets to land and park on the jam-packed airport tarmac. Canadian customs officials advised her that no one would be allowed to disembark or remove luggage due to security concerns and the need to properly process arrivals. Bass, her crew, and passengers remained on the airplane as flight attendants scavenged for any blankets and snacks and played movies to help pass the time. "We camped out on the airplane," remarked Beverley.

Overnight, Canadian officials mobilized emergency personnel while the entire town of about nine thousand residents pitched in to aid nearly seven thousand people and nineteen pets. Residents brought extra blankets, diapers, baby formula, and other necessities to the marooned aircraft. The next morning, Bass's crew and passengers were permitted to exit the plane, without their baggage, after seven hours in the air and twenty-one hours on the ground. Bass was flabbergasted to find tables of hot meals and desserts at the terminal, realizing that Ganderites stayed up all night cooking for their unexpected guests.

Striking school bus drivers staffed their buses to deliver passengers to emergency shelters and local motels. Store owners threw open their doors and distributed necessaries freely, like bottled water and toiletries. Pharmacies processed thousands of prescription medications for free. Local people gathered extra pillows, bedding, and clothing and invited the "plane people" into their homes. Phone and email centers were established so stranded visitors could connect with loved ones. A local man loaned Bass his new pickup truck to drive back and forth every day for her daily briefings to passengers sheltered at a Knights of Columbus hall. Despite this stressful situation, Bass admired the compassion and self-lessness of the Ganderites to help strangers during those five fateful days. Her new mantra became "'WWTGD? What would the Ganderites do?' And when I answer that question, it is 'Be kind, be nice, pay it forward and do the unexpected when nobody is watching.'"

When she flew back, Beverley was grateful to be home in Texas with her husband, Tom, a portfolio manager for Brown Brothers Harriman, whom she wed in 1989, and her two children. In spite of the challenging experience, Beverley remained anxious to return to the skies. "I wasn't going to let the terrorists ruin what I have loved my entire life," she explained. Seven years later, Bass retired from American with a string of aviation achievements and a spotless flying record at age fifty-six.

In 2011, the Ganderites held a 9/11 commemorative ceremony and invited the plane people to attend. Bass went back for the reunion, the only pilot grounded at Gander who participated. At that observance, Bass met with two Canadian writers, Irene Sankoff and David Hein, who interviewed a hundred or so people about Gander's 9/11 story under a Canadian government grant.

Beverley's conversation with the married writing duo captivated them as she related the story of her Florida upbringing, her slow, but determined climb from charter flights to the rank of captain at American, and her heartfelt experiences in Gander. Mesmerized by her narrative, they talked for nearly four hours. By the end of their conversation, the couple joked that they were prepared to write *Beverley Bass, the Musical.*

In June 2015, the musical *Come from Away* premiered at the La Jolla Playhouse in California with Bass and her family in the audience. The musical weaves together the various accounts of the Ganderites and stranded visitors, including a trailblazing female pilot, a stand-in for Bass and the other pilots who landed in Gander. One climactic song, "Me and the Sky," directly tracks Beverley's life story from her childhood dreams of flying to her determined advances in her aviation career, to the tragic events of 9/11. "My husband and I were in tears, and we missed 75 percent of the show," Beverley admitted. The success of the musical led to more tryouts in Seattle, Toronto, and Washington, D.C., in 2015 and 2016 and two benefit concert performances at a hockey rink in Gander. Bass grew close to the cast members and donated her 9/11 flight jacket, wings, and service pin to them before the Broadway premiere in 2017.

In New York City, the musical became an instant hit and earned seven Tony nominations, winning a Tony for Musical Direction, with Beverley at the awards show to cheer its success. The musical has been translated into various languages and become a global sensation. With her free-flying privileges on American, Beverley attended numerous openings, including premieres in Toronto, London, Melbourne, and Dublin, and bashfully admits that she has seen the show about 165 times. Calling it a 9/12 musical, Bass stated that "[i]t is the most emotionally uplifting play you can ever imagine. It's not about the sadness of 9/11. It's about the goodness that came out of it." Reflecting the generosity of the Ganderites, the musical has donated millions to charities, part of the town's "pay it forward" spirit.

The theatrical show catapulted Bass into the limelight with numerous articles, interviews, and videos about her life and connection to the award-winning musical. Audience members often ask for her autograph, and she continues to mentor and inspire the next generation of female airline pilots, including her daughter, Paige, a first officer flying Boeing 737s for American. Bass also wrote a children's book, *Me and the Sky: Captain Beverley Bass, Pioneering Pilot*, a picture-book autobiography that encourages children to follow their dreams.

Beverley still advocates for more women in aviation, setting a goal of 21 percent female airline pilots by 2030. Forty-five years later, the organization that Beverley co-founded, ISA+21, has nine hundred members from more than ninety carriers worldwide and focuses on scholarships, mentoring, and advocacy for women airline pilots. Bass remains an active pilot, flying an Embraer Phenom 100 for clients, and enjoys relaxing at her homes in Texas and Pine Island, Florida.

Capt. Bass remains an active pilot, flying an Embraer Phenom 100 for private clients. (*Courtesy of Beverley Bass*)

Her advice to young people thinking about a career in aviation: "You can't do it halfway. You have to be excellent at your job." She adds, "Being the best means showing the most dedication." That little girl who once leapt off a washing machine to fly would be proud of the incredible determination and awe-inspiring achievements of Capt. Beverley Bass.

"When I told my friends that I wanted to become a pilot, they laughed at me. But my mother taught me that there was no limit to what I could become."

—Capt. Patrice Clarke Washington
(September 11, 1961–)

CHAPTER 10

CAPT. PATRICE CLARKE WASHINGTON

Embry-Riddle Alum Helps Diversify Commercial Aviation

WHEN SHE WAS FIVE YEARS OLD, PATRICE CLARKE ENJOYED THE FIRST of many flights from her hometown of Nassau, The Bahamas, to Miami. A flight attendant gave her a pair of plastic pilot wings to mark the occasion. Looking out her cabin window, she brimmed with wonder as the plane rose into the sky and flew over shimmering blue waters. Patrice never lost that sense of awe about a flight taking her to an entirely new place. Her family trips to Miami for summer vacations and for Christmas and Easter breaks only increased her desire to see as much of the world as possible.

To some, that childhood dream to explore the globe might seem an unlikely reality for the oldest daughter of a single mother. At a young age, Patrice's parents split up and her father, Nathaniel, largely disappeared from her life. Her mother, Peggy, worked six days a week as a nurse's aide and restaurant manager to support her three daughters. A strong family network on the island helped to further nurture the girls. Despite these challenges, Peggy refused to narrow any of her daughters' ambitions. She instilled in them a strong work ethic, the importance of perseverance in the face of obstacles, and a trust in their faith to achieve their goals.

During career week activities at school, Clarke thought she might become a flight attendant with the airlines. But ultimately, she decided to pursue a career as a pilot. Her friends mocked her choice since Patrice was a girl and no role models for female pilots existed in her community. Clarke noted that "my head was never filled with the boy thing/girl thing. I wasn't told that 'the boys take out the garbage and the girls do the dishes.' Because there were no boys in our house, we did it all."

As high school graduation neared, Patrice applied to Embry-Riddle Aeronautical University, with its renowned aviation and aerospace programs, in Daytona Beach, Florida. Peggy was shocked at the high price of obtaining a college degree and pilot certification. But she didn't reject Patrice's career goals and redoubled her efforts to support her daughter's education with her close family network also pitching in to help fund the tuition.

In 1979, Clarke arrived at Embry-Riddle and wondered what she had done. Reflecting on her first day at the school, she remarked, "I was basically in a state of shock. I was pulling into the campus in a taxi. Of course, school hadn't started yet, so there's not a whole lot going on, and it's wintertime and it's gray out. I remember sitting in the back of this taxi, thinking, 'What am I doing here?'"

When she enrolled, Clarke was the first Black student to attend the school and often the only female student in her classes. Aside from courses in aerodynamics, meteorology, and physics, she undertook 210 hours of flight instruction. Patrice worried that her English language skills might be too limited for the demanding aeronautical science program. Yet she remembered her mother's example of focusing on what needed to be done and making the necessary efforts to overcome obstacles.

At times, Clarke felt lonely, but contended that she did not face much discrimination or harassment at the school. "I am quiet. I stay in the background so I don't get noticed a lot. But when I need to assert myself, I can," she said. Taking a page from her mother's book, she added, "I'm the kind of person who does what she has to do to get the job done." In April 1982, Patrice got the job done, becoming the first Black female student to graduate from Embry-Riddle with a bachelor's degree in aeronautical science and a commercial pilot's certificate. After graduating, the Bahamian citizen earned US residency and began searching for pilot jobs with the airlines.

Unfortunately, that year, the US economy faced a serious recession and pilot opportunities were difficult to find, especially for a woman of color. The airline industry in the United States had an extensive history of discrimination against women and Black pilots, although both groups had long proven their abilities to fly planes. Initially, many airlines would not hire a pilot unless that candidate had flown planes in the military. Many qualified women who were pilots were blocked from aviation employment because women were not permitted to be pilots in the armed services. The airlines rejected applicants from the Women Airforce Service Pilots (WASPs), who served in World War II, because the military considered them to be civilian pilots. The WASPs would not receive veteran's status until 1977 after decades of congressional lobbying.

Yet male African American pilots with military credentials, such as the Tuskegee Airmen of World War II, were also unable to find post-war employment in aviation. The airlines applied a variety of discriminatory practices to bar Black male military pilots, claiming that passengers would be unwilling to fly with a Black pilot or citing the challenges of layovers for Black pilots seeking meals and hotels in "Jim Crow" segregated states in the South. Despite an industry claim to rescind the exclusion of Black pilots in 1957, discrimination persisted in aviation. Marlon Green, a former US Air Force pilot and Korean War veteran, waged a six-year legal battle all the way to the US Supreme Court to legally strike down the exclusion of Black pilots in 1963. Civil rights litigation and Equal Employment Opportunities Commission (EEOC) and Department of Justice enforcement actions

The famed Tuskegee Airmen of World War II were unable to secure pilot jobs with airlines due to discriminatory laws and practices. (*Photo by US Air Force*)

against the airlines continued into the 1970s and 1980s, pushing the industry to cease its discriminatory policies and increase diversity in its ranks.

Having grown up in The Bahamas, Patrice was accustomed to seeing Black professionals in all walks of life. It disturbed her that African Americans had to sue to employ their piloting skills in her adopted country. Disappointed, she returned home to The Bahamas to seek aviation opportunities. In September 1982, Trans Island Airways (TIA) hired her as the first professional female pilot in The Bahamas for ten dollars an hour.

Loving to fly, she felt elated to receive her first pilot's check for nine dollars and eighty cents for an hour-long trip. With TIA, Clarke flew charter flights in six-seater Piper Aztecs and ten-seater Britten-Norman Islanders to Grand Cayman, Haiti, and South Florida from The Bahamas. For two years flying for TIA, she continued to train and study for exams and qualified to fly Boeing 737 and Boeing 747-8 jets. Patrice also became an active member of the Caribbean chapter of The Ninety-Nines, the well-known international organization of licensed female pilots.

At TIA, she further honed her piloting skills and often tested her abilities in dangerous thunderstorms that commonly rock the region. One of her closest calls came on a charter flight to Eleuthera in 1984. As she piloted a twin-engine Islander, one engine died 5,500 feet over the Caribbean far from any airport. With passengers on board, Clarke maintained her composure as she guided the plane to a safe landing on time in Eleuthera.

In October 1984, she made the leap to first officer with Bahamasair, the national airline of The Bahamas, becoming the airline's first female pilot. *Ninety-Nines News* trumpeted this major accomplishment in its newsletter. With Bahamasair, Patrice flew primarily Boeing 737s to South Florida with some longer flights to Atlanta and New York. In a few instances, passengers were startled or concerned about seeing a Black female pilot. In one case, a passenger refused to fly when they saw her in the cockpit. Yet she persevered and logged more than one thousand hours flying Boeing 737s.

Although Clarke appreciated the opportunity to fly bigger planes, she itched to pilot longer flights to new locations. Patrice noted she "got tired doing the same thing, which was flying The Bahamas and South Florida. After you've done that so many times, it gets old." She went looking for her next major flying opportunity in the States, hoping to expand her travel options.

In May 1988, United Parcel Service (UPS) hired her as a flight engineer. Back then, UPS employed 1,650 pilots, of which 59 were African Americans and 86 were women. When she joined UPS, Patrice found that "people started making me aware that I could be making history." Clarke became the first Black female pilot for UPS as well as for any major US air service. In addition, she was only one of eleven Black female commercial pilots in the entire country at that time. Subsequently, she joined the Organization of Black Aerospace Professionals (OBAP), finding camaraderie and support from other African Americans pursuing careers in the aviation industry.

At UPS, Patrice flew four-engine DC-8s as part of a three-person crew, hauling about 100,000 pounds of cargo on mostly night flights out of Louisville, Kentucky. In January 1990, UPS upgraded her to first officer and she enjoyed flying to different places, including Sydney, Australia, and Cologne, Germany. Yet one of her most memorable flights was a trip to Anchorage, Alaska. Having grown up in a tropical climate, Clarke found herself tearing up as the plane flew over Alaskan glaciers that she had learned about in elementary school. Despite the taxing physical and mental stress of long flights, she still thrilled to "the joy of climbing aboard an aircraft, and one hour later being in a totally new and exciting environment."

At an OBAP convention, she met Ray Washington, a captain with American Airlines. While dating and in their early married life, they juggled their demanding flight schedules, sometimes able to spend only five days together in a month while other months able to see each other every day. But they made it work and wed in February 1994, becoming the first and only African American couple to fly for major airlines. Yet another major achievement awaited Clarke Washington later that year.

On December 14, 1994, she flew a DC-8 from Louisville to Atlanta under the scrutiny of a Federal Aviation Administration (FAA) aviation safety inspector and a UPS flight standards supervisor. She had already undergone a twenty-five-hour flight review by an FAA-sanctioned UPS supervisor. When Clarke Washington touched down in Atlanta, she officially was promoted to captain, becoming the first Black female to earn that status at a major US air service. At age thirty-three, she had logged more than eight thousand hours of flying time to achieve this position. The newly minted captain viewed the flight as routine until a bevy of reporters

In 1994, Clarke Washington became the first Black female captain for a major US air service. (*Photo by Carolyn Russo, NASM A03353*)

and photographers greeted her return flight to Louisville. Stepping off the plane to a flood of bright camera flashes felt "more unnerving" than the actual record-making flight as she stepped into aviation history once again. UPS splashed a poster ad in newspapers heralding her achievements. Subsequently, Clarke Washington and UPS donated her captain's cap, coat, shirt, trousers, and belt to the Smithsonian's National Air and Space Museum to commemorate her groundbreaking accomplishments.

Throughout her aviation career, Clarke Washington found most of her peers to be "very gracious and encouraging." She stated that "I feel it is necessary to point out that not all of our male counterparts are sexist or discriminatory, but in every group there are a few rotten apples."

In dealing with discrimination as a trailblazing Black female pilot, Patrice often reminded herself about the tremendous struggles faced by her predecessors in flight, especially the first African American female pilot, Bessie Coleman. In 1995, Patrice and other African American pilots, their supporters, and airplane buffs established the Bessie Coleman Foundation to help encourage and promote Black females in the aviation industry. The foundation later evolved into the Bessie Coleman Aerospace Legacy (BCAL), which offered a BCAL Scholarship and BCAL Academy to youth underrepresented in science, technology, engineering, and math (STEM) fields and a "Bessie Coleman Breakfast" honoring Black women who achieved success in aviation fields.

Furthermore, as an active member of OBAP, Patrice participated in the organization's weeklong aviation camps for fifty seventh- and eighth-graders, held throughout the country. To participate, OBAP selected students with good grades, an interest in aviation, and a compelling essay. With a passenger plane provided by UPS, Patrice accompanied the mostly Black campers to Washington, D.C., for a visit to the Smithsonian's National Air and Space Museum in 1997. For many of the students, this flight was their first time on an airplane. When they arrived at the airport, members of the Tuskegee Airmen welcomed them and a police escort led the group to the museum. The students enjoyed an exhibit about pioneers in aviation that also featured their chaperone, Capt. Patrice Clarke Washington.

Based on her series of aviation firsts, Clarke Washington was honored with the Female Trailblazer Award from the National Black Coalition of Federal Aviation Employees in 1995. In 2000, Turner Broadcasting System selected Clarke Washington for one of its Trumpet Awards, which recognized the accomplishments of leaders in the African American community. In 2008, Patrice and her husband, Ray, were inducted into OBAP's Founders and Pioneers Hall of Fame. Due to her many aviation successes, Clarke Washington became an in-demand guest speaker at professional conferences, meetings, colleges, and schools to encourage women and people of color to pursue STEM degrees and a career in the aviation industry.

As of January 2023, only 9.2 percent of professional pilots and flight engineers are women, and only 2.3 percent are African Americans. Research has shown that some of the key barriers to diversifying the airline industry are the lack of role models, the high costs of flight instruction and college degrees, a dearth of aviation career information, and an isolating work environment. While some progress has been made, more concerted efforts need to be adopted to help even the playing field and to attract more women and minorities to aeronautical careers.

Throughout her career, Patrice spread her love of flight and encouraged young people, especially those underrepresented in aviation, to pursue careers at all levels in the industry. Capt. Clarke Washington told her audiences to "[d]ream good dreams for yourself, work hard, persevere, surround yourself with positive people, and know that one day your dreams too will come true." That young Bahamian girl on her first flight to Miami truly worked hard and overcame numerous obstacles to do just that.

"I was taken into the air and I was taken by the air. Flying opened a door into a whole new world."

—Patty Wagstaff
(September 11, 1951–)

CHAPTER 11

PATTY WAGSTAFF

Three-Time Aerobatic Champ Thinks Outside "The Box" in St. Augustine

MILLIONS OF SPECTATORS HAVE LOOKED SKYWARD IN AWE OF THE amazing rolls, loops, and snaps of aerobatic champion and air show favorite Patty Wagstaff. In her nearly forty-year career, Patty has earned just about every award and accolade for her smooth and aggressive style of precision aerobatic flying. Her renowned flight school in St. Augustine trains aerobatic athletes and helps pilots at all levels to hone their airmanship skills.

A fan of the sport might assume that Patty started flying at an early age with a laser-like focus on becoming an aerobatic pilot. But in a world where many pilots solo in their teens, Wagstaff made the first entry into her flight log at age twenty-eight. Once she embraced flying, Patty declared, "I just don't want to fly straight level. I want to fly upside down." Like her aerobatic flying routines, Patty's path to legendary status was not straight level, but filled with unexpected twists and turns.

Throughout her childhood, Patty lived a nomadic lifestyle. Her parents, Robert Combs, an Air Force B-25 pilot, and his wife, Rosalie, a former model, zigzagged the country for different military assignments and then moved often for Robert's civilian piloting jobs with various chartered airways. Eventually, a captain opportunity with Japan Airlines took the young family to Tokyo and then to Yokohama.

In her 1997 autobiography, *Fire and Air, A Life on the Edge*, Patty wrote that some of her happiest childhood memories centered on time flying with her dad or talking about airplanes with him. She quizzed her father about his upcoming check rides, updated his flight manuals, and sat in the cockpit with him. He even once allowed her to briefly take the controls of a Douglas DC-6 circling Mount Fuji. She admired her dad's career and later her younger sister Toni's desire to follow in his footsteps. But as a teenager, she could not imagine exercising the dedicated effort and rigid discipline needed to become an airline pilot.

Initially, Patty earned a business degree from Yokohama National University. In her twenties, she traveled and held various administrative and hospitality positions in Japan, the United States, and Australia. After about four years in Australia, she decided to move to Alaska to be closer to her family. Her sister, Toni, about to graduate high school, was learning to fly. Little did Patty know that her move to Alaska in 1978 would set the stage for her future success.

With her administrative skills, Patty worked with a nonprofit organization, the Bristol Bay Native Association (BBNA), in Dillingham, Alaska. BBNA helped to administer funds and lands from a legal settlement with Indigenous Alaskans. The people and the work fascinated Patty, who traveled to various remote communities on charter flights to help assess and prioritize projects.

In 1979, she met Robert "Bob" Wagstaff, a well-respected attorney and avid pilot, who operated law offices in Anchorage and Dillingham. He invited her to join him for a flight on his Cessna 185 on floats with its 300-horsepower Continental engine and offered to teach Patty how to fly. That day, she felt a rush of energy in her fingertips as Bob let her handle the plane's controls. Patty wrote that "[a]lmost effortlessly, I turned the airplane from the left to the right, banking over the lush valley below and climbing to feel on a par with the height of the distant mountains. I no longer doubted what I wanted to do with my life. In that instant it was revealed. I wanted to fly."

Patty relished being a student, and Bob was a patient instructor and cautious pilot. Ever-changing wind and weather conditions made Alaskan bush flying unpredictable and risky for both of them. They explored the

Alaskan bush with its pristine waterways, blue glaciers, and varied wildlife and vegetation, sometimes flying to distant villages for Patty's nonprofit work. She made her first logbook entry on June 29, 1979, and Bob encouraged her to obtain her private license on land planes. Flying lessons were expensive, so Patty took out student loans for flight instruction to obtain her licenses and ratings toward becoming a paid flight instructor.

Taking lessons in Dillingham and Anchorage, she flew a wide range of planes, including a Cherokee 180, Cessna 150 and 152, and Beech B-19 Sundowner before soloing in that Sundowner on March 27, 1980. A fast learner, she earned her private pilot's license on September 10, 1980, a day before her twenty-ninth birthday. Less than a year later, she earned her seaplane rating in August 1981 and then her instrument rating in November 1982. Subsequently, she earned her commercial license, multi-engine rating, and certified flight instructor status and began helicopter training in 1983. Patty started teaching students and earning money at two different flight schools at Anchorage's Merrill Field Airport.

As she amassed her flight credentials, Patty held no interest in becoming an airline pilot or forever serving as a flight instructor. Hoping to challenge her skills further, she looked into aerobatic flying (often referred to as "akro"), despite having never attended an air show or witnessed any aerobatic stunts. Beginning in June 1982, Patty enrolled in a ten-hour course with Darlene Dubay, an Anchorage aerobatics flight instructor. She soon found that she loved doing aerobatic tricks in her instructor's 150-horsepower red Bellanca Decathlon. "My wild side took to aerobatics like one who had been kept in darkness and was suddenly led into blinding light," she said.

Dubay also introduced Patty to the concept of "the box," a small cube of airspace in which highly skilled aerobatic pilots precisely maneuver their planes to earn their scores in competitions. In air meets, the box is typically a 1,000-meter square of airspace (about 3,300 feet) with white markings on the ground establishing the boundaries or "corners" of the box. At first, Patty was flabbergasted that any pilot could execute maneuvers within this cramped cube of air. Yet she continued to practice aerobatic maneuvers and sought Dubay's feedback on her progress even after the course ended.

Dubay's lessons confirmed Patty's growing belief "that the air is my element." She penned that "[i]mmersed in dizzying spins, rolls, loops, stalls—every conceivable realm of rotating, revolving, turning, rushing flight—I felt as if I had found something for which I had long been searching." In 1983, she took further aerobatic lessons in Fort Worth, Texas, with air show legend Duane Cole, a two-time US aerobatic champion, who founded the Cole Brothers Air Show. Cole immediately recognized Patty's innate talent as he coached her through more challenging spins and rolls in a Bellanca Decathlon 5066 Uniform.

At that time, Patty welcomed the opportunity to push her piloting skills to new heights, but she had not seriously considered aerobatics as a long-term career. But attending the Abbotsford International Airshow in British Columbia with Bob irrevocably changed her life. At her first air show, Patty watched the aerobatic pilots readying for their routines and instantly recognized that being corralled behind the audience barricade frustrated her. "Just as I had felt as a kid at the circus when I wanted to jump into the ring with the horses and be a bareback rider . . . I didn't want to be a spectator; I wanted to be a part of their lifestyle, their scene," she later reflected. Her realization was only further solidified when she then flew to Fond du Lac, Wisconsin, to watch precision flying at the International Aerobatic Club (IAC) Championships.

Her competitive spirit whetted, Patty bought her first aerobatic airplane—a red, white, and blue 189-horsepower Super Decathlon monoplane. Logging her first flight on March 3, 1984, she continued to hone her aerobatic skills. In May 1984, Patty was invited to participate in Alaska's largest air show at Gulkana Airport as a member of her local IAC chapter. With Cole's guidance, she created her first air show routine, featuring Cuban Eights, Reverse Half Cuban Eights, a Triple Loop, and various rolls. At the show, she learned from her peers about the importance of not only being a good pilot, but also being a successful air show entertainer and interacting with the crowds. Patty was pleased to receive a whole three hundred dollars for her efforts, not much for the time and costs of training and maintaining an aerobatic airplane. Yet she was on her way to forging a new career.

Just more than two years after her first aerobatic lesson, Patty formed her own air show company in July 1984. She flew in several other Alaskan air shows in Anchorage, Fairbanks, Skwentna, and Soldotna, enjoying the freedom of air show routines and comparing them to the "lyrical rhythm of modern dance." However, Patty knew that the best way to sharpen her aerobatic skills meant facing the formal challenges and high stress of "the box" in air competitions.

Patty embraced the rigors and meticulous precision of competitive aerobatic flying to refine her airmanship skills. Often pulling ten positive Gs and seven negative Gs in her performances, she knew the importance of good nutrition and hydration and remained in excellent physical shape by hiking, mountain biking, English-style horseback riding, and lifting weights.

Anxious about having her flying skills evaluated and graded, she finished twenty-third in the intermediate level at her first air competition, the 1984 IAC Championships in Fond du Lac. Yet the competition gave her the opportunity to seek advice from more experienced aerobatic pilots and to scope out the newest designs in aerobatic aircraft. That trip also marked an important personal turning point as Patty and Bob wed at a small courthouse ceremony in Oshkosh on August 10, 1984.

Wagstaff geared up for her first US National Aerobatic Championship ("nationals") at Grayson County Airport in Sherman, Texas, in September 1984. At the nationals, aerobatic competitors are divided into five categories based on their skill level: Primary, Sportsman, Intermediate, Advanced, and Unlimited. Since 1972, US female and male pilots compete equally against each other at the nationals. However, international competitions hold separate female and male competitions for gendered-awards, even though both sets of pilots complete the same program. Thus, a women's and a men's team are selected from the ranks of the Unlimited category for the US Aerobatic Team to compete in the World Aerobatic Championship (WAC). Patty hoped to place high enough to be considered for a slot on the US women's team and reached out to Duane Cole for further coaching.

The demanding annual competition involves three separately judged routines in the box; the compulsory, the freestyle, and the unknown. The compulsory, or known, flight involves accomplishing certain mandatory maneuvers depending upon one's category. The freestyle allows the pilot to develop a routine from a menu of established aerobatic maneuvers. The unknown specifies a particular sequence of maneuvers published only twenty-four hours in advance, requiring competitors to memorize the routine without being able to practice it in advance of their scoring round. In 1984, Wagstaff was disappointed when the competition got rained out, forcing her to wait until 1985 to compete for a spot on the US Aerobatic Team.

Yet her time at the canceled 1984 contest was not a complete wash-out. She met pilot Ron Fagen, who offered her half ownership of a Pitts S-1S biplane to fly in the remaining fall 1984 and 1985 air show and competition season. With a year before the next nationals, Wagstaff knew it would take seventy to eighty hours to master her Pitts biplane. In fall 1984, Patty took spin and recovery training with Texas aerobatic spin master Gene Beggs in a Pitts S-2A, learning advanced akro techniques.

In 1985, she sought out three-time national aerobatic champion Clint McHenry in Pompano, Florida, for coaching in his 180-horsepower, two-seater Pitts. His grace and precision in his flight routines inspired Patty to push harder to reach the Unlimited level and think more creatively in developing her freestyle presentation. Dedicated to learning her craft, Wagstaff also received coaching from Betty Stewart, a two-time women's world champion and a prior US champion. From her advanced akro training, Patty recognized that an excellent aerobatic pilot "feels the airplane and wears it like a glove."

After coaching from some of the best aerobatic pilots, Patty won first place as a foreign pilot in the Canadian National Aerobatics Championships and went on to compete in ten more air contests in the Midwest. Before heading to the nationals, Wagstaff bought out Fagen's remaining half interest in the Pitts S-1S. Filled with excitement and determination, Patty successfully battled the intense pressure of the high-stakes competition. Astonishingly, she won a fifth spot on the US Aerobatic Team on her first trip to the 1985 nationals, after only three years of aerobatic training. She became a member of the US female team at WAC 1986 in South Cerney, England, at Mildenhall Air Force Base. Returning to

The record-setting Wagstaff is a six-time member of the US Aerobatic Team and the first female, as well as a three-time winner of US National Aerobatic championships. (*Courtesy of Patty Wagstaff*)

Alaska after the nationals, Wagstaff stopped to refuel and participate in an air show at the former Women's Airforce Service Pilots (WASPs) air base in Sweetwater, Texas, grateful to these early female pilots for helping pave the way for American women in aviation.

To compete on the international stage, Patty upgraded her plane to a Pitts S1-T with a 200-horsepower engine. Bouncing between Alaska and Arizona, Patty practiced with her new plane over the desert landscape of Arizona's Avra Valley, seeking to perfect clear lines and angles and working on flying wing-to-wing in team formation. When she arrived at WAC 1986, Wagstaff received a chilly reception from some of her female teammates who felt threatened by this talented rookie. Their attitudes only galvanized Patty's desire to become an elite athlete, a world-class competitor. In the end, she placed seventh overall in the women's division, quite impressive for the new kid on the block at her first global meet.

Steadily progressing at the 1987 nationals, Wagstaff switched out her recently acquired Pitts S-2S plane for a German-built Extra 230, with its four-cylinder Lycoming engine and wooden wings, just five weeks before the contest. She learned to fly her new plane in Tampa, Florida—Betty Skelton's former stomping grounds. At the 1987 nationals, Patty finished sixth overall and earned the highest score out of all of the female pilots in only her third trip to that competition. She won her first Betty Skelton First Lady of Aerobatics Trophy as the top female pilot in the nationals. Wagstaff was now a force to be reckoned with on the aerobatic competition circuit.

Each season, Patty participated in about ten air competitions and ten air shows from March to November. Unfortunately, air competitions did not offer prize money, only awards, and were stressful events that demanded perfect maneuvers within the rigid limits of the box. Naturally creative, Wagstaff excelled in the freestyle presentation at these air contests and enjoyed freestyle routines at more laid-back air shows, including being the second woman, after Betty Skelton, to perform the inverted ribbon cut. Unlike the pressure-cooker environment of air competitions, air shows felt more like a friendly family reunion to Patty where the emphasis was on enjoying camaraderie and offering spectators a thrilling show. Yet air shows paid meager amounts to participants, often less than half of the costs of owning, maintaining, and storing aerobatic planes and a pilot's coaching, conditioning, and travel. Patty spent a great deal of her time courting sponsors and managed to stay afloat as a full-time aerobatic pilot with financial support from her sponsors.

In 1989, Wagstaff continued to excel at the nationals, ranking fourth overall and achieving the highest score of any of her female competitors. Her former coach and top-scoring male, Clint McHenry, would lead the US men's team, and Patty would captain the women's team at WAC 1990 in Switzerland. Wagstaff won the Skelton Trophy for a second time. Eventually, Patty made the US Aerobatic Team every year from 1985 to 1996, including being a part of the first-place US women's team in 1988 that defeated the dominant Soviet women's team.

At WAC 1990, the Wagstaffs negotiated with inventive aerobatic plane designer Walter Extra to purchase his prototype Extra 260 with its Lycoming AEIO 540 engine and high-performance composite MT-propeller. In March 1991, Patty began training for the nationals, working at mastering her new plane and undertaking conditioning exercises to handle the intense g-forces of competition. At the 1991 nationals, Patty blew away the field, winning gold medals for her compulsory, freestyle, and unknown performances. She earned twenty-eight perfect tens from the judges compared to her nearest competitor, who secured only seventeen perfect scores. Beating both male and female pilots, Patty became the first and only woman at that time to win the nationals, receiving the Mike Murphy Cup as the overall winning pilot and the Betty Skelton Trophy as the top female finisher.

Thrilled to have won the nationals and her place in aerobatic history, Wagstaff knew that her barrier-breaking victory would present new challenges. She noted that "[w]inning makes it easier to dedicate yourself to excellence and harder to defend your position. You are on the top and it is as if a bull's-eye were painted on the middle of your back. You become the one that everyone else wants to beat." She continued to practice with her Extra 260 and developed more complex and demanding aerobatic routines. Patty managed to persuade McHenry to coach her again in El Reno, Oklahoma, before the 1992 nationals.

In her Extra 260, Wagstaff defied gravity as she zoomed vertically in the air. (*Courtesy of Patty Wagstaff*)

At the competition, a fellow male pilot mentioned to Patty that she would have to repeat her 1991 win, otherwise, people would claim that a woman winning nationals was a matter of luck, a fluke. Undaunted, Patty would go on to win nationals in 1992 in her Extra 260 and again in 1993 in her Extra 300S. She would be awarded the Mike Murphy Cup three times and the Betty Skelton Trophy six times. Reflecting on her wins, Patty expressed gratitude to the legacy of pioneering female pilots who preceded her. "From them and from my own experience, I learned that an airplane doesn't know or care the gender of the person flying it, nor is the allure of speed and motion limited to the realm of the male."

With her groundbreaking dominance at the nationals, the Smithsonian Institution's National Air and Space Museum (NASM) sought out her experimental Extra 260 in 1993, hanging her plane in the NASM's Pioneers of Flight Gallery in 1994, next to Amelia Earhart's Lockheed Vega. Patty's flight suit, 1991 US National Aerobatic Champion trophy, and three gold medals are also displayed at NASM, and the museum presented NASM's Award for Current Achievement to Wagstaff in 1994. The International Council of Air Shows (ICAS) then awarded her its highest honor, the ICAS Sword of Excellence, in 1995. In worldwide competitions, Patty won gold, silver, and bronze medals and became the top-scoring US pilot, female or male, at WAC 1996, winning the Charlie Hillard Trophy, then retiring from air competitions.

But retiring from air contests did not mean retiring from flying. Wagstaff continued her hectic pace of air show performances, earned her helicopter rating, and served as a demo pilot for Raytheon's turbine-powered T-6A Texan II for nine years. Hollywood came knocking, too, and she became a Screen Actors Guild (SAG) member and the first pilot in the United Stuntwomen's Association (USA). Wagstaff served as an aerial coordinator for the movie *Up Close and Personal* and a stunt pilot in the films *Drop Zone* and *Forever Young* and the TV shows *Lois and Clark* and *Fortune Hunter* as well as being profiled in the Disney documentary film *America's Heart & Soul*. Patty also spent three wildfire seasons as an air attack pilot flying an OV-10A Bronco and aiding aerial firefighters from June to mid-November for CalFire, California's Department of Forestry and Fire Protection.

After several years in Tucson, Patty decided to relocate to Florida to join a lively aerobatic community. Since 1993, she had traveled to Florida to pick up her planes from an Extra distributor in St. Augustine. Wagstaff knew the Moser family had created a vibrant aerobatic network in the area. Ernie Moser, a retired US Air Force colonel, created "Colonel Moser's Air Circus" in the 1960s. His flying circus drew aerobatic pilots, parachute stunt performers, and wing-walkers to St. Augustine, and the troupe barnstormed in air shows throughout the southeast. His son, Jim, continued the family tradition after Ernie's retirement. Wagstaff wanted to share in the camaraderie of this close-knit aerobatic community and found it "important to be close to the scene." In 1997, Patty moved initially to Fernandina Beach, continuing her demanding roster of precision flying at air shows throughout North America.

In 2014, she found office space and an available hangar at the Northeast Florida Regional Airport and opened her flight school, Patty Wagstaff Aviation Safety, LLC, in St. Augustine, Florida. Aside from her busy air show schedule, Patty and her team of instructors offer aerobatic, airmanship, and upset and recovery training courses in a Super Decathlon and Extra 300L to help pilots at varying skill levels to fly more confidently and safely. In addition, she began serving as an honorary warden with Kenya's Wildlife Service in 2001, helping Kenyan pilots to improve pilot safety in their low-altitude poacher surveillance flights. Wagstaff still flies about 300 hours every year and has logged more than 12,000 hours of flight time in her career.

At this point in her life, Wagstaff has earned a mountain of aviation awards and been inducted into numerous aviation Halls of Fame, including Arizona Aviation Hall of Fame (1991), Women in Aviation International (WAI) Pioneer Hall of Fame (1997), National Aviation Hall of Fame (2004), International Aerobatic Club Hall of Fame (2005), ICAS Foundation Airshow Hall of Fame (2006), and International Aerospace Hall of Fame (2007). Patty has nothing left to prove.

Yet Wagstaff continues to thrill crowds at air shows across the globe and firmly believes that these performances provide important positive opportunities for the public to become exposed to and interested in aviation. She wrote that her "greatest joy as an air show pilot is inspiring children and having them respond to me. You never know when you will inspire one person with the desire to learn to fly or at least to appreciate aviation."

Although she never set out to be a role model, Patty recognizes that many admire her accomplishments and hopes that more women enter the field of aerobatic flying. In May 2023, Patty established the Patty Wagstaff Aviation Foundation, Inc., a nonprofit organization aimed at advancing and developing budding pilots for careers in aeronautics and promoting aviation safety and airmanship skills. Through her foundation, she plans to help students, regardless of age or gender, to enroll in upset training courses at their selected flight school in order to improve their competency and safety as pilots. Her stunning record of aerobatic achievements and her newly formed foundation will serve as lasting testimonials to Patty Wagstaff's legacy as a trailblazing aerobatic pilot.

"What I treasure most of all, though, are the quiet moments in the middle of the night, as we fly among the stars."

—Capt. Linda Pfeiffer Pauwels

(March 10, 1963–)

CHAPTER 12

CAPT. LINDA PFEIFFER PAUWELS
A Latina Pilot Marks Firsts in the Cockpit and in Poetry

CAPT. LINDA PAUWELS FACED HER FIRST IN-FLIGHT EMERGENCY
before she was ever born. Her parents, Jerzy "Jorge" Pfeiffer, a Polish-
born naturalized Argentinian citizen, who spoke six different languages, and Mabel Gaspard Pfeiffer, an Argentinian schoolteacher,
loved to travel and explore new places and cultures. In 1962, the adventurous couple self-financed a trip to Texas and Oklahoma to promote
the beauty and industry of their home country of Argentina. Newspaper, television, and radio interviews reported excitedly about their visit,
an unusual outreach effort from Latin Americans in that era. Her dad
brought back a cowboy hat to mark the trip. On their return flight to
Buenos Aires, the airplane experienced a serious mechanical issue and
passengers were ordered to brace for an emergency landing in Panama
on a foamed runway. At the time of the incident, Mabel was six months
pregnant with her first child, Linda.

Jorge's unexpected death at age thirty-nine left Mabel struggling to
support her two young children, six-year-old Linda and two-year-old
Walter. In hopes of better economic opportunities, Mabel relocated her
young family to Miami in 1970. Unable to find a teaching position, the
single mother worked two jobs to try to make ends meet, reluctantly
sending her children back to Argentina to live with different relatives at

various times. The long periods of separation from her mother were very stressful and painful for Linda during her childhood.

Yet Linda's maternal grandparents, Francisca Rodriguez and Carlos Gaspard, unable to complete sixth grade, ardently encouraged education for family members. Linda also credited her paternal grandmother, Tamara Stylinska, a survivor of the Auschwitz concentration camp, and her paternal grandfather, Polish Army Gen. Franciszek Edward "Radwan" Pfeiffer, a decorated hero of the Warsaw Uprising of 1944, for her grit and "warrior soul." Her early hardships and family influences instilled in her a lifelong thirst for learning and a spirit of perseverance.

A stellar student fluent in Spanish, English, and French, Linda initially thought about going into medicine and began studying for the medical school entrance exams in Argentina. At age sixteen, she traveled to Miami, where her mother held an agent's position with traffic and operations for Transportes Aereos Centro Americanos (TACA) Airlines. Fascinated by the airport environment, Linda fibbed about her age, claiming to be seventeen, and nabbed a summer job at Wardair Canada, a privately owned Canadian airline. With her French-language skills, Linda's role required her to deliver flight plans from a teletype to waiting pilots in the cockpit. "It was a 747, and as I was looking at the cockpit, I just thought this is the most amazing thing, and I want to do this," she remembered.

But her newly discovered interest in flying faced a lot of naysayers who doubted this choice for a teenager with no piloting background and few financial resources and the limited opportunities for women in aviation. Yet her persistence and drive took these discouraging words as a challenge to strive for her goal. Flight school tuition was far too expensive, so Linda saved her money to rent single-engine planes. She paid an independent instructor to teach her how to fly at Opa Locka Airport, an airfield originally founded by aviation pioneer Glenn Curtiss in the 1920s. At age sixteen, she soloed, and she earned her private pilot's license by age seventeen. The day she passed her flight exam, Linda met another flight instructor and pilot, Frederick Pauwels, who conversed with her in French. They married the following year in June 1981 with a honeymoon trip transporting a small plane from Florida to Chile. Yet a bad economy for aviation led Frederick to take a manager's position at a concrete plant in Martinique for two years, placing Linda's aviation plans on a temporary hold.

Returning to Miami in 1983, Linda received a scholarship to attend Miami Dade College, earning her associate in science degree as a professional pilot and flight engineer in 1985. While attending school, she worked two jobs while Frederick flew for commuter carriers and then non-scheduled cargo carriers. She then trained for a pilot position with commuter carrier Air New Orleans, but she never got to fly with the airline when it lost its financing for new aircraft.

Disappointed, Linda persisted in her efforts to find a piloting role. She learned from a fellow male pilot, with similar qualifications, that Southern Air Transport (SAT), a cargo carrier with civilian and military contracts, was hiring. Sending in her resume, Pauwels reached out to SAT about an interview. A Latina secretary for SAT's director of operations warned her that the cargo carrier would not hire women pilots. Undaunted, Linda promised "to come down to your office and sit on your doorstep until I get an interview."

Her persistence paid off when SAT relented and granted her an interview a few days later. Within three weeks, SAT hired her as a co-pilot on a civilian version of Lockheed's C-130 military aircraft. At age twenty-two, Pauwels became the first female pilot in SAT's nearly forty-year history as a commercial cargo carrier. For three years, her piloting duties for SAT took her across the globe for extended periods of time, including lengthy trips to Europe, Africa, and South America. "All of a sudden, you find yourself flying over the Tower of Pisa and you can't believe it," she declared. Pauwels continued to log about seventy hours every month for SAT, including flights on 160-ton Boeing 707s.

In 1988, SAT promoted Pauwels, at age twenty-five, making her the youngest female in the world to captain a Boeing 707 cargo jet for a commercial air service. Known for her wit, SAT colleagues lined up on the ramp to moon Linda after her promotion as she taxied by them in Atlanta, a funny gesture that made her feel a sense of true belonging. Pauwels took great pride in her work, especially United Nations' humanitarian missions, where she delivered supplies for earthquake-ravaged

Ecuador or blankets to children in Ethiopia. However, prolonged global flights were not conducive to her hopes of starting a family, so she began to apply to domestic airlines.

That same year, Linda made a move to American Airlines (American), which needed more pilots after purchasing Central and South American routes out of Miami International Airport (MIA) from Eastern Airlines. She started as a flight engineer for Boeing 727s, monitoring the engines, fluid levels, and mechanical systems in the cockpit during flights. A year later, Pauwels became the first female flight engineer check airman, responsible for training, evaluating, and supervising American's probationary flight engineers at MIA. Her brother, Walter, also became a pilot for American, and her mother, Mabel, continued to work at MIA into her eighties.

As she progressed through the ranks at American, Pauwels was elevated to first officer, adding the Airbus A-300 and Boeing 757, 767, and 777 to her repertoire of aircraft. Linda took on each new aircraft with a mix of excitement and confidence. In discussing her sensation of flying, Pauwels believes that "the pilot becomes one with the machine. . . . A unitive experience, a mystical feeling. You lose yourself in a way."

While Linda continued at American, Frederick landed a pilot position with Japan Airlines in 1993. Despite the scheduling challenges of a two-pilot marriage, the Pauwels welcomed their first child, Nathalie, in 1992 and a son, Patrick, in 1994. Under FAA regulations, Linda was not allowed to fly during her first pregnancy, but the rules had changed to allow her to fly for the first six months during her second pregnancy. She recalled a funny encounter after having just returned from her first maternity leave and still nursing. On a flight to Bogota from Miami, Pauwels was being requalified to pilot an Airbus A-300. When Linda landed at Bogota, she advised the check airman evaluating her piloting skills that she needed to excuse herself to go pump. Puzzled, he asked her about what was wrong with the pump. Was there a malfunction in the hydraulic pump? Linda quelled his safety concerns and explained that as a new mother she needed to pump breast milk. The check airman laughed at his own mistaken understanding, realizing that more women pilots meant a need to keep pace with changing pilot concerns.

Pauwels became the first Latina captain for American, its first female check airman, and an FAA-designated examiner on American's initial Boeing 787s. (*Photo by Stephen Gould/CC BY-SA 4.0*)

By 2000, she became the first Latina captain for American, piloting a McDonnell Douglas MD-80. She would later serve as a captain on Airbus A-320s and Boeing B-787 Dreamliners. In one memorable instance, she accompanied another pilot to pick up a brand-new Boeing 787. She felt a tremendous sense of responsibility in signing for the delivery of a $270 million-plus aircraft on behalf of American. Pauwels remembered breathing in its new airplane smell as they flew the jet on its maiden voyage.

Based in California in the early 2000s, she also became active with the Allied Pilots Association (APA), the collective bargaining organization for American's unionized pilots, and served on various national committees. As a member of the APA's Communications Committee, she received media training and became one of the official spokespersons for the APA, starting in 2001. Then the terrorist attacks on 9/11 unexpectedly threw Pauwels into the spotlight. As the only female APA spokesperson, she responded to a barrage of media requests and underwent a gauntlet of live interviews about pilot safety and security issues to educate a deeply shaken public. During this intense period of media scrutiny, Pauwels represented her community of pilots in a calm, authoritative manner.

Contrary to her own sense of humility, Pauwels's accomplishments as a Latina pilot started to become better recognized in the wake of her APA appearances promoting airline safety. Both *Hispanic Business Magazine* and *Hispanic Magazine* placed her on their lists of the 100 Most Influential Latinas in the nation. The US Department of Transportation invited her to be its keynote speaker at its Hispanic Heritage Month Observance opening ceremony in Washington, D.C., in September 2002. She spoke eloquently about her family roots, her ability to overcome obstacles, and the importance of the nation unifying to build a stronger and more secure air transportation network after the 9/11 tragedies.

A couple of months after her speech, US Representative Loretta Sanchez of California entered a tribute to Pauwels into the Congressional Record on November 14, 2002, extolling her many firsts in aviation, her role as the only woman spokesperson for the APA, her dedication to safer air travel, and her efforts to promote women and Hispanics in aviation. In addition, Sanchez noted Pauwels's piloting excellence after a successful emergency landing of a Los Angeles-to-Chicago flight in Sioux City, Iowa, after engine failure, one of two that Pauwels had expertly handled during her career. The *Orange County Register* also selected Pauwels to write their first aviation column, From the Cockpit, published in the paper's travel section to review aviation issues of public interest and to answer reader questions about aviation.

With a thirst for learning, Linda returned to her studies and earned a bachelor's of science degree in professional aeronautics and a certificate in aviation safety from Embry-Riddle Aeronautical University (ERAU) in Daytona Beach, Florida, in 2004. Her alma mater, Miami Dade College, then inducted her into their Hall of Fame in 2005 for her pioneering efforts in transportation. Yet her high-flying career almost came to a grinding halt when health issues upended her medical certification to fly and placed her on medical leave. Linda wondered if she would ever fly again, so she began considering alternatives after more than twenty years as a pilot.

Not content to sit around while recuperating, Pauwels considered her many years training and evaluating her peers and pursued a master's degree in education from Azusa Pacific University. Her 2006 master's thesis explored the mind-body connection and addressed the impacts of a yoga-based physical education program on elementary schoolchildren's health and behaviors. She received a fellowship at the University of Southern California in health journalism and enrolled in a PhD program at ERAU focusing on the benefits of meditation and other holistic practices to reduce pilot job stress. Pauwels noted that "[i]t is important, especially in high stress professions, that you balance out some of the rigors of the profession with something else." Fortunately, her own wellness rebounded and she returned to flying.

Yet she was not done making aviation history. In 2015, she attained another historic mark as the first Latina check airman on the Airbus A-320 at MIA for nearly two years. As a check airman, she served as an experienced aircraft pilot who evaluates and qualifies other commercial pilots on that particular aircraft, either in the cockpit or on a flight simulator. Pauwels would then relocate to the Dallas–Fort Worth area to act as the first female check airman and an FAA-designated examiner for pilots on the initial cadre of Boeing 787s, continuing in that role for seven years. Yet Linda maintained a second residence in the Miami area as her husband, Frederick, retired from Japan Airlines, served as a flight instructor for Atlas Air.

Aside from making aviation history once more in 2015, that year also marked Linda's creation of a new discussion thread, "Morning Haiku," on the APA's forum for American pilots. Having long researched and studied the mind-body connection, Pauwels thought that the discussion board could use a dose of poetry for pilots who work under regimented, stressful conditions. She contended that "[p]ilots live in a world of structure where we fly by the rules. But poetry deconstructs some of that rigidity." At first, she received some pushback from pilots who complained about poetry being posted on a workplace forum, while others enjoyed reading the poems. The discussion thread gained increased interest and participation with other pilots contributing some of their favorites throughout the years, from medieval times to contemporary poems.

Having always loved language and writing, Linda began to secretly pen poetry focusing on haiku for its ability to convey a depth of information and meaning in so few words, likening it to the communication style of pilots in the cockpit. She posted her poems on the discussion board, and other pilots contributed their original works too. She also wrote essays about her experiences as a Latina pilot, or "pilotina," for *Latinas in Aviation* in 2020 and *Today's Inspired Latinas Volume IX: Life Stories of Success in the Face of Adversity* in 2021. Latina pilots comprise only about 1 percent of the estimated 7 percent of female pilots in the United States. Pauwels hoped her essays and promotion of these books would encourage other Hispanic women to seek out careers in aviation.

When COVID struck, many of Pauwels's peers endured lengthy furloughs as air travel plummeted. Concerned about the financial stress on her fellow pilots, Linda decided to curate five years of posted poetry from the discussion thread into a book and invite the children of pilots, many of whom were homebound due to the pandemic, to draw art to accompany the poems. Working quickly, Linda gathered together the materials in just a few weeks.

Beyond Haiku: Pilots Write Poetry, a collection of poems from more than forty American pilots and accompanying artwork from pilots' children, aged six to seventeen, was published in December 2020. "This book deconstructs some of that rigidity and allows the people on the other side of the cockpit doors to see that there is a softer side to the men and women who fly," Pauwels said. The book was the first of its kind and more than a thousand dollars in proceeds were donated to the APA's Emergency Relief and Scholarship Fund to aid pilots and their families impacted by the pandemic.

In the wake of the poetry book, Linda felt honored to be invited to participate as a poet-in-residence with ESCRIBE AQUÍ/Write Here, The Betsy Hotel's 7th Annual Celebration of IberoAmerican Artists in Miami Beach in August 2021. The Betsy's Writers Room previously hosted more than a thousand artists and creatives, including Poet Laureates, MacArthur Genius Winners, and National Book Award winners. Now Pauwels, a pilot and poet, found herself in a new community of exceptional artists and writers.

The success of Pauwels's first book led to expanding the call for haikus and other short poems in a second collection, entitled *Beyond Haiku: Women Pilots Write Poetry*, addressing six distinct themes. Pauwels reached out to a wide range of pilot groups, including The Ninety-Nines, Women in Aviation International, and ISA+21. Enthusiastic about this new collaboration, Linda also contacted the American Society of Aviation Artists for assistance on the artwork and to review contributions from teen artists for the book.

With her journalistic training and research skills, Pauwels wondered if female pilots from other eras had written poetry. She was shocked to find an academic paper about Amelia Earhart's dream of becoming a writer, having drafted short stories and poems before her aviation fame. Very private about her creative writing, only one poem, *Courage*, was published during her lifetime without her consent. Linda contacted Professor Sammie Morris, Purdue University's head of Archives and Special Collections and director of its Virginia Kelly Karnes Research Center, about Earhart's unpublished poetry in a collection of her papers donated to Purdue. Earhart served as a visiting faculty member for aeronautical engineering and

135

Purdue permitted eight of Earhart's poems, including five unpublished ones, to appear in Pauwels's second poetry collection, *Beyond Haiku: Women Pilots Write Poetry.* (*Photo by Harris and Ewing, Library of Congress, LC-DIG-hec-40747*)

career counselor for female students at Purdue in 1935. Decades after her tragic death, several of Earhart's poems appeared in academic journals, but her works had not been distributed to a broader public audience.

To Pauwels's surprise, the Purdue Research Foundation agreed to allow eight of Earhart's poems, five of which had never been published, to appear in the book. Pauwels also garnered permissions from the Smithsonian's National Air and Space Museum for a poem from 1936 Bendix Trophy Race champion Louise Thaden and from the University of Texas in Dallas for WWII poems collected in the personal scrapbook of Women's Auxiliary Ferrying Squadron (WAFS) pilot Delphine Bohn. Upon a request from Professor Morris, Linda was honored to agree to gift her papers to Purdue's archives for her groundbreaking role in aviation history and poetry.

Honoring female aviation pioneers, Pauwels would captain an all-female flight crew to mark International Women's Day in March 2021.

She followed in the footsteps of American's first female captain, Beverley Bass, who led the first all-female flight crew in 1986. The event was further barrier-breaking when the ground crew, including check-in agents, cargo personnel, and air traffic control, along with TSA officers and firefighters, all women, conducted a water cannon salute. Pauwels expressed her gratitude to all of the women who had "broken barriers in aviation, from Beverley Bass to Willa Brown and Bonnie Tiburzi, forging a path for me and my colleagues at American. We want young women and girls who aspire to become aviators or work in the airline industry to know their dream is within reach, and that gender, race and ethnicity isn't a barrier."

In December 2021, the poetry of fifty-eight female pilots from ten countries and illustrations from artists from ten nations was published in the second *Beyond Haiku* book. Aware of the high costs of flight training and having benefited from a college scholarship years before, Pauwels directed the proceeds of the second book to scholarships for young women interested in aviation. The Girl Scouts of Tropical Florida requested a thousand copies to inspire the next generation of female pilots.

In May 2023, Pauwels returned to line flying in her captain's role and continues to balance her piloting and family life in Texas and Florida along with her creative writing and editing of pilot poetry and stories. She co-edited a collection of aviation short stories, *Beyond Haiku: Pilot Stories*, and is planning two more pilot poetry books, one from military pilots and another from pilots in different stages of their career. With her love of languages, Linda has also studied Sanskrit and Mandarin as American expands its flights into China.

Her advice to young people wondering about a future in aviation is not to give in to self-doubt. "If you see yourself doing this, don't talk yourself out of it. If it's something that appeals to you, if it's something that you think would be extremely cool . . . Don't give in to the 'buts.' . . . Don't limit yourself. Look at the possibilities out there."

Living up to her own recommendation, Capt. Linda Pauwels was not afraid to take risks and prevailed over personal and economic hardships to pursue her dreams and to become both a groundbreaking Latina pilot and poet who flies among the stars.

"There I was as a five-year-old, looking up at these big, bad F-4s just making noise and just looking awesome. I told my mom, 'I want to do that someday.'"

—Lt. Col. Christine Mau Kelley (ret. USAF)

(February 26, 1975–)

CHAPTER 13

LT. COL. CHRISTINE MAU
KELLEY (RET. USAF)
Air Force Pilot Zooms into Aviation History in Fighter Jets

WHEN YOU'RE FIVE YEARS OLD, YOU DO NOT THINK IN TERMS OF LIMITS. As a child, Christine Callahan loved watching F-4 fighter jets zooming overhead from nearby Marine Corps Air Station El Toro in California. She wanted to fly fighter jets, not your typical childhood goal. Perhaps her interest in fighter jets came baked into her family genes. Her father, a commercial pilot for Continental Airlines, served as a C-130 pilot in the Air Force for seven years during the Vietnam War and then another thirteen years with the California Air National Guard. During World War II, her maternal grandfather, Willis Miller, piloted a B-24 bomber over Nazi Germany and occupied France and Holland. Yet her mother cautioned Christine that women could not be fighter pilots, at least not yet.

At age eleven, her viewing of the 1986 film *Top Gun* heightened her desire to become a fighter pilot. Her dream remained unrealistic as US military policy barred women from flying combat aircraft. But Christine, who considered herself to be "determined and super stubborn," was not easily deterred from her goal. She possessed a strong competitive streak and excelled in gymnastics, volleyball, and softball and made good grades in her junior high and high school studies. In her high school research on female pilots and fighter aircraft, she discovered the stories of the Women's Airforce Service Pilots (WASPs).

SHE SOARS

During World War II, the WASPs ferried 12,650 aircraft of seventy-seven different types of military planes, including about 50 percent of all of the military's fighter planes. From November 1942 through December 1944, 1,074 female pilots served in the WASPs at more than 100 military bases, including Eglin Army Air Base (Niceville), Buckingham Army Air Field (Fort Myers), Marianna Army Air Base (Marianna), and Tyndall Army Air Base (Panama City) in Florida. Yet these female pilots were considered civilian employees even though they underwent military-style training, discipline, and living conditions. Thirty-eight WASPs lost their lives carrying out their wartime duties. When the WASPs disbanded, those women pilots fought for more than three decades for veteran's status, which was finally granted in 1977.

The WASPs' history inspired Christine as she pursued her fighter pilot goal. As a junior in high school, she decided to pursue a college education at the US Air Force Academy, even though she had never flown a plane. In January 1993, Christine received an appointment to the academy. Her timing was excellent as the biggest barrier to her dream of becoming a fighter pilot was about to be lifted.

After congressional approval and guidance from a presidential commission, Secretary of Defense Les Aspin charged all military service branches with opening combat aviation positions to qualified women. On April 28, 1993, Gen. Merrill A. McPeak, chief of staff of the US Air Force, directed that women were now eligible to fly any Air Force aircraft.

When Mau began Basic Cadet Training in June 1993, the long-held barrier to female fighter pilots no longer existed. In July 1993, Lt. Jeanne Marie Leavitt became the first woman to train as a US Air Force fighter pilot, successfully completing her training in an F-15E Strike Eagle in 1994. This change in policy recognized an already well-established fact—the WASPs had proven their gender's ability to pilot military aircraft more than fifty years earlier. Ultimately, Lt. Leavitt rose to the rank of major general, and Mau later considered her to be both a mentor and friend.

At the academy, Christine had a few opportunities to fly gliders, soloing in a glider at age nineteen, and T-3A Firefly trainers. After four years, Christine graduated in 1997 with a bachelor of science in biology and aerospace physiology and was commissioned as a second lieutenant.

Actual pilot training became an option for cadets only after graduating from the academy. Mau would have to pass a rigorous pilot screening process to be accepted into Undergraduate Pilot Training (UPT).

All academy applicants had to jump through various hoops to qualify for UPT. Each candidate had to meet strict medical requirements, such as possessing excellent overall health, 20/20 vision, certain height and weight minimums, and acceptable depth perception scores. Christine found the depth perception test to be very challenging, but she passed it each time. Candidates also had to demonstrate an aptitude for piloting an airplane, a Slingsby T-3A Firefly, and show piloting promise through an evaluation of academic, military, and athletic standards as well as successful completion of the Air Force Officer Qualifying Test (AFOQT).

Although women could now train on combat aircraft, many female applicants could not meet certain height and weight minimums. With cockpits engineered for the average man's height, pilot applicants were required to be between five feet, four inches to six feet, six inches with a sitting height of thirty-four to forty inches. Approximately 44 percent of the US female population aged in their twenties did not qualify to become pilots based on height alone. Pilot candidates were also required to meet certain weight standards, designed primarily for males in the 5th to 95th percentile weight range, to be able to fly aircraft with ejection seats. Some candidates applied for weight waivers, while others received them without their knowledge. Thus, Mau and a small cadre of women became eligible for pilot training.

After completing the rigorous screening process, Christine's hard work and determination paid off. With her high total screening score, she chose Euro-NATO Joint Jet Pilot Training (ENJJPT) at Sheppard Air Force Base because of its focus on training fighter pilots. Six months after graduating from the academy, she became only one of four females in a training program of more than three hundred male pilots. It was hard not to stick out in her group. But she brushed off the remarks of naysayers and continued her laser focus on her pilot training.

At pilot training, some of her classmates had previously earned private pilot licenses or had achieved their instructor ratings. These peers possessed a great deal of experience and confidence in their flying abilities

Determined from a young age to become a fighter pilot, Mau stands before an
F-35A Lightning II at Eglin Air Force Base, Florida, in 2017. (*US Air Force photo by
Staff Sgt. Peter Thompson*)

while Christine had to work intensely at learning piloting basics. At age
twenty-three, Mau made her first powered solo flight in a twin-engine
Cessna T-37 Tweet jet, the Air Force's primary training aircraft, and then
trained in T-38s for another six months.

Her pilot training instructors regularly evaluated each student's
piloting skills under exacting standards. Like any student, Mau had her
good days and bad ones, but she kept her focus and determination on
achieving her goal. "I put on my horse blinders and just kept pushing
through," she said. "My instructors critiqued everything, from the way I
walked to the plane to the way I spoke on the radio. You had to have thick
skin to get through pilot training."

Over time, she gained confidence in her skills and excelled in her
pilot training from 1998 to 1999. It was not until graduation that Christine found out that she ranked as number two overall in her class.

Having performed so well at ENJJPT, Mau graduated as a distinguished graduate, enabling her to receive further training on her top

choice of aircraft, the F-15E Strike Eagle. She considered the F-15E to be "the most impressive airplane at that time." The eight-month F-15E training course became her first experience flying combat jets and she found it to be both fun and difficult. "Every minute that you're airborne is challenging and demanding and requires a lot of your attention and focus. I love that challenge," she said.

In 2000, Christine became the third woman assigned to the 492nd Fighter Squadron at RAF Lakenheath, England. From that base, she initially deployed to Kuwait and participated in Operation Southern Watch, and then from Turkey for Operation Northern Watch in Iraq, combat missions to patrol and enforce no-fly zones. Mau, call sign "Grinder," found some pushback based on her gender at her first operational assignment. She noted that "[t]here was a lot of resistance to some of the cultural changes that came from having women in combat squadrons." Despite her combat experiences, a few "old dinosaurs" in her first operational unit made it a point to tell her that she would never truly become a fighter pilot because of her gender.

Yet she thought back to the limitations placed on the WASPs in the 1940s. Mau was grateful for the breadth of her opportunities in the Air Force and to the "WASPs for their sacrifice and service during World War II that was completely devalued, underappreciated and swept under a rug at the end of the war. . . . These ladies put up with a lot." Aware of the headwinds faced by her predecessors, Mau let her grit and performance of her pilot duties speak for themselves.

After serving three years at Lakenheath, Mau was assigned to Seymour Johnson Air Force Base in North Carolina. At that base, she played a pivotal role in instructing new F-15E pilots and weapon systems officers and providing supplemental support to students having difficulties in achieving positive training outcomes. As a F-15E instructor pilot, Mau discovered she had a real knack for teaching. "I love instructing students. It's a passion of mine," she said. Christine would carry that passion for teaching throughout her twenty years in the Air Force and into her post-retirement career.

While in the Air Force, Mau married and gave birth to two daughters. "No one really knows what to do with a pregnant fighter pilot," she quipped. Grounded during her pregnancies due to safety concerns, Mau lost no time in being productive, securing non-flying director positions and earning a master's of aeronautical science and aviation management from Embry-Riddle Aeronautical University in 2009 with a perfect 4.0 grade point average (GPA) and a master's of military operational art and science studies from the USAF Air Command and Staff College with a 3.88 GPA. Like any new parent, Mau relied upon a strong support network of family and friends to help balance her parenting role with her demanding job.

The mother of two would then take on a new assignment at Mountain Home Air Force Base in Idaho. Her time at that base led to a deployment in Afghanistan for Operation Enduring Freedom where Mau would further make her mark in aviation history. In March 2011, then Maj. Mau participated in the first all-female combat mission. The women planned the mission, prepared the aircraft, launched the flight, and piloted the jets in support of troops under fire in the Kunar Valley.

Leading the all-female team, Mau reflected that "[i]t was the coolest, most surreal experience. I kind of felt like the WASPs may have felt during World War II." Their mission call sign was "Dudette 07," playing off the normal F-15E combat call sign of "Dude." Although coinciding with Women's History Month, some crew members did not realize that fact until after the mission was completed. The all-female team was surprised at the level of national and international news coverage. Some were excited about a media light being shown on the efforts of female Air Force members, while Mau considered the mission part of just doing her job. Christine recognized that "[f]lying is a great equalizer. The plane doesn't know or care about your gender as a pilot, nor do the ground troops who need your support. You have to perform."

To Mau, her most memorable combat sortie involved strikes on the key leadership of the Haqqani terrorist network and the recovery of a large supply of US military weapons and uniforms. She appreciated the depth of cohesive teamwork of ground fighters, drone pilots, and four F-15E aircrew in accomplishing the mission.

After her deployment to Afghanistan, Christine returned to Mountain Home Air Force Base as an instructor, including training Singaporean aircrews on how to fly their nation's F-15SG fighter jets. Mau then moved into a new role as a squadron commander for the 4th

In 2013, Lt. Col. Mau became the first and only female F-35 pilot in the world. (*US Air Force photo by Staff Sgt. Peter Thompson*)

Operations Support Squadron at Seymour Johnson Air Force Base. Less than 2 percent of Air Force officers are ever selected to serve as squadron commanders, and Mau joined that elite group in 2013. In her new commander position, she supervised nearly three hundred Air Force personnel, oversaw daily base operations and joint exercises, and managed a $58 million construction and repair budget.

But Mau was not quite done with making aviation history yet. In summer 2015, Christine was chosen as the first female F-35 Lightning II pilot as well as deputy commander of the 33rd Operations Group at Eglin Air Force Base in the Florida Panhandle. The F-35 jet possesses impressive speed and altitude capabilities along with advanced sensors and stealth technologies. Christine would be the first woman of eighty-eight pilots trained in the new sophisticated jet from the Air Force, Navy, Marine Corps, and allied forces.

For nearly sixteen years, Mau had flown the two-seater F-15E, and now she began her training transition to the single-seater F-35. She found the dome-shaped flight simulator for the F-35 truly realistic, completing fourteen simulators before stepping into the cockpit on May 7, 2015. Mau stated that "[i]t wasn't until I was taxiing to the runway that it really struck me that I was on my own in the jet. It felt great to get airborne. The jet flies like a dream."

Used to the chatter of the two-seater F-15E, Christine grew accustomed to hearing mainly the sound of her own breathing in the F-35 cockpit. "For a while, that was my happy place. I would just listen to myself breathe," said Mau. One of her favorite moments in the F-35 involved a large force exercise where she could fully appreciate the jet's unique power and capabilities compared to other military aircraft. Excelling in her F-35 piloting skills, Mau once again became the teacher, instructing new pilots on the jet's cutting-edge capabilities. For about two years, Mau served as the world's only female F-35 pilot.

In January 2017, the National Aeronautic Association (NAA) awarded its 2016 Katherine and Marjorie Stinson Trophy to the much-decorated Lt. Col. Mau. The Stinson sisters were among the first group of certified female pilots in the United States, broke numerous aviation records, and established a flying school in Texas to train American and foreign pilots for pilot licenses. Named after the pioneering aviation sisters, the award honors a living person who has shown "an outstanding and enduring contribution to the role of women in the field of aviation, aeronautics, space, or related sciences." The selection committee pointed to Mau's extensive Air Force career as a groundbreaking pilot and fighter jet instructor for choosing her to receive this prestigious aviation award.

Nearing retirement, Mau had successfully completed ten base assignments and five deployments, flying more than 2,500 hours, including 500 combat hours, in more than five different aircraft in her twenty-year career. "Retiring makes me a little emotional," said Mau. "Flying fighters is all I ever wanted to do. Every day I kind of pinch myself when I realize this is my job. I was flying home the other day and looked over my shoulder and said to myself 'yeah, this is awesome.'"

After retiring in 2017, her passion for flying and teaching continues in her new civilian role as a Lockheed Martin F-35 Training Instructor at the Academic Training Center (ATC) at Eglin Air Force Base. She hopes to see more opportunities for women and minorities as military pilots. "I want the Air Force to have the best pilots, bottom line. In order to get the best pilots, we need to recruit the best people. If we want to come up with the best solutions to problems and continue to be an innovative force, we need to have people who think differently and look at problems differently," said Mau.

Recently remarried in 2023, Christine Kelley continues to balance life as a wife, a mother of two teenaged girls, an instructor, and her active support for expanded opportunities in aviation. By both her life example and advocacy, she wants to inspire more young people to pursue a career in aviation. She serves as a guest speaker at aviation conferences, WASPs reunions, and local schools to promote aviation careers to young people.

Kelley's advice to would-be pilots boils down to three key points: "grow thick skin, ignore those that don't support you, and persevere." She notes that "[f]eedback hurts sometimes, and in the flying business, you will always get feedback. So, growing thick skin will allow you to accept, process, and implement feedback to make you a better pilot." Christine adds that "[t]here will always be haters and naysayers in life. It doesn't matter what field you are in. They are usually small-minded, jealous, or bigoted people. Therefore, it's imperative to learn to ignore them. Find people who support you; people who will mentor and encourage you." Lastly, she advises future pilots that "[t]he perseverance piece is just a fancy term for grit, and a synonym for the saying, 'never give up!' You will absolutely fail at some things in life. But without those failures, you will never achieve greatness. . . . As you work through these challenges and requirements, your confidence in yourself will grow."

Christine Kelley is living proof of the advice she offers to future pilots. Through her groundbreaking efforts, she has earned her place as a trailblazing female pilot, having flown some of the world's most sophisticated combat jets. Yet she also owns and enjoys flying general aviation airplanes to transport her family and friends or just for fun. She even checked a big item off her personal bucket list, flying one of the old war birds, a North American P-51 Mustang, used extensively during World War II—a tip of her wings to the sacrifices and wartime service of her grandad and the pioneering WASPs.

"Perhaps many generations from now, pilots will be training to go places in the Milky Way galaxy, flying in ships yet to be imagined."

—Col. Eileen Collins (ret. USAF)
(November 19, 1956–)

CHAPTER 14

COL. EILEEN COLLINS (RET. USAF)

Don't All Moms Fly the Space Shuttle?

ONE OF AMELIA'S SCARVES. FEMALE ENDURANCE CHAMP BOBBI TROUT'S pilot's license, signed by Orville Wright. A WASPs' wings pin. Mementos from the unheralded Mercury 13. Lt. Col. Collins brought those keepsakes aboard *Discovery* as it roared off the launchpad at the Kennedy Space Center (KSC) in Florida, the sixty-seventh flight of the space shuttle program. The intense g-forces of acceleration pressed down on Eileen Collins nearly as much as the weight of history from decades of pioneering female pilots who paved the way for her in this moment.

Grateful to her predecessors, Eileen personally invited the eleven surviving Mercury 13 members, who nicknamed themselves the First Lady Astronaut Trainees (FLATs) in the 1960s, to the groundbreaking launch. Seven of the FLATs witnessed her flight into the history books as the first female pilot of NASA's space shuttle program, more than thirty years after their space hopes were dashed. As *Discovery* streaked into orbit, the soft-spoken Collins felt that she carried forward not only their dreams, but the aspirations of all women pilots trying to break barriers. She wrote that "[c]urrent and future women pilots are counting on me to do a perfect job up here."

That's a lot of pressure and responsibility to place on anyone's shoulders. Yet Eileen had grown accustomed to overcoming a myriad of challenges in her long climb to reach this point. The second of four children of James Collins, a city surveyor, and Rose Marie O'Hara, a police department typist, Eileen grew up in subsidized housing in the economically struggling city of Elmira, New York. Her hometown, dubbed the "Soaring Capital of America," drew glider pilots for takeoffs from its windswept ridges looming more than eight hundred feet above the Chemung Valley. For inexpensive entertainment, Eileen's family watched quiet gliders climbing from Harris Hill or noisy light planes taking off and landing at Elmira Corning Regional Airport.

A shy child, Eileen worked with a speech therapist at her Catholic school to overcome a debilitating stutter. As early as the fourth grade, she daydreamed about space travel after watching reruns of the *Buck Rogers* television series. An avid reader, Collins also became fascinated with the Gemini astronauts and viewed them as her aspirational heroes, unaware that women were then barred from space flight. Young Eileen fancied the idea of growing up "to be a lady astronaut . . . As my backup plan, if I couldn't be an astronaut, I would marry one."

In her early teens, she discovered the aviation section of her local library, where her mother often took her four children. Excelling in math and science at school, she ate up any book that dealt with pilots and planes, especially the exploits of military fliers in World Wars I and II and the daring exploits of aviation pioneers, such as Charles Lindbergh, Amelia Earhart, and Jackie Cochran. She noted that "[m]y mom sowed the seeds of my lifelong passion for flight just by taking me to the library." Eileen also credited her outgoing mother for "the explorer gene," since she was often taking her kids to see new places, such as Niagara Falls and other state parks.

In her senior year of high school, Eileen made an appointment with a local recruiter even though her dad strongly objected to her plans to join the Air Force. When the recruiter did not show up, she left dejected and uncertain about her future. But Collins later realized it was a lucky break, since only officers with bachelor's degrees were trained to fly, with astronaut pilots drawn primarily from those ranks.

She set out on a new path, attending Corning Community College. Eileen stitched together grants, a loan, and savings from various part-time jobs to pay her tuition, including waiting tables at a pizza joint, serving as a physical therapy aide at a hospital, and selling various sporting and consumer goods at a catalog showroom. She continued to devour any magazine article or book on aviation, from pilot biographies to airplane design, especially the fighter jets of the 1950s, to military leadership and history, including the Women's Airforce Service Pilots (WASPs) who ferried planes during World War II.

A solid "B" student in high school, Collins became more focused on her college studies and earned an associate degree in math in May 1976. She knew her next step required obtaining a bachelor's degree, but money was tight. She applied for and received an Air Force ROTC scholarship to Syracuse University in September 1976. That same year, the Air Force announced that women could train as pilots for noncombat missions, with an inaugural cohort of ten female trainees. Eileen hoped this change in policy meant that she might one day become an Air Force pilot.

During her basic training in summer 1976, Collins loved the physical and mental challenges and won top academic honors in her cohort. On one of the cadet field trips, Collins sat for the first time in an airplane cockpit of an A-7 Corsair II. She soaked in the moment, smelled the pungent fuel and marveled at the switches and circuitry, wondering if she would ever be able to pilot such a plane. At a group trip to Reese Air Force Base in Lubbock, Texas, she reveled in her first flight in a light military trainer aircraft, a Cessna T-37 Tweet, with a flight instructor and got hooked on flying.

When the first female trainees earned their Air Force wings, Collins decided to take flying lessons the following summer to improve her chances of flight duty. With $1,000 in savings, she took private lessons in a two-seater Cessna 150 at Elmira-Corning Regional Airport, where she once gazed up at planes in her childhood. A quick study, Collins made her first solo flight at the age of twenty.

During her final college semester in 1978, she was originally destined for a computer engineer's role due to her bachelor of arts degree in mathematics and economics. But her ROTC department head nominated

Collins for one of the eight open slots nationwide for the next Air Force training round of female pilots. After passing the basic flight screening program, Collins was assigned to Undergraduate Pilot Training (UPT), one of four women in a class of forty trainees, at Vance Air Force Base, in Enid, Oklahoma. Female pilots were still a novelty and Collins drew quite a few stares in her flight suit at the base's grocery store. She learned of pushback from some pilots' wives not wanting female pilots on long flights with their husbands. Collins made it clear that she wasn't looking for a husband, exclaiming that she was "'married' to my plane!"

In her first week at the base, Eileen was excited to learn that the first potential group of NASA female astronauts were undergoing parachute training at the base, including Dr. Sally Ride, who made history as the first American woman in space in 1983. Eileen later bought a small home in Enid that backed onto a large wheat field. In the still darkness of the night, she took to exploring the stars above with two telescopes, learning about different constellations from astronomy magazines and books and enjoying being an amateur stargazer and a member of an astronomy book club.

Aside from classroom studies at Vance, Collins spent many practice hours in a flight simulator for Cessna T-37 and Northrup T-38 Talon jets, memorized checklists, and visualized flight options while seated in a chair with her eyes closed. Collins possessed the focus to be a good operational pilot and found it to be "an interesting combination of complete situational awareness of everything going on around you in this precise moment, while simultaneously thinking about what you are going to do next." After several months flying an actual jet with an instructor, Collins soloed in a T-37 jet for the first time in November 1978 at the age of twenty-two.

By March 1979, Collins was flying T-38 supersonic jets, the same aircraft NASA pilots trained on, capable of accelerating to more than 850 mph, faster than the speed of sound. She loved making cloverleaf loops in the jet with its precise right-angle turns. By the ending of her T-38 training, Eileen felt that she "was strapping the airplane onto *myself*, not strapping myself into the plane. The T-38 became an extension of *me*." With her skillful flying, she continued as a T-38 pilot and the base's first female T-38 instructor in March 1980. After three years of flying and teaching, Collins racked up more than a thousand hours in the T-38.

Although she hoped to fly fighter jets, the military's combat exclusion policy barred women from any kind of combat-related aircraft. Eileen reluctantly settled on her twenty-first choice for flight duty, serving as a co-pilot on a Lockheed C-141 Starlifter cargo-transport plane at Travis Air Force Base, California. That plane ended up being a much more challenging aircraft than she had initially expected, requiring her to lead and collaborate with a much larger and varied crew—valuable experience for any future NASA missions.

While flying the C-141, she also transported personnel and supplies and evacuated medical students from Grenada during Operation Urgent Fury in October 1983, earning combat awards despite the Air Force's combat exclusion policy. Eight months later, she was promoted to a command position as a C-141 pilot, flying relief missions in Central America and delivering humanitarian aid after natural disasters across the globe. No longer married only to her plane, Eileen met and dated fellow C-141 pilot and Air Force Academy graduate Pat Youngs while at Travis.

After seven years flying jets, Collins sought a new challenge and reached out to the Air Force Academy in Colorado Springs about math or science teaching positions. The academy agreed to bring her on as an assistant professor, paying for her to complete a master's degree program first. In eleven months, Collins completed a master's degree in operations research at Stanford University, applying mathematical and quantitative data analysis to decision-making, and she joined the academy's teaching staff in August 1986. Happily, Youngs received an appointment as the school's golf coach three weeks before Collins's arrival, and they married in 1987.

Serving as a math professor, Collins overcame her apprehension about public speaking and enjoyed training young cadets to use math and computer programming as problem-solving tools. When not in class, she trained student pilots on a Cessna T-41 Mescalero, a military adaptation of the civilian Cessna 172 Skyhawk. Yet still keeping her eyes on the NASA prize, Eileen completed a master's degree in space systems management from Webster University in 1989.

Collins applied twice to the Air Force Test Pilot School (TPS) but was not selected due to administrative service and assignment policies.

With her commanding officer approving a waiver, her third time was a charm as she was accepted into TPS, only the second female pilot in Air Force history to do so. Right on the heels of her acceptance into TPS, NASA issued a call for astronaut applications, the first time since June 1987. Collins worried that the NASA application process might distract from her current academy duties and her upcoming TPS training. Yet she decided it was now or never and sent in a stack of forms to NASA.

With little time to catch her breath, Eileen started her yearlong advanced training at Edwards Air Force Base, California, in June 1989. The highest-ranking officer in her entering class, Maj. Collins also became the first female class commander in TPS history, honing her leadership skills and learning to delegate duties to her peers.

Collins once again flew T-38s and added other jets to her resume, including Lockheed P-3 Orion turboprop surveillance aircraft, Northrop F-5 Tiger Fighter jets, and McDonnell Douglas F-4 Phantom II and General Dynamics F-16 Fighting Falcon supersonic jets. At TPS, she recognized the key differences between her prior role as an operational pilot and her new role as a test pilot. Based on a test pilot's creativity and evaluation of an airplane, she found that "test pilots *write* the rules for an aircraft. Operational pilots *follow* those rules."

Only four months into her TPS training, she was invited to interview with NASA at the Johnson Space Center (JSC) in Houston, Texas. She felt more excited than nervous to explore JSC and meet astronauts in this weeklong screening process in October 1989. Most of the week was spent in psychological exams and medical screenings. She passed the extensive testing regimen, including an extreme claustrophobia screening that required her to remain inside a dark, three-foot inflated ball for thirty minutes. Curled up in a fetal position, Collins fell asleep and napped her way to passing that evaluation.

Her last major assessment remained the in-person interview before a board of twelve people, some of whom were current and former astronauts, including John Young, who walked on the moon and served as a commander of STS-1 (Space Transportation System-1), the space shuttle's first flight in 1981 in the orbiter *Columbia*. Their questions ranged from mundane inquiries about her high school years and what car she drove to her thoughts on various aircraft and whether she ever faced fear in an airplane. Several of the interviewers pressed her about serving as either a mission specialist or a pilot for NASA. Despite her many years as a pilot, Collins stated she would accept either role in order to become a NASA astronaut. Like anyone, she wondered if she made the cut after the interview, heading back to Edwards to continue her TPS training and awaiting NASA's decision.

After a morning A-37 flight on January 16, 1990, Collins noticed a message tacked to the school's message board asking her to contact NASA. Her heart pounding, she dialed the number and learned from John Young that she would be NASA's first female pilot candidate for the space shuttle. Eileen told her husband, Pat, but kept the news confidential to allow NASA to make a formal announcement.

Two days later, NASA identified 23 astronaut candidates out of 1,945 applications with 11 civilians and 12 military officers, including thirty-three-year-old Maj. Eileen Collins. Only seven candidates were assigned to co-pilot training, six men and Collins, the first woman ever selected for this role. Her family, friends, and colleagues were surprised, unaware of Eileen's long-hidden astronaut dream. She would still need to successfully complete her final six months of TPS before heading to JSC. A couple of days after the NASA announcement, Collins watched the space shuttle *Columbia* land on an Edwards's runway and knew her dream of space travel lay within her grasp.

A month after graduating from TPS, Eileen reported to JSC and joined her fellow astronaut candidates ("ASCANs" for short) in NASA Group 13 on July 16, 1990. An intense media spotlight fell on Collins over her gender-shattering pilot's role. Her unprecedented story served as a bit of good news after a rocky year for NASA, including near disastrous mirror flaws on the $1.5 billion Hubble Space Telescope, disciplinary actions against two astronaut commanders—one for flying a stunt plane in a fatal collision at a weekend air show and another for flying a T-38 too close to a commercial airliner—and the grounding of space shuttles *Atlantis* and *Columbia* over persistent fuel leaks.

During that year, Collins and the other ASCANs spent many hours in classroom and simulator sessions training on the shuttle's complex systems. In some ways the program revisited some of Collins's earlier military training, such as abbreviated land and water survival courses and parachute and parasail training at Vance, her former base. As a former instructor, Collins performed well in flying T-38s and undertook extensive simulator and Gulfstream II Shuttle Training Aircraft (STA) final approaches and landings. She qualified as a shuttle pilot after five hundred successful STA final approaches and landings and also became scuba-certified for water landings. On July 29, 1991, Eileen earned her silver wings after her twelve-month training. By year's end, Collins was itching to make more substantial contributions to NASA.

After initially being assigned to work on shuttle systems, NASA later named Collins to serve as a KSC astronaut support person (ASP), nicknamed a "Cape Crusader." The role meant providing direct support to shuttle crews and undertaking practical work on shuttle vehicles as well as demanding regular commuting between Florida and Texas, where her supportive husband, Pat, flew for Delta Airlines. From February 1992 to June 1993, Collins served as a Cape Crusader on ten missions at KSC. Eileen felt honored to serve on KSC closeout crews that helped shuttle astronauts put on their gear for the flight and strapped them into their seats before closing the spacecraft's hatch. Collins wrote, "[t]his was an emotional time, when you stop to consider that the closeout crew were the last people these astronauts would see until they returned from space."

With her love of astronomy, Eileen was excited to learn she was slated to serve as pilot for a Hubble repair mission, set to launch in December 1993. Yet another experienced shuttle pilot was named to the flight, rather than Collins, after NASA officials determined that no rookie astronauts would serve on this high visibility mission. Despite the crushing news, Collins knew how she handled this distressing disappointment would speak volumes about her. She continued to maintain a positive attitude and to keep training hard for her first mission.

The ever-patient pilot would have to wait until 1995 to become one of those astronauts strapped into a space shuttle. Her first shuttle flight, STS-63, focused mainly on a rendezvous between space shuttle *Discovery* and the Russian space station *Mir*, in a show of post–Cold War collaboration. NASA wanted more opportunities to work with the Russians on *Mir* and to undertake various experiments in anticipation of construction of the International Space Station (ISS). The trip marked a series of firsts—the first trip of a NASA spacecraft to *Mir*, the first African American man and first British-born man to undertake a spacewalk, and the first woman to serve as a pilot in the shuttle's fourteen-year history, Collins.

In preparation for her first trip, Collins, Cmdr. Jim Weatherbee, and the rest of the *Discovery* crew traveled to Russia for ten days to meet their counterparts at the Gargarin Cosmonaut Training Center at Star City. Although *Discovery* would not dock with *Mir*, its rendezvous would help establish the flight, navigation, and communication procedures for future docking missions. Initially, the Russians wanted *Discovery* to remain one thousand feet away from *Mir* out of an abundance of caution about the one-hundred-ton shuttle accidentally colliding with its space station. Continued negotiations brought that distance down to ten meters or about thirty-three feet, to replicate the distance of final maneuvers of future docking shuttles.

Despite two scrubbed launches, Collins soared into orbit from KSC on February 2, 1995, as the first female shuttle pilot. Although the shuttle commander lands the ship, the pilot is the systems expert on the spacecraft and undertakes an extensive checklist of critical duties after launch and during touchdown, including lowering the landing gear and deploying the drag chute to slow the shuttle down on the runway.

During the mission, *Discovery*'s crew carried out numerous tasks, including using a robotic arm to deploy a satellite, undertaking the planned spacewalk, and completing twenty experiments, including a much-ballyhooed test of a fluid delivery system that found that soda tastes the same in space as on Earth. Yet the mission's main goal was almost dashed when a leaky jet thruster threatened the planned close rendezvous with *Mir* about 250 miles above Earth.

Fortunately, the leak exhausted itself and *Discovery* began to orchestrate its orbital dance with *Mir*. Weatherbee maneuvered the ship while Collins navigated their approach, and the two spacecrafts came within thirty-eight feet of each other. In the end, the eight-day STS-63 mission successfully achieved all of its major objectives and landed safely at KSC.

After circling the globe 129 times and traveling more than 4.8 million miles, Collins became a veteran shuttle pilot and officially inscribed her name into aviation history.

Shortly after her return from space, Collins became pregnant with her first child, Bridget. Under NASA policies, a pregnant pilot had the option to fly T-38s during their first trimester, but no later to protect their health and that of their unborn child. Collins chose to fly while she still could under NASA rules. But Collins wasn't grounded for too long, with NASA announcing her selection for STS-84 on space shuttle *Atlantis*, scheduled for May 1997.

Unlike other missions, the launch remained on schedule for its liftoff from KSC. On this nine-day mission with an international crew, Collins would again serve as shuttle pilot and have the opportunity to dock at *Mir*, delivering 6,500 pounds of supplies and swapping out one NASA astronaut for another. Collins would also bring her test pilot expertise to maneuvering *Atlantis* within a very slim airspace corridor to help test equipment for docking procedures for future ISS missions.

A veteran pilot of STS-63, Eileen felt more relaxed this trip, snapping lots of photos, taking time to explore *Mir*, and dining and toasting her counterparts with cognac aboard *Mir* to the sounds of Russian folk music. One evening, Collins enjoyed the thrill of watching the colorful Earth rotate in a sea of space darkness, her "most profoundly remarkable" experience as an astronaut. "Feeling like a flying angel, I was momentarily astonished when I realized the giant sphere below me was an oasis in the middle of nowhere," she wrote. As the mission came to an end, Collins secured the hatch between *Atlantis* and *Mir* before guiding the ship away from the station.

Even before *Atlantis* landed at KSC, word circulated that NASA planned to select Collins as the first female commander of a space mission in NASA's forty-year history. Having completed two missions as a shuttle pilot, Eileen became eligible for the commander's role. On March 5, 1998, NASA announced Collins's elevation to commander of STS-93 at a White House ceremony with President Bill Clinton, First Lady Hillary Clinton, and Dr. Sally Ride, the first female NASA astronaut. With Pat and her cousin in attendance, Collins, now age forty-two, spoke of her humble beginnings and her childhood dream of space travel. She expressed her heartfelt gratitude to her family as well as female aviation pioneers, WASPs, Mercury 13, and other women pilots and astronauts that laid the groundwork before her.

Despite the inevitable surge of media attention, Collins stuck to her usual practice of keeping the focus on the mission. STS-93's main objective was to transport and deploy the largest, heaviest payload in space shuttle history, the twenty-ton, fifty-seven-foot Chandra X-ray Observatory. Named after Nobel Prize–winning astrophysicist Subrahmanyan Chandrasekhar, the massive telescope would map and analyze X-ray emissions given off by stars, galaxies, black holes, supernovae, and other celestial bodies, offering scientists a glimpse back in time billions of years, to the earliest days of the universe.

Before heading to the KSC launch, Collins dealt with the usual press inquiries about her role as a barrier-breaking female commander. "Eventually, having women in these roles won't be news anymore. It will be accepted and expected. I'm setting a precedent for women to follow. With that in mind, I want to do the best job that I can," she told reporters at a pre-launch news conference. Downplaying her historic role, she quipped that her daughter thought, "everybody's mommy flies the space shuttle," having grown up around other NASA astronaut families. Yet despite her reluctance to take center stage, Eileen made history once again when space shuttle *Columbia* successfully launched from KSC on July 23, 1999, under her command, after two scrubbed launches due to mechanical and weather delays.

However, shorted circuitry and hydrogen fuel leaks left *Columbia*, one of the oldest shuttles in the program, seven miles short of its planned orbit. Having trained extensively for various flight scenarios, Collins and her crew managed the problem and successfully used the shuttle's robot arm to send Chandra off into space, the third of four planned space observatories, and also completed a series of microgravity experiments. Unbeknownst to Collins and her crew at the launch, these various mechanical problems could have caused a deadly explosion aboard *Columbia*. Fortunately, the members of STS-93 accomplished their mission objectives and Collins safely landed *Columbia* at Cape Canaveral.

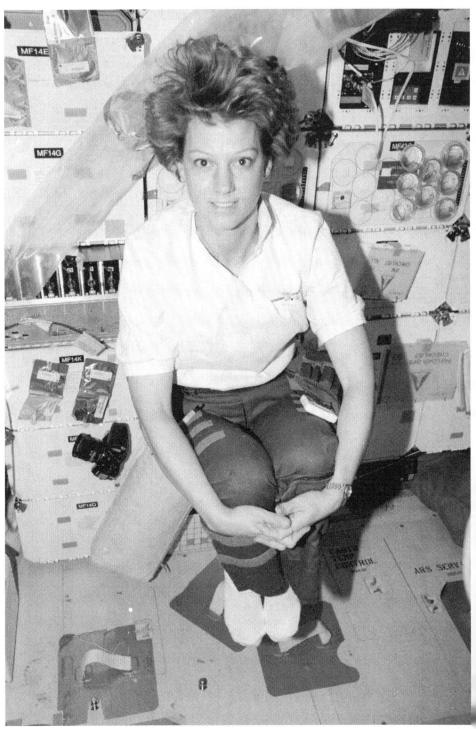

Becoming the first female commander of a NASA space mission, Collins floats weightless on space shuttle *Columbia* in 1999. (*Courtesy of Lyndon B. Johnson Space Center/National Archives NAID: 23178677*)

But the discovery of bare uninsulated wiring grounded the entire shuttle fleet until December 1999.

The challenges of the mission were compounded by the dizzying demands of post-launch media and publicity events that awaited Collins. Eileen participated in forty-seven press interviews in her first week back, with the press dubbing her "Janeway" after the cool, collected female commander in *Star Trek: Voyager* TV series. Eileen also made appearances on a number of popular TV talk shows, including *The Tonight Show*, *Today*, *The Oprah Winfrey Show*, and *Live with Regis and Kathie Lee*. She even rang the opening bell at the New York Stock Exchange. Collins had to balance this whirlwind of publicity with her official post-mission reporting duties, putting in long hours for NASA.

After the hoopla of STS-93 subsided, she returned to a variety of administrative roles, including NASA's chief information officer (CIO), shuttle branch chief, and safety branch chief after giving birth to her second child, Luke. She remained at her Texas home base but made frequent trips to KSC in Florida for readiness reviews and launch briefings. In 2001, NASA announced that Collins would serve as commander again on STS-114, flying *Atlantis* to the ISS to rotate crew members and to deliver needed equipment and supplies at the end of 2002. Eileen quietly told family and close friends that STS-114 would be her last space mission, with plans to move to Florida and make way for budding shuttle pilots.

Yet tragedy struck on February 1, 2003, when space shuttle *Columbia* disintegrated upon reentry, taking the lives of its seven crew members. The nation was shocked and saddened by the untimely deaths of the *Columbia* crew while Collins and the NASA community grieved the personal loss of their friends. The Columbia Accident Investigation Board undertook an intensive review of the mechanical and organizational issues that contributed to the terrible incident, faulting foam insulation shedding from external fuel tanks that damaged the shuttle's wings and cultural management flaws that misjudged certain flight risks. The board's report handed down numerous recommendations, including fifteen critical safety upgrades required before any next mission. Over the next twenty-nine months, NASA spent $1.5 billion making fifty modifications to the shuttle fleet.

Collins delayed her plans to relocate to Florida and instead prepared to serve as *Discovery's* commander on NASA's "return to flight" (RTF) mission in 2005. The STS-114 mission involved testing safety improvements and a fifty-foot robotic arm extension for shuttle inspections, experimenting in spacewalks with techniques for heat shield repairs, and delivering twenty-nine tons of supplies to the ISS. She spent many hours practicing the rendezvous pitch maneuver, a balletic move of manually and slowly turning the shuttle nose-over-tail to allow an inspection of *Discovery's* heat shield.

Eileen also understood the symbolic significance of the mission in bolstering public confidence in NASA and the important benefits of space travel, despite its risks. She further recognized the need to support her family and that of her crew about the overall safety of the updated shuttle fleet with family visits to training facilities, practice in flight simulators, and tours of T-38s to allay concerns. Collins publicly made it clear that she would not fly *Discovery* unless she believed that the necessary safety improvements were completed in the aftermath of the *Columbia* accident.

On July 27, 2005, *Discovery* launched from KSC with 200,000 spectators in attendance after a two-and-one-half-year pause in the shuttle program. With more than 110 cameras and sensors trained on the launch, some concerns arose over falling foam debris and a chip on heat-resistant tiles near the landing gear. Fortunately, Shuttle Cmdr. Collins flawlessly executed the pitch maneuver just four hundred feet away from the ISS, giving the ISS crew an unparalleled opportunity to photograph and video the shuttle's underbelly for any damage. The new robotic arm also undertook a five-hour survey of the ship to provide additional data on *Discovery's* condition. During the fifteen-day mission, Collins took time to enjoy the freedom of floating around the massive station's various modules and labs on her first and only visit to the ISS.

Before parting from the ISS, the crew of both ships held a solemn ceremony for the fallen *Columbia* astronauts in English, Japanese, and Russian. *Discovery's* crew brought along mementos to mark the RTF after the tragic incident. Collins and her fellow astronauts reflected on the lives of *Columbia's* crew and paid tribute to their sacrifices in pursuit of expanding the bounds of space exploration and human knowledge.

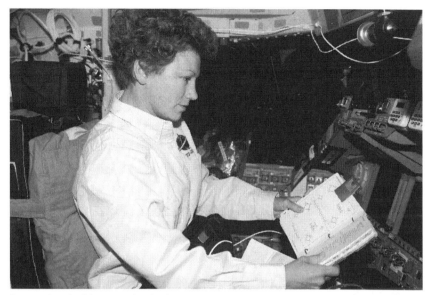

Space shuttle *Discovery* Cmdr. Collins checks display procedures during NASA's "return to flight" in 2005 after the 2003 *Columbia* tragedy. (*Courtesy of Lyndon B. Johnson Space Center/National Archives NAID: 23398662*)

With bad weather at KSC, Collins was diverted to Edwards Air Force Base, her old TPS stomping grounds, and landed the shuttle with its twin sonic booms for her last time on August 9, 2005. Although the meticulous commander was not completely satisfied with her landing speed, NASA and the country breathed a sigh of relief that the *Discovery* astronauts had returned safely. Yet concerns about the shedding of foam insulation would put the shuttle program on hold once more.

Having logged more than 6,751 hours in thirty different types of aircraft, Collins retired from the Air Force in 2005 and NASA in 2006. Flying her first shuttle mission at age thirty-eight, Collins completed her last shuttle flight at age forty-eight, having exceeded her space travel goals. She wrote, "I'm amazed I made it to the pinnacle of my dreams. I flew in space—not just once, but four times." Totaling up her time with NASA, Eileen wryly noted that out of nearly sixteen years, she spent thirty-eight days, eight hours, and twenty minutes in space—about .66 percent of her time with the agency—with the rest focused on training and administrative tasks. Clearly, Collins made aviation history in that slim window of time.

Throughout her storied career, she earned numerous military and NASA service and leadership medals and honors and won numerous aviation awards, including the Katherine Wright Award (2011), the Harmon Trophy (2020), and the Wright Brothers Memorial Trophy (2020). Various artifacts from her career are in the collections of the National Air and Space Museum. Collins has been inducted into many Halls of Fame, including the National Women's Hall of Fame (1995), National Aviation Hall of Fame (2009), KSC's United States Astronaut Hall of Fame (2013), Texas Aviation Hall of Fame (2020), and International Air and Space Hall of Fame (2021). Her alma mater, Corning Community College, named its observatory after her, and the entry boulevard to Syracuse Hancock International Airport bears her name. Each summer, Elmira's National Soaring Museum operates an Eileen Collins Aerospace Camp to introduce young girls to aviation, math, and science.

Modest about her unprecedented role, Collins thought that being first was not as critical as more women shuttle pilots in the future, stating "[f]or me, the important thing is we're going to have a second and a third and there are going to be more women and it's not going to be a big deal anymore." Two more female shuttle pilots, Navy Cmdr. Susan Still Kilrain and Air Force Col. Pam Melroy, followed in Collins's wake before the shuttle program ended in August 2011. Other female pilots have flown into space with SpaceX commercial flights, including Dr. Sian Proctor, the first Black female to pilot a spacecraft, and US Navy Col. Nicole Aunapu Mann, the first Indigenous female astronaut and commander.

For now, Eileen's feet are firmly planted on the ground, serving on boards and panels, acting as a guest speaker and aerospace consultant, being an expert commentator on space launches, writing her 2021 autobiography, *Through the Glass Ceiling to the Stars*, and raising her family in Texas.

Yet Collins still looks forward to more firsts for women in space, noting that "[w]e haven't had a woman on the moon yet or on Mars." Perhaps a friendly challenge from barrier-breaking pilot and shuttle commander Col. Eileen Collins to the next space-age generation of trailblazing female pilots.

REFERENCES

CHAPTER 1
Ruth Law

"Air 'Thrillers' at Fair; Ruth Law Stands on Top of Plane as It Loops the Loop." *New York Times*. September 28, 1921. https://nyti.ms/3IC9YE6.

"Aviation Industry Took Flight Here." Staten Island Advance. silive.com. September 12, 2010. https://www.silive.com/memories_column/2010/09/aviation_industry_took _flight_here.html.

"Aviatrix Practices Thrilling Death Dip." *Daytona Beach Daily News*. December 16, 1915. NewspaperArchive.com. https://access.newspaperarchive.com/us/florida /daytona-beach-daily-news-Dec-16-1915-p-10/.

"Big Crowd Sees Flying Exhibition." *Daytona Beach Daily News*. January 13, 1913. NewspaperArchive.com. https://access.newspaperarchive.com/us/florida/daytona -beach-daily-news-Jan-13-1913-p-16/.

"Big Plane for Ruth Law; Curtiss Factories to Make Machine Capable of Crossing Country." *New York Times*. December 17, 1916. https://nyti.ms/45ugC8Y.

Bowden, Denny. "Casey Stengel's Near 'Murderous' Prank and His 'Suicide' in 1915 Daytona." Volusia History—Retracing Florida's Past. March 31, 2014. https:// volusiahistory.wordpress.com/2014/03/31/casey-stengels-near-murderous-prank -and-his-suicide-in-1915-daytona/.

"Brooklyn Ball Players Are Passengers of Ruth Law." *Daytona Beach Daily News*. March 15, 1915. NewspaperArchive.com. https://access.newspaperarchive.com/us/florida /daytona-beach/daytona-beach-daily-news/1915/03-15/page-8/.

Brotemarkle, Dr. Ben. "Racing on the Beach." Florida Frontiers. September 13, 2016. https://myfloridahistory.org/frontiers/article/131.

"Challenge Is Issued for Automobile Race on Beach." *Daytona Beach Daily News*. January 8, 1913. NewspaperArchive.com. https://access.newspaperarchive.com/us/flor ida/daytona-beach-daily-news-Jan-08-1913-p-14/.

Cochrane, Dorothy and Ramirez, P. "Ruth Law: Record Setting Early Aviator." National Air and Space Museum/Smithsonian. November 2, 2021. https:// airandspace.si.edu/stories/editorial/ruth-law-record-setting-early-aviator.

Demers, Daniel J. "It's a Bird! It's a Plane! . . . It's a Baseball?" DanielDemers.com. 2011. http://www.danieldemers.com/BASEBALL-PAGE1.php.

REFERENCES

"Editor of Grit Shows His Grit." *Daytona Beach Daily News*. February 12, 1915. NewspaperArchive.com. https://access.newspaperarchive.com/us/florida/daytona-beach -daily-news-Feb-12-1915-p-19/.

Edwards, John Carver. *Orville's Aviators: Outstanding Alumni of the Wright Flying School, 1910–1916.* Jefferson, NC: McFarland and Company, 2009.

Erisman, Fred. *In Their Own Words: Forgotten Women Pilots of Early Aviation.* West Lafayette, IN: Purdue University Press, 2021. muse.jhu.edu/book/78999.

"Girl Dies in Stunt Boarding Airplane from Running Auto." *New York Times*. October 5, 1921. https://nyti.ms/3BRiDhZ.

Gobourne, Terry. "RR Ruth Law Thrills a Nation 300K." YouTube video, 25:27. August 10, 2017. https://www.youtube.com/watch?v=D045tjSRRvw&list=PLlILD-lep63TSGt_DfrxQ-EEQPQCwQgR5eO&index=3.

Halifax Country Productions. "Ruth Law—Early Aviator." YouTube video, 4:02. August 20, 2017. https://www.youtube.com/watch?v=PubkuRTY1s8.

Historyans. "Ruth Law and Her Curtiss Pusher." YouTube video, :35. July 20, 2011. https://www.youtube.com/watch?v=ABLNKINAcrM.

Holden, Henry. *Great Women in Aviation #5—Ruth Law—First Female Enlisted Army Aviator.* Statesville, NC: Black Hawk Publishing Co., 2012.

Law, Ruth. "Ruth Law's Story of Her Long Flight." *New York Times*. November 20, 1916. https://nyti.ms/3pW5OAb.

Lebow, Eileen F. "Star Quality" and "Superstar II." In *Before Amelia: Women Pilots in the Early Days of Aviation*, 179, 201–24. Dulles, VA: Brassey's Inc., 2002.

McGraw, Eliza. "Ruth Law Awed the Country before Amelia Earhart Even Took to the Skies." *Washington Post*. January 6, 2019. Gale General OneFile. https://link .gale.com/apps/doc/A568489343/GPS?u=11947_gcpl&sid=bookmark-GPS&xid =798e24af.

McGraw, Eliza. "This Ace Aviatrix Learned to Fly Even Though Orville Wright Refused to Teach Her." *Smithsonian Magazine*. March 22, 2017. https://www .smithsonianmag.com/smithsonian-institution/ace-aviatrix-learned-fly-even -though-orville-wright-refused-teach-her-180962606/.

Moczygemba, Sarah. "Ruth Law: The Aviatrix's Florida Connection." The US Caribbean and Florida Digital Newspaper Project. August 19, 2017. https://ufndnp .domains.uflib.ufl.edu/ruth-law-the-aviatrixs-florida-connection-ufndnp/.

Moore, M. Ashley. "The Clarendon Takes Flight with Ruth Law." YouTube video, 4:54. January 11, 2015. https://www.youtube.com/watch?v=jiXaiHI1sRY.

mreman47. "Ruth Law & Pioneer Aviator." Pioneers of Aviation (blog). February 11, 2020. https://av8rblog.wordpress.com/2020/02/11/ruth-law-pioneer-aviator/.

"Native of Omaha, Neb., Takes Aerial Flight." *Daytona Beach Daily News*. March 27, 1915. NewspaperArchive.com. https://access.newspaperarchive.com/us/florida /daytona-beach-daily-news-Mar-27-1915-p-8/.

"News of the Hotels." *Daytona Beach Daily News*. January 20, 1913. NewspaperArchive. com. https://access.newspaperarchive.com/us/florida/daytona-beach-daily-news -Jan-20-1913-p-6/.

REFERENCES

"News of the Hotels." *Daytona Beach Daily News.* January 25, 1913. NewspaperArchive .com. https://access.newspaperarchive.com/us/florida/daytona-beach/daytona -beach-daily-news/1913/01-25/page-6/.

NewspaperArchive.com. https://access.newspaperarchive.com/us/florida/daytona-beach -daily-news-Mar-17-1915-p-8/.

"No More Grapefruit for Manager Robinson." *Daytona Beach Daily News.* March 17, 1915.

Paterson, Searle. "The Incredible Ruth Law." NewOrleans. November 1, 2022. https:// www.myneworleans.com/the-incredible-ruth-law/.

"Rodman and Ruth Law Take Their Sibling Rivalry to Crazy Heights." New England Historical Society. Last modified 2022. https://newenglandhistoricalsociety.com /rodman-and-ruth-law-take-their-sibling-rivalry-to-crazy-heights/.

"Ruth Law at White House; Sees President and Thinks She Will Get an Army Commission." *New York Times.* November 24, 1917. https://nyti.ms/3WyNOIC.

"Ruth Law Back to Enlist; Will Join Army Aviation Corps after Flying in Europe." *New York Times.* April 5, 1917. https://nyti.ms/3BSqOuA.

"Ruth Law's First Flight of Season on Christmas Day." *Daytona Beach Daily News.* December 21, 1914. NewspaperArchive.com. https://access.newspaperarchive .com/us/florida/ daytona-beach-daily-news-Dec-21-1914-p-12/.

"Ruth Law Flies 590 Miles without Stop." *New York Times.* November 20, 1916. https://nyti.ms/41YhCiF.

"Ruth Law Gets a Medal; Aero Club Makes Award for Her Chicago–New York Flight." *New York Times.* March 31, 1917. https://nyti.ms/3WxQp5C.

"Ruth Law Lands Here from Chicago in Record Flight." *New York Times.* November 21, 1916. https://nyti.ms/4331eyW.

"Ruth Law Made Air Flights over Ebbets Field." *Daytona Beach Daily News.* March 12, 1915. NewspaperArchive.com. https://access.newspaperarchive.com/us/florida /daytona-beach-daily-news-Mar-12-1915-p-4/.

"Ruth Law Not Coming to Daytona; Will Go into French Aviation." *Daytona Beach Daily News.* January 15, 1917. NewspaperArchive.com. https://access.newspape rarchive.com/us/florida/daytona-beach/daytona-beach-daily-news/1917/01-15 /page-2/.

"Ruth Law Reaches Paris Says Report." *Daytona Beach Daily News.* February 7, 1917. NewspaperArchive.com. https://access.newspaperarchive.com/us/florida/daytona -beach-daily-news-Feb-07-1917-p-9/.

"Ruth Law Seeks Airplane. Wants Fast Machine for San Francisco–New York Flight." *New York Times.* December 11, 1916. https://nyti.ms/3MV6OOk.

"Ruth Law Sees Curtiss; Hopes to Have Him Build Her Ocean-to-Ocean Aeroplane." *New York Times.* December 10, 1916. https://nyti.ms/3OEiNRp.

"Ruth Law to Enlist Men; In Army Uniform She Will Seek Military Aviators in Chicago." *New York Times.* April 30, 1917. https://nyti.ms/428Sg1z.

"Ruth Law to Fly for Loan; Plans Transcontinental Trip to Advertise the Liberty Bonds." *New York Times.* May 30, 1917. https://nyti.ms/3ICc32S.

REFERENCES

"Ruth Law Will Try Transatlantic Flight; Aviatrix Coming Here to Consult Curtiss, Who Is Building a New Biplane for Her." *New York Times*. May 28, 1919. https://timesmachine.nytimes.com/timesmachine/1919/05/28/issue.html.

Skelley, Billie Holladay. "Ruth Law—Queen of the Air: Challenging Stereotypes and Inspiring a Nation." Ninety-Nines. n.d. Accessed March 6, 2023. https://www.ninety-nines.org/ruth-law.htm.

Smithsonian National Air and Space Museum. "Pioneering Women in Aviation." YouTube video, 3:06. October 9, 2019. https://www.youtube.com/watch?v=jnF3Yt_uaOM.

Smithsonian National Air and Space Museum. "Stories from the Archive—The Yamada Diary and Ruth Law's Scrapbook." YouTube video, 3:35. January 13, 2021. https://www.youtube.com/watch?v=kfpg7cFy5l8&list=PLlLDlep63TSG7c SUPYvoYQUO_bzrGD8s_&index=3.

"Superbas Up in Air; Several of Them and Mrs. Aitchison in Flights with Ruth Law." *New York Times*. March 13, 1915. https://nyti.ms/3MSlayE.

"Thrill World but Their Dad Is Not So Much Impressed." *Wichita Eagle*. November 1, 1919. https://www.newspapers.com/clip/9211065/laws-father/.

"Triplane for Ruth Law; Woman Flier Goes to Seacoast for Experimental Flights." *New York Times*. January 2, 1917. https://timesmachine.nytimes.com/timesmachine/1917/01/02/118127454.html?pageNumber=9.

United States Bureau of Labor Statistics. Washington, DC. CPI Inflation Calculator. Accessed March 8, 2023. https://data.bls.gov/cgi-bin/cpicalc.pl.

"War Lures Ruth Law. Aviatrix Sails for Europe to Study the Fighting Aircraft." *New York Times*. January 14, 1917. https://nyti.ms/432FCCy.

"Weather Man Kind to Some Players." *Daytona Beach Daily News*. March 5, 1915. NewspaperArchive.com. https://access.newspaperarchive.com/us/florida/daytona-beach-daily-news-Mar-05-1915-p-12/.

"W. H. Peters Enjoys a Soar in the Air with Miss Law." *Daytona Beach Daily News*. January 21, 1913. NewspaperArchive.com. https://access.newspaperarchive.com/us/florida/daytona-beach-daily-news-Dec-21-1914-p-12/.

Wikipedia. "Aero Club of America." Last modified April 7, 2023. https://en.wikipedia.org/wiki/Aero_Club_of_America.

Wikipedia. "Ruth Law Oliver." Last modified March 29, 2023. https://en.wikipedia.org/wiki/Ruth_Law_Oliver.

"Wilson Greets Ruth Law." *New York Times*. December 3, 1916. https://nyti.ms/3Ow5 fHH.

"Woman to Give Flights at Clarendon." *Daytona Beach Daily News*. January 7, 1913. NewspaperArchive.com. https://access.newspaperarchive.com/us/florida/daytona-beach-daily-news-Jan-07-1913-p-1/.

CHAPTER 2

Dessie Smith Prescott

Belleville, Bill. "Making the PBS Film 'In Marjorie's Wake': Navigating the Territory between the Hero's Journey and a Floating Opera." *Journal of Florida Studies*:

REFERENCES

Volume 1, Issue 1 (2011). https://www.journaloffloridastudies.org/files/JFSBelle
ville%20X.pdf.

Berra, Monica. "Marjorie Kinnan Rawlings and Cracker Culture." YouTube video, 9:45.
April 2013. https://www.youtube.com/watch?v=AdByZIJAZwc.

"Dessie's Legacy." *Citrus County Chronicle*. November 30, 2008. https://newspapers.uflib
.ufl.edu/UF00028315/01448/images/1.

"Dessie Smith Prescott Memorial Is Set for Today." *St. Petersburg Times*. April 25, 2002.
Gale General OneFile. https://link.gale.com/apps/doc/A85075169/GPS?u
=11947_gcpl&sid=bookmark-GPS&xid=3decc5c3.

Federal Aviation Administration. "A Brief History of the FAA." Accessed March 21,
2023. https://www.faa.gov/about/history/brief_history.

Federal Aviation Administration. "Records of the Federal Aviation Administration
[FAA]." Accessed March 20, 2023. https://www.archives.gov/research/guide
-fed-records/groups/237.html#237.2.

Florida Women's Hall of Fame. "Dessie Smith Prescott, Crystal River, FL." Accessed
March 20, 2023. https://flwomenshalloffame.org/bio/dessie-smith-prescott/.

"Governor Jeb Bush Selects Three for Induction into Florida Women's Hall of Fame."
PR Newswire. November 4, 1999. Gale OneFile: Business. https://link.gale.com
/apps/doc/A57227957/GPS?u=11947_gcpl&sid=bookmark-GPS&xid=17a5cca1.

Hyman, Ann. "Woodswoman Hailed as Florida's Treasure." *Florida Times Union*. December 5, 1999. Gale OneFile: Florida Newspaper Database. https://link.gale.com/apps
/doc/A58078662/GPS?u=11947_gcpl&sid=bookmark-GPS?&xid=73488b68.

Johnson, Carrie. "Dessie Prescott, a Florida Original, Dies." *St. Petersburg Times*. April
22, 2002. Gale General OneFile. https://link.gale.com/apps/doc/A84991818
/GPS?u=11947_gcpl&sid=bookmark-GPS&xid=e77991da.

Johnson, Carrie. "Dessie Prescott's Long, Remarkable Life Is Recalled." *Tampa Bay
Times*. April 26, 2002. https://www.tampabay.com/archive/2002/04/26/tribute
-to-a-true-pioneer-dessie-prescott-s-long-remarkable-life-recalled/.

Kennedy, Nancy. "Marking History: Sign Honors Prescott." *Citrus County Chronicle*.
May 14, 2011. https://ufdc.ufl.edu/UF00028315/02412/images/0.

Kindy, David. "For Pilot Bessie Coleman, Every 'No' Got Her Closer to 'Yes.'" *Smithsonian Magazine*. January 21, 2022. https://www.smithsonianmag.com/smithsonian
-institution/for-pilot-bessie-coleman-every-no-got-her-closer-to-yes-180979416/.

Klinkenberg, Jeff. "Pioneer Woman." *St. Petersburg Times*. September 2, 2008. Gale
General OneFile. https://link.gale.com/apps/doc/A184339296/GPS?u=11947
_gcpl&sid=bookmark-GPS&xid=d8a62b7c.

Marjorie Kinnan Rawlings Society. "Remembering Dessie." Accessed March 21, 2023.
https://rawlingssociety.org/docs/2014/October%202014.pdf.

McCarthy, Kevin. *Dessie Smith Prescott: An Illustrated Biography*. Orlando, FL: Independently Published, 2019.

McCutchan, Ann. *The Life She Wished to Live, A Biography of Marjorie Kinnan Rawlings*.
New York: W. W. Norton and Company, 2021.

Pieklik, Dave. "Home to History." *Citrus County Chronicle*. April 23, 2003. https://ufdc
.ufl.edu/UF00028315/00093/images/2.

REFERENCES

Poole, Leslie Kemp. "In Marjorie's Wake: A Film Voyage into Florida's Nature Consciousness." *Florida Historical Quarterly*: Vol. 90: No. 3, Article 7 (2011). https://stars.library.ucf.edu/fhq/vol90/iss3/7.

Prescott, Dessie Smith. "Interview with Dessie Smith Prescott," by Leland Hawes. *Alachua County General Oral History Collection*. March 30, 1990. https://original-ufdc.uflib.ufl.edu/UF00093305/00001.

Rawlings, Marjorie Kinnan. "Hyacinth Drift." In *Cross Creek*, 354–70. New York: Touchstone Edition, Simon and Schuster, Inc., 1996.

Sanchez, Jorge. "Old Timers Got by with Fishing Pole, Hoe." *St. Petersburg Times*. November 19, 2001. Gale General OneFile. https://link.gale.com/apps/doc/A80179514/GPS?u=11947_gcpl&sid=bookmark-GPS&xid=ba0e1268.

Sigler, David, Citrus County Chronicle Online. "Dessie's House." YouTube video, 13:15. May 9, 2011. https://www.youtube.com/watch?v=Ke_VqyJgPnM.

Sullivan, John J. "One a Day in Tampa Bay: B-26 Bomber Training at MacDill Air Base during World War II." *Tampa Bay History*: Vol. 11: Iss. 1, Article 5 (1989). https://digitalcommons.usf.edu/tampabayhistory/vol11/iss1/5.

Susman, Carolyn. "The Florida Women's Hall of Fame, a College President, a Tennis Champ and a Florida Pioneer." *Palm Beach Post*. November 15, 1999. Florida Newspaper Database. https://link.gale.com/apps/doc/A62318124/GPS?u=11947_gcpl&sid=bookmark-GPS&xid=c61b3c44.

Worthington, Eryn. "A Pioneering Legend." *Citrus County Chronicle*. March 22, 2014. https://ufdc.ufl.edu/UF00028315/03427/images/1.

CHAPTER 3
Elizabeth "Bessie" Coleman

"5 Paths to Aviation Immortality." *Plane & Pilot*. September 2022. Gale General OneFile. https://link.gale.com/apps/doc/A736684740/GPS?u=11947_gcpl&sid=bookmark-GPS&xid=ebad8dac.

Alexander, Kerri Lee and Ljungren, Rebecca. "Bessie Coleman." National Women's History Museum. 2018, modified December 2022. https://www.womenshistory.org/education-resources/biographies/bessie-coleman.

American Masters PBS. "Bessie Coleman: First African American Aviator—Unladylike2020." YouTube video, 9:07. March 4, 2020. https://youtu.be/4fSwHryVWZE.

Associated Press. "Two Lives Lost in Accident." *Key West Citizen*. May 1, 1926. NewspaperArchive.com. https://access.newspaperarchive.com/us/florida/key-west/key-west-citizen/1926/05-01/.

Baker, Elizabeth. "Orlando International Displays Bessie Coleman Exhibit for Black History Month." *Passenger Terminal Today*. February 8, 2023. https://www.passengerterminaltoday.com/news/airport/orlando-international-displays-bessie-coleman-exhibit-for-black-history-month.html.

Barone, Gabrielle. "Bessie Coleman: Barnstorming through Barriers." Smithsonian National Air and Space Museum. June 15, 2018. https://airandspace.si.edu/stories/editorial/bessie-coleman-barnstorming-through-barrier.

REFERENCES

Bean, Shawn C. *The First Hollywood, Florida and the Golden Age of Silent Filmmaking.* Gainesville: University Press of Florida, 2008.

"Bessie Coleman: April 30, 1926." *Jet.* May 1, 1995. Gale General OneFile. https://link.gale.com/apps/doc/A16878956/GPS?u=11947_gcpl&sid=bookmark-GPS&xid=a2992c72.

"Bessie Coleman, Aviation Pioneer." Chicago History Museum. Accessed April 24, 2023. https://www.chicagohistory.org/bessie-coleman-aviation-pioneer/.

"Bessie Coleman, Hall of Fame Induction Video," San Diego Air and Space Museum, 6:36. 2014. https://storage.googleapis.com/hof-video/BessieColeman.mp4.

"Bessie Coleman." National Aviation Hall of Fame. Accessed April 22, 2023. https://nationalaviation.org/enshrinee/bessie-coleman/.

"Bessie Coleman." National Women's Hall of Fame. Accessed April 22, 2023. https://www.womenofthehall.org/inductee/bessie-coleman/.

"Bessie Coleman." San Diego Air and Space Museum. Accessed April 22, 2023. https://sandiegoairandspace.org/hall-of-fame/honoree/bessie-coleman.

"Bessie Coleman." Smithsonian National Air and Space Museum. Accessed April 23, 2023. https://airandspace.si.edu/explore/stories/bessie-coleman.

"Bessie Coleman Stamp Set for April 27th." *Stamps.* April 1, 1995. Gale General One-File. https://link.gale.com/apps/doc/A16833142/GPS?u=11947_gcpl&sid=bookmark-GPS&xid=b3d4925c.

Blakemore, Erin. "The First Black Woman Aviator Had to Leave the U.S. in Order to Achieve Her Dreams." *Timeline.* March 19, 2018. https://timeline.com/bessie-coleman-first-black-female-pilot-4eb9102e202c.

CBS Evening News. "All-Black Female Airline Crew Honors Bessie Coleman." You-Tube video, 1:33. August 17, 2022. https://www.youtube.com/watch?app=desktop&v=oBvsQLgzZOc.

"Celebrating the Centennial of Bessie Coleman as the First Licensed African American Woman Pilot." *States News Service.* June 15, 2021. Gale General OneFile. https://link.gale.com/apps/doc/A665283557/GPS?u=11947_gcpl&sid=bookmark-GPS&xid=8a2f1734.

Dickinson, Joy Wallace. "Daring Pilot Bessie Coleman Flew into Hearts of Orlandoans in '20s." *Orlando Sentinel.* February 21, 2021. https://www.orlandosentinel.com/features/os-fe-joy-wallace-dickinson-20210221-cx6dmvzu55bondu2dya4zsehra-story.html.

Doolittle, Gardner, dir. *The Legend: The Bessie Coleman Story.* Hosted by Aneva Walker. Holland, OH: Dreamscape Media, LLC, 2018. DVD.

"Elizabeth 'Bessie' Coleman—Hall of Fame." Lone Star Flight Museum. Accessed May 9, 2023. https://lonestarflight.org/hall-of-fame/elizabeth-bessie-coleman/.

"Elizabeth 'Bessie' Coleman, the 'Daredevil Aviatrix,' 'Queen Bess.'" Accessed April 22, 2023. https://orlando.novusagenda.com/AgendaPublic/AttachmentViewer.ashx?AttachmentID=58283&ItemID=36903.

"Fly Girls—Bessie Coleman 1892–1926." The African American Experience 1892–1926. PBS. Accessed April 22, 2023. https://www.pbs.org/wgbh/americanexperience/features/flygirls-bessie-coleman/.

REFERENCES

Grabowski, Amelia. "Bessie Coleman: Five Stories You May Not Know." Smithsonian National Air and Space Museum. June 14, 2021. https://airandspace.si.edu/sto ries/editorial/bessie-coleman-five-stories-you-may-not-know.

"Hall of Fame: Bessie Coleman (1892–1926)." *SP's Aviation*. November 26, 2011. Gale OneFile: Military and Intelligence. https://link.gale.com/apps/doc/A273475466 /GPS?u=11947_gcpl&sid=bookmark-GPS&xid=0fc5d77b.

Henderson, Shirley. "Flying High with Female Pilots: African-American Women Are Taking Control in the Cockpit." *Ebony*. April 2006. Gale General OneFile. https://link.gale.com/apps/doc/A143436340/GPS?u=11947_gcpl&sid=book mark-GPS&xid=06c04a7e.

History of the World Podcast. "The Bessie Coleman Story—Her Life, Her Death." YouTube video, 8:54. February 13, 2021. https://www.youtube.com/watch?v =Snhyzvmro1A.

Indian Pueblo Cultural Center. "Bessie Coleman Aerospace Legacy." Indigenous Connections and Collections Library Blog (blog). November 5, 2022. https://indian pueblo.org/indigenous-connections-collections-2/.

Kee, Dr. Beverly. "95 Years Since Aviator Bessie Coleman Fell into History." *Florida Star*. May 1, 2021. https://ufdc.ufl.edu/uf00028362/01541.

Kee, Dr. Beverly. "Bessie Coleman Flying the Blues." *Florida Star*. October 23, 2021. https://ufdc.ufl.edu/uf00028362/01566.

Kee, Dr. Beverly. "Bessie Coleman Flying the Blues." *Florida Star*. October 9, 2021. https://ufdc.ufl.edu/uf00028362/01564.

Kee, Dr. Beverly. "Bessie Coleman Flying the Blues: The Life and Times of Pioneering Aviatrix." *Florida Star*. October 2, 2021. https://ufdc.ufl.edu/uf00028362/01563.

Kindy, David. "For Pilot Bessie Coleman, Every 'No' Got Her Closer To 'Yes.'" *Smithsonian Magazine*. January 21, 2022. https://www.smithsonianmag.com/smithsonian -institution/for-pilot-bessie-coleman-every-no-got-her-closer-to-yes-180979416/.

Lewis, Katelyn. "National Women in Aviation Week: Six Aviatrixes and Their Impact on Florida." *LAL Today*. March 9, 2021. https://laltoday.6amcity.com/national -women-aviation-week-fl#bessie-coleman.

London, Martha. *Bessie Coleman—Bold Pilot Who Gave Women Wings*. North Mankato, MN: Capstone Press, 2020.

Lupack, Barbara Tepa. *Richard E. Norman and Race Filmmaking*. Bloomington: Indiana University Press, 2014.

National Aviation Hall of Fame. "Bessie Coleman." YouTube video, 6:39. December 16, 2019. https://www.youtube.com/watch?v=GZJgMlqwhHo&t=15s.

"Negro Aviatrix Arrives. Bessie Coleman Flew Planes of Many Types in Europe." *New York Times*. August 14, 1922. https://www.nytimes.com/1922/08/14/archives /negro-aviatrix-arrives-bessie-coleman-flew-planes-of-many-types-in.html.

Rich, Doris L. *Queen Bess: Daredevil Aviator*. Washington, DC: Smithsonian Books, 1993.

Rudd, Thelma. "Bessie Coleman—Yesterday, Today and Tomorrow." The Official Website of Bessie Coleman. Accessed April 24, 2023. http://www.bessiecoleman.org /bio-bessie-coleman.php.

REFERENCES

Schaller, K. B. "Soaring Above: Elizabeth (Bessie) Coleman (1893–1926), Stunt Pilot: First American of Any Gender or Ethnicity to Earn an International Aviation License." *Indian Life*. November–December 2017. Gale General OneFile. https:// link.gale.com/apps/doc/A560835562/GPS?u=11947_gcpl&sid=bookmark-GPS &xid=9890fae4.

Scott, Phil. "The Blackbirds Take Wing: William Powell Believed Aviation Would Transform Modern Life—And Enable African Americans to Escape Racial Segregation." *Aviation History*. March 2011. Gale General OneFile. https://link.gale.com /apps/doc/A247157762/GPS?u=11947_gcpl&sid=bookmark-GPS&xid=d830ca72.

Slotnick, Daniel. "Overlooked No More: Bessie Coleman, Pioneering African-American Aviatrix." *New York Times*. December 11, 2019. https://www.nytimes.com/2019/12 /11/obituaries/bessie-coleman-overlooked.html?searchResultPosition=1.

Smithsonian National Air and Space Museum. "Bessie Coleman: The Centennial of a Pioneering Pilot." YouTube video, 51:58. November 2, 2021. https://youtu.be /1Pxyfrd_1gA.

Smithsonian National Air and Space Museum. "Pioneering Women in Aviation." YouTube video, 3:06. October 9, 2019. https://www.youtube.com/watch?v=jnF3Yt _ua0M.

Sokoni, Opio. "Bessie Coleman—Flying the Blues Pt. 1." YouTube video, 13:53. April 6, 2011. https://www.youtube.com/watch?v=oUdgJrfJjI8.

Sokoni, Opio. "Bessie Coleman—Flying the Blues Pt. 2." YouTube video, 9:39. April 6, 2011. https://www.youtube.com/watch?v=kVI9txHlnLE.

Sokoni, Opio. "Jacksonville Must Never Forget Brave Bessie Coleman." *Florida Star*. February 6, 2016. https://ufdc.ufl.edu/uf00028362/01286.

Sokoni, Opio. "Opio Sokoni's St. Philips Episcopal Church Speech about Aviatrix Bessie Coleman." Bessie Coleman: Flying the Blues (blog). April 28, 2013. http:// bessiecolemanflyingtheblues.blogspot.com/2013/04/.

"Sports Black History Edition: Bessie Coleman." *Florida Star*. March 1, 2008. https:// ufdc.ufl.edu/uf00028362/00806.

St. Fleur, Nicholas. "Bessie Coleman. How This Pilot Inspired People to Fly to Greater Heights." National Geographic Kids. Accessed April 22, 2023. https://kids.national geographic.com/history/article/bessie-coleman.

Swedberg, Nick. "Tribute for Bessie Coleman, Black Female Aviators Planned at Lincoln Cemetery." *Chicago Tribune*. April 13, 2016. https://www.chicagotribune .com/suburbs/daily-southtown/ct-sta-lincoln-cemetery-coleman-st-0414-2016 0413-story.html.

"The Bessie Coleman Aerospace Legacy Scholarship." Aviation Youth Empowerment Foundation. Accessed May 2, 2023. https://www.ayefoundation.org/scholarships.

The History Guy. "Bessie Coleman, Barnstorming Pioneer." YouTube video, 13:28. February 10, 2020. https://www.youtube.com/watch?v=XCgdU2oHt_0.

Toth, Maria Lynn. "Daredevil of the Sky: The Bessie Coleman Story." *Los Angeles Times*. February 10, 2006. https://web.archive.org/web/20121105072047/http://www .latimes.com/features/kids/readingroom/la-et-story10-feb10-2006,0,7374705 ,full.story.

REFERENCES

"Trailblazing Women to Be Honoured on US Coins." *Coin Collector*. September 2022. Gale General OneFile. https://link.gale.com/apps/doc/A736483588/GPS?u =11947_gcpl&sid=bookmark-GPS&xid=0323130b.

"Two Killed as Airplane Falls Over 1,000 Feet." *Sarasota Herald*. May 1, 1926. News paperArchive.com. https://access.newspaperarchive.com/us/florida/sarasota/sara sotahe ald/1926/05-01/.

Unique Coloring. "Bessie Coleman: The First Black Female Pilot Ever!" YouTube video, 12:33. March 15, 2020. https://www.youtube.com/watch?v=4tgR3znEpNE.

Valdes, Nicolette. "Bessie Coleman—The World's First Black and Native American Aviatrix—The Way We Were." *Community Newspaper*. March 20, 2023. https:// www.yourcommunitypaper.com/articles/the-way-we-were-bessie-coleman-the -worlds-first-black-and-native-american-aviatrix/.

White, Claytee D. "Bessie Coleman (1892–1926)." Black Past (blog). February 12, 2007. https://www.blackpast.org/african-american-history/coleman-bessie-1892-1926/.

Wikipedia. "Bessie Coleman." Last modified May 5, 2023. https://en.wikipedia.org/wiki /Bessie_Coleman.

"Women Fly." Great Aviation Quotes. Accessed March 13, 2023. https://www.aviation quotations.com/womenflyquotes.html.

CHAPTER 4
Ruth Rowland Nichols

"100 Most Influential Women in the Aviation and Aerospace Industry." Women in Aviation International. Accessed May 10, 2023. https://www.wai.org/100-most -influential-women-in-the-aviation-and-aerospace-industry##.

"Air Pioneer Killed in Crash of Plane." *New York Times*. April 2, 1932. https://nyti.ms /42nW14v.

Alex. "Ruth Nichols Aviatrix." Flight Birds (blog). March 2, 2022. https://flightbirds .net/ruth-nichols-aviatrix/.

Associated Press. "Ace Airwoman Seriously Injured When Plane Crashes in New York: Was Taking Off for Florida Trip." *Panama City Herald*. October 21, 1935. News paperArchive.com. https://access.newspaperarchive.com/us/florida/panama-city /panama-city-herald/1935/10-21/page-9/.

Associated Press. "Fast Flight Ahead." *Sarasota Herald-Tribune*. January 23, 1958. News paperArchive.com. https://access.newspaperarchive.com/us/florida/sarasota/sara sota-herald-tribune/1958/01-23/page-7/.

Associated Press. "First New York–Miami Non-Stop Flight Made by Ruth Nichols of Rye with 2 Companions." *New York Times*. January 5, 1928. https://nyti.ms /44W1pxs.

Associated Press. "Flyers from Gotham Here in 12 Hours." *Sarasota Herald*. January 5, 1928. NewspaperArchive.com. https://access.newspaperarchive.com/us/florida /sarasota/sarasota-herald/1928/01-05/.

Associated Press. "Girl Aviator Tells of Hop." *Sarasota Herald*. January 6, 1928. News paperArchive.com. https://access.newspaperarchive.com/us/florida/sarasota/sara sota-herald/1928/01-06/page-10/.

REFERENCES

Associated Press. "Injured Woman Is Improving." *Panama City Herald*. October 23, 1935. NewspaperArchive.com. https://access.newspaperarchive.com/us/florida /panama-city/panama-city-herald/1935/10-23/page-15/.

Associated Press. "Nichols Wrecks Plane but Is Unhurt." *Sarasota Herald*. November 4, 1932. NewspaperArchive.com. https://access.newspaperarchive.com/us/florida /sarasota/sarasota-herald/1932/11-04/page-7/.

Associated Press. "Ruth Nichols Breaks Record." *Sarasota Herald*. December 2, 1930. NewspaperArchive.com. https://access.newspaperarchive.com/us/florida/sarasota /sarasota-herald/1930/12-02/.

Associated Press. "Ruth Nichols Feels Flying, Business as Well as Sport." *Key West Citizen*. June 6, 1931. NewspaperArchive.com. https://access.newspaperarchive.com /us/florida/key-west/key-west-citizen/1931/06-06/.

Associated Press. "Ruth Nichols Finds Enough Romance in Air for Present." *Key West Citizen*. June 3, 1931. NewspaperArchive.com. https://access.newspaperarchive .com/us/florida/key-west/key-west-citizen/1931/06-03/.

Associated Press. "Ruth Nichols Holds Her Altitude Record." *Sarasota Herald*. April 24, 1931. NewspaperArchive.com. https://access.newspaperarchive.com/us/florida /sarasota/sarasota-herald/1931/04-24/page-4/.

Associated Press. "Ruth Nichols Is Not on Way Still." *Key West Citizen*. June 18, 1931. NewspaperArchive.com. https://access.newspaperarchive.com/us/florida/key-west /key-west-citizen/1931/06-18/.

Associated Press. "Ruth Nichols Plane Burns; She Escapes." *Sarasota Herald*. October 26, 1931. NewspaperArchive.com. https://access.newspaperarchive.com/us/florida /sarasota/sarasota-herald/1931/10-26/.

Associated Press. "Ruth Nichols Sets Woman's Record to Coast with Flying Time of 16 Hours 59 Minutes." *New York Times*. December 2, 1930. https://nyti.ms/42qSX7E.

Associated Press. "U.S. Airliner Crash Lands in Sea; 9 Killed." *Sarasota Herald Tribune*. August 15, 1949. NewspaperArchive.com. https://access.newspaperarchive.com /us/florida/sarasota/sarasota-herald-tribune/1949/08-15/.

Cochrane, Dorothy and Ramirez, P. "Breaking Records and Making History with Striking Stunts." Smithsonian National Air and Space Museum. October 30, 2021. https://airandspace.si.edu/stories/editorial/breaking-records-and-making-history -striking-stunts.

Curtis, Olga. "Moon—Here I Come." *Sarasota News*. January 30, 1958. Newspaper Archive.com. https://access.newspaperarchive.com/us/florida/sarasota/sarasota -news/1958/01-30/page-5/.

Davis-Monthan Airfield Register. "Ruth Nichols." *People* (blog). Modified June 23, 2014. https://dmairfield.org/people/nichols_ru/index.htm.

"Death Ruled Suicide." *New York Times*. October 20, 1960. https://nyti.ms/3LTrqoi.

Douglas, Deborah G. "American Women and Flight Since 1940" (2004). History of Science, Technology, and Medicine, 1. https://uknowledge.uky.edu/upk_history _of_science_technology_and_medicine/1.

Duson, W. W. "Debutante Paid $10 for First Air Thrill; Now Plans to Fly Lindbergh Trail Alone." *Key West Citizen*. May 5, 1931. NewspaperArchive.com. https:// access.newspaperarchive.com/us/florida/key-west/key-west-citizen/1931/05-05/.

REFERENCES

Erisman, Fred. "In Their Own Words: Forgotten Women Pilots of Early Aviation." *Purdue Studies in Aeronautics and Astronautics*, 1 (2021). https://docs.lib.purdue.edu/psaa/1.

Finlay, Mark. "Simultaneous Record Holder: The Life & Times of US Aviation Pioneer Ruth Nichols." SimpleFlying (blog). February 15, 2023. https://simpleflying.com/ruth-nichols-history/.

"Fliers to Organize Air Country Clubs." *New York Times*. July 5, 1928. https://nyti.ms/3pwx5cx.

"From Frost to Flowers." *Sarasota Herald*. January 6, 1928. NewspaperArchive.com. https://access.newspaperarchive.com/us/florida/sarasota/sarasota-herald/1928/01-06/page-4/.

"Hall of Fame: Ruth Nichols (1901–1960)." *SP's Aviation*. November 30, 2021. Gale OneFile: Military and Intelligence. https://link.gale.com/apps/doc/A687301530/GPS?u=11947_gcpl&sid=bookmark-GPS&xid=a2bd71de.

History Mystery Man. "1 Plane+1 Woman=Aviation Record Setting Pioneer Ruth Nichols!!!" YouTube video, 14:05. April 26, 2019. https://www.youtube.com/watch?v=tzaro2XIUJo.

Laneri, Raquel. "How This 'Fly Girl' Rose to Fame—And Then Lost It All." *New York Post*. August 4, 2018. https://nypost.com/2018/08/04/this-fly-girl-almost-beat-amelia-earhart-across-the-atlantic/.

Massock, Richard. "Ruth Nichols, Who Quit Drawing Room for Plane, to Fly Alone Route Lindy Traveled." *Key West Citizen*. May 21, 1931. NewspaperArchive.com. https://access.newspaperarchive.com/us/florida/key-west/key-west-citizen/1931/05-21/.

Massock, Richard. "Ruth Nichols Flew Despite Objection of Entire Family." *Key West Citizen*. May 25, 1931. NewspaperArchive.com. https://access.newspaperarchive.com/us/florida/key-west/key-west-citizen/1931/05-25/.

Meikle, Olivia and Nelson, Katie, hosts. "Episode 31: The Fly Girl Ruth Nichols." What'sHerName (Podcast). January 14, 2019. https://whatshernamepodcast.com/ruth-nichols/.

"Miss Nichols Borne Out to Sea by Gale." *New York Times*. March 7, 1931. https://nyti.ms/44NQHZz.

National Aviation Hall of Fame. "Ruth Rowland Nichols." Accessed May 10, 2023. https://nationalaviation.org/enshrinee/ruth-rowland-nichols/.

"Nichols, Ruth (1901–1960)." Women in World History: A Biographical Encyclopedia. *Encyclopedia.com*. May 4, 2023. https://www.encyclopedia.com/women/encyclopedias-almanacs-transcripts-and-maps/nichols-ruth-1901-1960.

Nichols, Ruth. "Lenten Guideposts, Written in the Skies." *Fort Pierce News Tribune*. March 23, 1960. NewspaperArchive.com. https://access.newspaperarchive.com/us/florida/fort-pierce/fort-pierce-news-tribune/1960/03-23/.

Nichols, Ruth R. "Ruth Nichols Soars Six Miles Above City, Setting New Record." *New York Times*. March 7, 1931. https://nyti.ms/44RMeoD.

Noronha, Joseph. "Hall of Fame—Ruth Nichols (1901–1960)." *SP's Aviation*. Issue: 11-2021. https://www.sps-aviation.com/story/?id=3041&h=Ruth-Nichols-1901---1960.

REFERENCES

O'Brien, Keith. *Fly Girls: How Five Daring Women Defied All Odds and Made Aviation History*. Read by Erin Bennett. Minneapolis: HighBridge, 2018.

O'Brien, Keith. "The Daredevil Fly Girl Who Challenged Amelia Earhart." *Daily Beast*. August 18, 2018. https://www.thedailybeast.com/the-daredevil-fly-girl-who-chal lenged-amelia-earhart.

"Personal Mention, Ruth Nichols, American Woman Champion Aviator for 1931." *Key West Citizen*. April 21, 1932. NewspaperArchive.com. https://access.newspaper archive.com/us/florida/key-west/key-west-citizen/1932/04-21/page-4/.

"Planes Are Sought for Civilian Relief." *New York Times*. May 27, 1940. https://nyti.ms /3pwCOix.

"Promoting Aviation: High-flying Women Pilots Provide Lift." *Key West Citizen*. October 29, 1986. NewspaperArchive.com. https://access.newspaperarchive.com/us /florida/key-west/key-west-citizen/1986/10-29/page-14/.

Roe, Dorothy. "Ruth Nichols Pioneer Pilot Still Flying." *Fort Pierce News-Tribune*. November 20, 1957. NewspaperArchive.com. https://access.newspaperarchive .com/us/florida/fort-pierce/fort-pierce-news-tribune/1957/11-20/page-3/.

"Ruth Nichols." Barron Hilton Pioneers of Flight Gallery, National Air and Space Museum. Accessed May 11, 2023. https://pioneersofflight.si.edu/content/ruth -nichols.

"Ruth Nichols: First Female Flying Boat Pilot." Glenn H. Curtis Museum. Accessed May 11, 2023. https://glennhcurtissmuseum.org/education/teaching-the-world -to-fly/.

"Ruth Nichols Hurt, Her Pilot Killed." *New York Times*. October 22, 1935. https://nyti .ms/430hmB1.

"Ruth Nichols' Records." *Key West Citizen*. December 24, 1930. NewspaperArchive.com. https://access.newspaperarchive.com/us/florida/key-west/key-west-citizen/1930 /12-24/page-8/.

"Ruth Nichols to Fly the Atlantic Alone." *New York Times*. April 22, 1931. https://nyti .ms/3IuhUaj.

"Ruth Rowland Nichols." The Ninety-Nines. Accessed May 10, 2023. https://www.ninety -nines.org/Bio-Ruth_Rowland_Nichols_66.htm.

Rye Historical Society. "Ruth Nichols: Rye's Aviatrix Flies High." Rye History (blog). March 31, 2016. https://www.ryehistory.org/stories/ruth-nichols-ryes-aviatrix -flies-high.

Suess, Jeff. "Female Pilot Competed with Amelia Earhart in Powel Crosley's Plane." *Cincinnati Enquirer*. April 10, 2021. Modified April 11, 2021. https://www.cin cinnati.com/story/news/2021/04/11/ruth-nichols-amelia-earhart-cincinnati -powel-crosley-plane/7115927002/.

Swopes, Bryan R. "6 March 1931." This Day in Aviation (blog). March 6, 2023. https:// www.thisdayinaviation.com/tag/ruth-nichols/.

"Two Oklahoma Flyers Winging Way to Europe, Miss Nichols Hurt." *Key West Citizen*. June 23, 1931. NewspaperArchive.com. https://access.newspaperarchive.com/us /florida/key-west/key-west-citizen/1931/06-23/.

"Two Women Fliers Hail Achievement." *New York Times*. May 22, 1932. https://nyti.ms /3VUtosX.

REFERENCES

United States Bureau of Labor Statistics. Washington, DC. CPI Inflation Calculator. Accessed May 18, 2023. https://data.bls.gov/cgi-bin/cpicalc.pl.

"Urges Aviation for Debutantes." *Sarasota Herald.* April 4, 1928. NewspaperArchive .com. https://access.newspaperarchive.com/us/florida/sarasota/sarasota-herald /1928/04-04/page-7/.

Wikipedia. "Ruth Rowland Nichols." Last modified April 13, 2023. https://en.wiki pedia.org/wiki/Ruth_Rowland_Nichols.

"Woman Aviator Found Dead Here." *New York Times.* September 26, 1960. https:// nyti.ms/3nYaqQS.

"Woman Flier Seen as Possible Suicide." *New York Times.* September 27, 1960. https:// nyti.ms/42D6b0U.

"Woman's 12,000-Mile Flight Disclosed Variety of Airports." *New York Times.* October 6, 1929. https://nyti.ms/3WuAFQQ.

"World-Mark Fliers Get Certificates." *New York Times.* January 31, 1932. https://nyti .ms/3ppHkz7.

CHAPTER 5

Jacqueline Cochran

Associated Press. "Chiles Picks Women for the Hall of Fame." *Northwest Florida Daily News.* November 7, 1992. NewspaperArchive.com. https://access.newspaper archive.com/us/florida/fort-walton-beach/northwest-florida-daily-news/1992 /11-07/page-14/.

Associated Press. "Miss Cochran Breaks 100-Kilometer Mark." *Sarasota Herald.* December 10, 1937. NewspaperArchive.com. https://access.newspaperarchive .com/us/florida/sarasota/sarasota-herald/1937/12-10/page-6/.

"Aviation Award Won by a Woman Flier." *New York Times.* February 19, 1938. https:// nyti.ms/3CaaPIn.

"Aviatrix Wins Honor." *New York Times.* February 9, 1954. https://nyti.ms/3IJ4J5c.

Chan, Hannah. "Breaking Barriers: Wasps of Color." Federal Aviation Administration. Accessed May 31, 2023. https://www.faa.gov/sites/faa.gov/files/about/history /pioneers/WASPs_of_Color.pdf.

Clark, Betty. "Make-Up Goes Sky High with Jacqueline Cochran." *Sarasota Herald Tribune.* September 27, 1938. NewspaperArchive.com. https://access.newspaper archive.com/us/florida/sarasota/sarasota-herald-tribune/1938/09-27/page-5/.

Cochrane, Dorothy and Ramirez, P. "Early African American Aviator Willa Brown." National Air and Space Museum/Smithsonian. November 4, 2021. https:// airandspace.si.edu/stories/editorial/early-african-american-aviator-willa-brown.

Delaney, Elizabeth. [Review of *Promised the Moon: The Untold Story of the First Women in the Space Race*, by S. Nolen]. *Australasian Journal of American Studies* 23, no. 2 (2004): 127–30. http://www.jstor.org/stable/41416016.

Florida Aviation Hall of Fame. "Current Inductees." Accessed June 1, 2023. https:// www.floridaairmuseum.org/home/florida-aviation-hall-of-fame/.

Florida Women's Hall of Fame. "Jacqueline Cochran, Panama City, FL." Accessed May 25, 2023. https://flwomenshalloffame.org/bio/jacqueline-cochran/.

REFERENCES

"Fly Girls. Jackie Cochran, 1906–1980." American Experience/PBS. Accessed May 25, 2023. https://www.pbs.org/wgbh/americanexperience/features/flygirls-jackie -cochran/.

Foster, Amy. "The Gendered Anniversary: The Story of America's Women Astronauts." *Florida Historical Quarterly* 87, no. 2 (2008): 150–73. http://www.jstor.org/stable /20700213.

Graham, Frederick P. "Miss Cochran Wins Bendix Air Race." *New York Times.* September 4, 1938. https://nyti.ms/3ozb8sZ.

"How an Early Black Pilot Soared above Setbacks." National Air and Space Museum/ Smithsonian. February 16, 2018. https://airandspace.si.edu/stories/editorial/how -early-black-pilot-soared-above-setbacks.

Hull, Michael D. "Jacqueline Cochran: Blazing a Trail for Women in Aviation Service." Warfare History Network (blog). Accessed May 30, 2023. https://warfarehistory network.com/jacqueline-cochran-blazing-a-trail-for-women-in-aviation-service/.

"Jacqueline Cochran and the Women's Airforce Service Pilots (WASPs)." Dwight D. Eisenhower Presidential Library, Museum, and Boyhood Home. Accessed May 30, 2023. https://www.eisenhowerlibrary.gov/research/online-documents/jacque line-cochran-and-womens-airforce-service-pilots-wasps.

Laclede, Kiersten. "Jacqueline 'Jackie' Cochran." National Museum of the United States Army. Accessed May 30, 2023. https://www.thenmusa.org/biographies/jacqueline -jackie-cochran/.

Ladevich, Laurel, dir. *American Experience: Fly Girls.* Narrated by Mary McDonnell. 2006. Boston, MA: Silverlining Productions. DVD.

Landdeck, Katherine Sharp. *The Women with Silver Wings: The Inspiring True Story of the Women Airforce Service Pilots of World War II.* New York: Crown, 2020.

Linder, Blake. "Today in History: The Sound Barrier Was Broken by a Woman for the First Time." *Roodepoort Record.* May 18, 2018. https://roodepoortrecord.co.za /2018/05/18/today-in-history-the-sound-barrier-was-broken-by-a-woman-for -the-first-time-web/.

Martin, Kalli. "Wings to Beauty: Aviation Pioneer Jacqueline Cochran." The National WWII Museum. March 26, 2021. https://www.nationalww2museum.org/war /articles/aviation-pioneer-jacqueline-cochran.

McQuiston, John T. "Floyd B. Odlum, Financier, 84, Dies." *New York Times.* June 18, 1976. https://nyti.ms/3ODZ04H.

"Miss Cochran First at Bendix Also." *New York Times.* September 4, 1938. https://nyti .ms/3WRfgS5.

"Miss Cochran Tops the Speed of Sound." *New York Times.* May 19, 1953. https://nyti .ms/43o9itI.

Motorsports Hall of Fame of America. "Jacqueline Cochran." Accessed June 1, 2023. https://www.mshf.com/hall-of-fame/inductees/jacqueline-cochran.html.

Museum of Florida History. "Jacqueline Cochran." Florida Division of Historical Resources. Accessed May 24, 2023. https://dos.myflorida.com/historical/museums /historical-museums/united-connections/women-in-history/jacqueline-cochran/.

National Aviation Hall of Fame. "Jacqueline Cochran." Accessed June 1, 2023. https:// nationalaviation.org/enshrinee/jacqueline-cochran/.

REFERENCES

Oakes, Claudia M. "United States Women in Aviation 1930–1939." *Smithsonian Studies in Air and Space*, no. 6 (1985). https://repository.si.edu/bitstream/handle/10088 /2672/SSAS-0006_Lo_res.pdf?sequence=2&isAllowed=y.

Patino, Frankie. "Well Behaved Women Rarely Make History: An Examination of the Life of Jacqueline Cochran." 2020. Electronic Theses, Projects, and Dissertations, 1065. https://scholarworks.lib.csusb.edu/etd/1065.

"Promoting Aviation: High-flying Women Pilots Provide Lift." *Key West Citizen*. October 29, 1986. NewspaperArchive.com. https://access.newspaperarchive.com/us /florida/key-west/key-west-citizen/1986/10-29/page-14/.

Reuters. "French Honor Miss Cochran." *New York Times*. July 22, 1951. https://nyti.ms /3MZFuhS.

Roberts, David. "Men Didn't Have to Prove They Could Fly, but Women Did." Smithsonian. August 1994. Gale General OneFile. https://link.gale.com/apps/doc /A15682286/GPS?u=11947_gcpl&sid=bookmark/GPS&xid=0c852da3.

Shipstead, Maggie. "When Jackie Cochran Flew This Jet, She Broke All Kind of Barriers." *Smithsonian Magazine*. December 2021. https://www.smithsonianmag.com /smithsonian-institution/jackie-cochran-flew-jet-broke-barriers-180979013 /#:~:text=When%20Jackie%20Cochran%20Flew%20This%20Jet%2C%20She %20Broke%20All%20Kind%20of%20Barriers,-The%20spirited%20aviator &text=On%20August%2024%2C%201961%2C%20a,near%20Edwards%20 Air%20Force%20Base.

Swopes, Brian R. "13 December 1937." This Day in Aviation (blog). December 13, 2022. https://www.thisdayinaviation.com/13-december-1937/.

Swopes, Brian R. "3 December 1937." This Day in Aviation (blog). December 3, 2022. https://www.thisdayinaviation.com/3-december-1937/.

Teitel, Amy Shira. *Fighting for Space: Two Pilots and Their Historic Battle for Female Spaceflight*. New York: Grand Central Publishing, 2020.

Tiede, Tom. "It May Be a Woman's World, but Space Is Man's Domain." *Panama City News*. September 5, 1969. NewspaperArchive.com. https://access.newspaper archive.com/us/florida/panama-city/panama-city-news/1969/09-05/page-5/.

United Press International. "Jacqueline Cochran, Pilot, Dies." *New York Times*. August 10, 1980. https://nyti.ms/43xMJ69.

Vance, Betty. "New Horizons May Be in Her Future." *Sarasota News*. August 26, 1956. NewspaperArchive.com. https://access.newspaperarchive.com/us/florida/sarasota /sarasota-news/1956/08-26/page-12/.

WASP on the Web. "Across the USA Where WASP Were Stationed During WWII." Wings Across America. Waco, TX. http://wingsacrossamerica.us/wasp/baselist .htm.

Wikipedia. "Jacqueline Cochran." Last modified May 18, 2023. https://en.wikipedia.org /wiki/Jacqueline_Cochran.

"Wins Flying Award Again." *New York Times*. September 12, 1940. https://nyti.ms/43 Ma3gD.

Womack, Marlene. "Cochran's Book: Millville Not 'Garden of Eden' for Everyone." *Panama City News Herald*. July 12, 1998. NewspaperArchive.com. https://access

.newspaperarchive.com/us/florida/panama-city/panama-city-news-herald/1998
/07-12/page-18/.
"WWII Female Pilots Honored with Gold Medal." All Things Considered. NPR.
National. March 10, 2010.

CHAPTER 6

Betty Skelton

"5,000 Attend Civil Air Patrol's Air Activities Show at Airport." *Sarasota Herald-Tribune.* February 21, 1949. NewspaperArchive.com. https://access.newspaper archive.com/us/florida/sarasota/sarasota-herald-tribune/1949/02-21/.

Ancestry.com. "Betty June Skelton in the 1940 Census." Accessed June 5, 2023. https://www.ancestry.com/1940-census/usa/Florida/Betty-June-Skelton_4p41b1.

Anderson, Andy. "Young Girl Prefers Florida Jail to Yankee Freedom." *Sarasota Herald-Tribune.* March 14, 1947. NewspaperArchive.com. https://access.news paperarchive.com/us/florida/sarasota/sarasota-herald-tribune/1947/03-14/page-5/.

Associated Press. "22-Year-Old Tampa Girl Sets Altitude Mark by Climbing to 25,760 Feet in Piper Plane." *Panama City News-Herald.* January 9, 1949. Newspaper Archive.com. https://access.newspaperarchive.com/us/florida/panama-city/panama-city-news-herald/1949/01-09/.

Associated Press. "Air Carnival Opens." *Panama City News Herald.* April 18, 1948. NewspaperArchive.com. https://access.newspaperarchive.com/us/florida/panama-city/panama-city-news-herald/1948/04-18/page-7/.

Associated Press. "Aviatrix Sets a Record." *New York Times.* January 9, 1949. https://nyti.ms/45G86DX.

Associated Press. "Aviatrix Sets Speed Record in Tampa Meet." *Sarasota Herald-Tribune.* March 17, 1947. NewspaperArchive.com. https://access.newspaper archive.com/us/florida/sarasota/sarasota-herald-tribune/1947/03-17/page-8/.

Associated Press. "Aviatrix Weds Auto Racer of Detroit." *Panama City News.* January 1, 1966. NewspaperArchive.com. https://access.newspaperarchive.com/us/florida/panama-city/panama-city-news/1966/01-01/page-2/.

Associated Press. "Betty Skelton Climbs to New Plane Record." *Sarasota Herald-Tribune.* May 20, 1951. NewspaperArchive.com. https://access.newspaperarchive.com/us/florida/sarasota/sarasota-herald-tribune/1951/05-20/page-3/.

Associated Press. "Betty Skelton, Tampa Flier, Back in America." *Sarasota Herald-Tribune.* August 10, 1949. NewspaperArchive.com. https://access.newspaperarchive.com/us/florida/sarasota/sarasota-herald-tribune/1949/08-10/.

Associated Press. "Brennand Wins Rich Finale in All-America Air Classic." *Panama City News Herald.* January 12, 1948. NewspaperArchive.com. https://access.news paperarchive.com/us/florida/panama-city/panama-city-news-herald/1948/01-12/page-2/.

Associated Press. "M. F. Thomas Victor in Economy Test Run." *Sarasota Herald-Tribune.* February 4, 1960. NewspaperArchive.com. https://access.newspaperarchive.com/us/florida/sarasota/sarasota-herald-tribune/1960/02-04/page-18/.

REFERENCES

Associated Press. "Pilot Shaken Up." *Sarasota Herald-Tribune*. October 3, 1947. News paperArchive.com. https://access.newspaperarchive.com/us/florida/sarasota/sara sota-herald-tribune/1947/10-03/.

Associated Press. "Stock Car Set to Race at Daytona." *Sarasota Herald-Tribune*. June 30, 1960. NewspaperArchive.com.https://access.newspaperarchive.com/us/florida /sarasota/sarasota-herald-tribune/1960/06-30/page-19/.

Associated Press. "Stunt Pilot Winner." *Key West Citizen*. January 14, 1948. Newspaper Archive.com. https://access.newspaperarchive.com/us/florida/key-west/key-west -citizen/1948/01-14/.

Associated Press. "Tampa Girl Flier Sets Height Mark." *Sarasota Herald-Tribune*. January 9, 1949. NewspaperArchive.com. https://access.newspaperarchive.com/us /florida/sarasota/sarasota-herald-tribune/1949/01-09/page-10/.

Associated Press. "Women Flyers Invade Havana." *Sarasota Herald-Tribune*. June 7, 1948. NewspaperArchive.com. https://access.newspaperarchive.com/us/florida /sarasota/sarasota-herald-tribune/1948/06-07/page-10/.

"Betty Skelton Thrills Britons." *Sarasota Herald-Tribune*. August 12, 1949. Newspaper Archive.com. https://access.newspaperarchive.com/us/florida/sarasota/sarasota -herald-tribune/1949/08-12/page-2/.

"Betty Skelton to Star in CAP Sunday Air Show." *Sarasota Herald-Tribune*. February 19, 1950. NewspaperArchive.com. https://access.newspaperarchive.com/us/flor ida/sarasota/sarasota-herald-tribune/1950/02-19/page-8/.

"Betty Skelton Used Pure-Premium for New Coast-to-Coast Record." *Panama City News*. October 30, 1956. NewspaperArchive.com. https://access.newspaper archive.com/us/florida/panama-city/panama-city-news/1956/10-30/page-8/.

"'Boundless: Betty Skelton' A Fox Sports Documentary Presented by NASCAR Race Hub, Earns International Motor Film Awards Nomination." Fox Sports (blog). July 28, 2022. https://www.foxsports.com/presspass/blog/2022/07/28/bound less-betty-skelton-a-fox-sports-documentary-presented-by-nascar-race-hub -earns-international-motor-film-awards-nomination/.

British Pathé. "Crowds Attend Air Show at Gatwick Airport (1949)." YouTube video, 2:24. November 10, 2020. https://www.youtube.com/watch?v=9z-PgwngWKk.

Cochrane, Dorothy. "Betty Skelton." International Motor Sports Hall of Fame of America. Accessed June 4, 2023. https://www.mshf.com/hall-of-fame/inductees /betty-skelton.html#:~:text=Motorsports%20Hall%20of%20Famer%20Art,way %20run%20of%20316%20mph.

Cochrane, Dorothy and Ramirez, P. "Meet Betty Skelton." National Air and Space Museum/Smithsonian. November 2, 2021. https://airandspace.si.edu/stories /editorial/meet-betty-skelton.

Florida Sports Hall of Fame. "Betty Skelton Frankman." Accessed June 2, 2023. https:// flasportshof.org/fshofmember/betty-skelton-frankman/.

Florida Women's Hall of Fame. "Betty Skelton Frankman, Winter Haven, FL." Accessed June 2, 2023. https://Flwomenshalloffame.Org/Bio/Betty-Skelton-Frankman/.

Frankman, Betty Skelton. NASA Johnson Space Center Oral History Project. Inter-view by Carol L. Butler. NASA Johnson Space Center. July 19, 1999. https://his

REFERENCES

torycollection.jsc.nasa.gov/JSCHistoryPortal/history/oral_histories/NASA_HQ
/Aviatrix/FrankmanBS/frankmanbs.htm.

Freedman, William M. "Woman Race Car Driver Helps to Add Facts to Chevrolet
Copy." *New York Times*. December 16, 1956. https://nyti.ms/3oNIMLJ.

GSEvents. "Betty Skelton Promo Video." YouTube video, 2:09. March 21, 2022. https://
www.youtube.com/watch?v=enjlIKFvhTQ.

GSEvents. "Women Shifting Gears Driven by Hemmings, Episode 41 with Pam
Miller, Lindsey Mandia and Cindy Sisson." YouTube video, 33:05. April 6, 2022.
https://www.youtube.com/watch?v=cFpHOgm28.

Hemmings. "The Producers of Betty Skelton: Boundless Share Their Inspiration from
This Racing Pioneer." YouTube video, 41:16. May 17, 2022. https://www.youtube
.com/watch?v=iGD4SY8LhHc.

Hevesi, Dennis. "Betty Skelton, Air and Land Daredevil, Dies at 85." *New York Times*.
September 10, 2011. https://www.nytimes.com/2011/09/11/us/11skelton.html
?searchResultPosition=1.

Hirschman, Dave. "Airplanes We Love: The Pitts Special at 75." *AOPO Pilot Magazine*.
July 1, 2020. https://www.aopa.org/news-and-media/all-news/2020/july/pilot
/airplanes-we-love-pitts-special.

Holden, Henry M. *Great Women in Aviation #1—Betty Skelton First Lady of Firsts
(Women in Aviation)*. Fernandina Beach, FL: Black Hawk Publishing Company,
2011.

Hughes, Mariah. "1956 Daytona Trophy Presented to Betty Skelton." *National Corvette
Museum* (blog). March 17, 2022. https://www.corvettemuseum.org/1956-daytona
-trophy-presented-to-betty-skelton/.

International Aerobatic Club. "Hall of Fame 1988 Betty Skelton Frankman." February
27, 2012. https://www.iac.org/node/1104.

International Motor Film Awards. "Betty Skelton—Boundless (trailer)." YouTube video,
3:35. April 16, 2023. https://www.youtube.com/watch?v=a4lLAwvYtxw.

Jensen, Tom. "Top-10 List: Dodges at Daytona." NASCAR Hall of Fame Curator's
Corner (blog). October 13, 2022. https://www.nascarhall.com/blog/dodges-at
-daytona.

Johnson, Joe. "Betty Skelton Interview." YouTube video, 2:56. March 8, 2017. https://
www.youtube.com/watch?v=q9tmiE7m2RI.

Koueiter, Michelle. "Corvette Evangelist, Aerobatic Pilot Betty Skelton Dies at 85."
Autoweek. September 8, 2011. https://www.autoweek.com/news/a1980766
/corvette-evangelist-aerobatic-pilot-betty-skelton-dies-85/.

Marchetti, Shalyn. "Betty Skelton: A Groundbreaking Aerobatics Star." *Plane and Pilot*.
March 17, 2022. https://www.planeandpilotmag.com/news/pilot-talk/betty-skelton
-a-groundbreaking-aerobatics-star/.

Marsh, Alton K. "Pilot Briefing—Betty Skelton Still Loves Speed." Aircraft Owners
and Pilots Association (blog). February 1, 2009. https://www.aopa.org/news-and
-media/all-news/2009/february/01/pilot-briefing-(4).

Motorsports Hall of Fame of America. "Betty Skelton." Accessed June 9, 2023. https://
www.mshf.com/hall-of-fame/inductees/betty-skelton.html.

REFERENCES

National Air and Space Museum. "Pitts Special S-1C." Accessed June 8, 2023. https://airandspace.si.edu/collection-objects/pitts-special-s-1c/nasm_A19850806000.

National Air and Space Museum, Smithsonian Institution. "Betty Skelton Collection." Accessed June 4, 2023. https://airandspace.si.edu/collection-archive/betty-skelton -collection/sova-nasm-2002-0002.

National Aviation Hall of Fame. "Betty Skelton Bio." YouTube video, 5:13. December 16, 2019. https://www.youtube.com/watch?v=_R3TjDyhsm4.

National Aviation Hall of Fame. "Betty Skelton Frankman." Accessed June 2, 2023. https://nationalaviation.org/enshrinee/betty-skelton-frankman/.

"Queen of the Skies." *Sarasota Herald-Tribune.* February 21, 1949. NewspaperArchive .com. https://access.newspaperarchive.com/us/florida/sarasota/sarasota-herald -tribune/1949/02-21/page-4/.

Schudel, Matt. "Betty Skelton, 'Fastest Woman on Earth,' Dies at 85." *Washington Post.* September 3, 2011. https://www.washingtonpost.com/local/obituaries/betty-skelton -fastest-woman-on-earth-dies-at-85/2011/09/03/gIQAyv83zJ_story.html.

Sheffield, Richard G. "Jet Fighter School II—More Training for Computer Fighter Pilots." FlightSimBooks.com (blog). Accessed June 6, 2023. https://www.flight simbooks.com/jfs2/chapter3-3.php.

Skelton, Betty. "Motor Maids—Steer Your Youngster Straight on Bike Safety." *Sarasota News.* March 23, 1957. NewspaperArchive.com. https://access.newspaperarchive .com/us/florida/sarasota/sarasota-news/1957/03-23/page-28/.

Tallman, Jill W. "Aerobatic Pilot Betty Skelton, 'First Lady of Firsts,' Dies." Aircraft Owners and Pilots Association (blog). September 6, 2011. https://www.aopa.org /news-and-media/all-news/2011/september/06/aerobatic-pilot-betty-skelton -first-lady-of-firsts-dies.

"Tampa Girl Stunt Pilot in CAP Show." *Sarasota Herald-Tribune.* February 13, 1949. NewspaperArchive.com. https://access.newspaperarchive.com/us/florida/sarasota /sarasota-herald-tribune/1949/02-13/page-11/.

The United States Navy Blue Angels. "History, Significant Events." Accessed June 4, 2023. https://www.blueangels.navy.mil/history/events.htm.

"Two Girls, a Chevy, and a Record!" *Eustis Lake Region News.* November 29, 1956. NewspaperArchive.com. https://access.newspaperarchive.com/us/florida/eustis /eustis-lake-region-news/1956/11-29/page-14/.

Wikipedia. "Betty Skelton." Last modified May 16, 2023. https://en.wikipedia.org/wiki /Betty_Skelton.

Wild Blue Adventure Company. "Aerial Aerobatics Options." Accessed June 6, 2023. https://www.wildblueadventurecompany.com/aerobatics-options/#:~:text=Ham merhead%20%E2%80%93%20An%20aerobatic%20maneuver%20in,ending%20 with%20another%20half%2Dloop.

Wilson, Earl. "Betty's a Fast Woman." *Sarasota Herald-Tribune.* December 19, 1956. NewspaperArchive.com. https://access.newspaperarchive.com/us/florida/sarasota /sarasota-herald-tribune/1956/12-19/page-17/.

"Writers Vote Pinella to Florida Hall." *Sarasota Herald-Tribune.* February 6, 1977. News paperArchive.com. https://access.newspaperarchive.com/us/florida/sarasota/sara sota-herald-tribune/1977/02-06/page-73/.

CHAPTER 7

Gladys "Penny" Thompson

"1930: Air Race Miami, the K K Culver Trophy and Fast Women!" TravelforAircraft (blog). August 1, 2012. https://travelforaircraft.wordpress.com/2012/08/01/k-k -culver-trophy-write/#:~:text=a%20particular%20air%20race%2c%20the,then%20 from%201946%20through%201950.

Allen, Ruth Stuart. "Comely Ninety-Nines All Ready to 'Fly Right' in June Air Show." *Miami Herald.* May 15, 1949. Newspapers.com. https://www.newspapers.com/.

"All Woman's Air Show Set Here Today." *Tampa Tribune.* March 16, 1947. Newspapers .com. https://www.newspapers.com/.

"Amelia Earhart's Mother to Present Plane Trophies for Air Show March 15–16." *Tampa Tribune.* March 11, 1947. Newspapers.com. https://www.newspapers.com/.

Associated Press. "Florida Auto in Powder Puff Air Show." *Sarasota Herald-Tribune.* June 3, 1949. NewspaperArchive.com. https://access.newspaperarchive.com/us /florida/sarasota/sarasota-herald-tribune/1949/06-03/page-6/.

Associated Press. "Woman Pilot Sets International Record." *Orlando Morning Sentinel.* March 17, 1947. https://ufdc.ufl.edu/uf00079944/00136.

Associated Press. "Women Compete in Continental Coverage Races." *Panama City News Herald.* June 2, 1949. NewspaperArchive.com. https://access.newspaperarchive.com /us/florida/panama-city/panama-city-news-herald/1949/06-02/page-11/.

Berning, C. G. "Navy Field to Be Named for Earhart." *Miami Herald.* August 9, 1947. Newspapers.com. https://www.newspapers.com/.

Boyd, Robert. "Women Aviators of the Past, Present and Future to Be Celebrated at Peter O. Knight Airport." ABC Action News. March 18, 2022. https://www.abc actionnews.com/news/region-hillsborough/women-aviators-of-the-past-present -and-future-to-be-celebrated-at-peter-o-knight-airport.

Bulit, David. "Richmond Naval Air Station." Abandoned Florida (blog). June 19, 2019. https://www.abandonedfl.com/richmond-naval-air-station/.

"Cross-Country Races to Mark Air Show Here." *Tampa Tribune.* February 25, 1947. Newspapers.com. https://www.newspapers.com/.

Douglas, Deborah G. "American Women and Flight since 1940." History of Science, Technology, and Medicine, 1 (2004). https://uknowledge.uky.edu/upk_history _of_science_technology_and_medicine/1.

Eckland, K. O. "The Powder Puff Derbies." K. O. Eckland's Aerofiles (blog). Accessed June 17, 2023. http://www.aerofiles.com/powderpuff.html.

"Fliers Reach Florida in Women's Air Race." *New York Times.* June 2, 1949. https://nyti .ms/3quLx50.

Florida Aviation/Aerospace Historical Society. "Class of 2020." *FAAHS Report.* April 6, 2022. http://www.floridaahs.org/uploads/1/7/2/0/17207228/fahs_reporthall_of _fame2022.pdf.

Florida Aviation Hall of Fame. "Current Inductees—Gladys 'Penny' Thompson." Accessed June 9, 2023. https://www.floridaairmuseum.org/home/florida-aviation -hall-of-fame/.

REFERENCES

Florida Press Association Hall of Fame. "Larry Thompson." Accessed June 13, 2023. https://flpress.com/hall_of_fame/larry-thompson/.

"Florida Women Pilots Plan Own Air Show." *Panama City News Herald.* January 12, 1947. NewspaperArchive.com. https://access.newspaperarchive.com/us/florida /panama-city/panama-city-news-herald/1947/01-12/page-5/.

"Flying Auto in Florida." *Sarasota Herald-Tribune.* June 7, 1949. NewspaperArchive. com. https://access.newspaperarchive.com/us/florida/sarasota/sarasota-herald -tribune/1949/06-07/page-10/.

"Hedgehopping over Florida." *Eustis Lake Region News.* April 8, 1948. Newspaper Archive.com. https://access.newspaperarchive.com/us/florida/eustis/eustis-lake -region-news/1948/04-08/page-12/.

History Miami Museum. "The First Historic Flights." Aviation in Miami, the First 100 Years (blog). Accessed June 16, 2023. https://historymiami.org/exhibition/avia tion-in-miami-the-first-100-years/#:~:text=Amelia%20Earhart,-In%201937 %2C%20Amelia&text=During%20her%20first%20visit%20in,to%20feel%20 safer%20about%20flying.

Homan, Lynn M. and Reilly, Thomas. *Wings over Florida.* Charleston, SC: Arcadia Publishing, 1999.

"It Flew into Town and Drove Out—Same Vehicle." *Key West Citizen.* June 3, 1949. NewspaperArchive.com. https://access.newspaperarchive.com/us/florida/key -west/key-west-citizen/1949/06-03/page-8/.

Jinks, Larry. "The Thompsons' Park: It Would Please Them." *Miami Herald.* November 23, 1975. Newspapers.com. https://www.newspapers.com/.

"Lady Birds Stretch Wings." *Miami Herald.* May 29, 1949. Newspapers.com. https:// www.newspapers.com/.

Landdeck, Katherine Sharp. *The Women with Silver Wings: The Inspiring True Story of the Women Airforce Service Pilots of World War II.* New York: Crown, 2020.

MacFie, David A. *Richmond Naval Air Station, 1942–1961.* Tequesta Volume XXXVII, 38. Historical Association of Southern Florida, 1977. https://ufdc.ufl.edu/uf0010 1446/00037.

"Mad as Hornets Are Flying WASPs." *Miami Herald.* January 12, 1947. Newspapers .com. https://www.newspapers.com/.

McRae, Evelyn. "Florida Chapter." *The Ninety-Nines Newsletter.* January 15, 1946. http://www.ninety-nines.org/pdf/newsmagazine/194601.pdf.

"Men Strictly Taboo in Women's Air Race." *Miami Herald.* March 28, 1948. News papers.com. https://www.newspapers.com/.

"More Than 300 Sets of Twins to Parade Today." *Miami Herald.* March 29, 1959. NewspaperArchive.com. https://access.newspaperarchive.com/us/florida/miami /miami-herald/1959/03-29/page-184/.

"Mrs. Earhart Will Attend Tampa Meet." *Miami Herald.* March 4, 1947. Newspapers .com. https://www.newspapers.com/.

"Navy Helps." *Eustis Lake Region News.* April 15, 1948. NewspaperArchive.com. https://access.newspaperarchive.com/us/florida/eustis/eustis-lake-region-news /1948/04-15/page-10/.

REFERENCES

"New Aviation Paper Starts." *Hollywood Sun-Tattler*. December 14, 1945. Newspapers .com. https://www.newspapers.com/.

"New Titles Won at All-Woman Air Show." *Tampa Bay Daily Times*. March 17, 1947. Newspapers.com. https://www.newspapers.com/.

"Ninety-Nines Invites WAVES." *Miami Herald*. April 9, 1948. Newspapers.com. https://www.newspapers.com/.

"Ninety Nines Swim Sunday." *Miami Herald*. March 19, 1949. Newspapers.com. https://www.newspapers.com/.

Oakes, Claudia M. *United States Women in Aviation 1930–1939*. Smithsonian Studies in Air and Space Number 6. Washington, DC: Smithsonian Institution Press, 1985.

"Park Honors Thompsons." *Miami Herald*. November 19, 1975. Newspapers.com. https://www.newspapers.com/.

"Peggy Lennox Captures Canada–Miami Air Race." *Miami Herald*. June 3, 1949. Newspapers.com. https://www.newspapers.com/.

Pennington, Gladys. "The All-Woman Air Show." *Tampa Times*. April 28, 1947. Newspapers.com. https://www.newspapers.com/.

Pennington, Gladys. "Florida Chapter." *The Ninety-Nines Newsletter*. January 15, 1946. https://www.ninety-nines.org/pdf/newsmagazine/194606.pdf.

Peters, Elise V. "Thumbnail Sketches of 1948–49 Candidates." *The Ninety-Nines Newsletter*. July 15, 1948. http://www.ninety-nines.org/pdf/newsmagazine/194807.pdf.

"Plans for the All Woman Air Show." *Miami Herald*. April 4, 1948. Newspapers.com. https://www.newspapers.com/.

"Ponciana Festival, Women's Air Meet Lure June Visitors." *Miami Herald*. May 30, 1948. Newspapers.com. https://www.newspapers.com/.

"'Powder Puff' Fliers Roar into Miami for Big Air Show." *Miami Herald*. June 3, 1949. Newspapers.com. https://www.newspapers.com/.

Reilly, Thomas and Homan, Lynn. "Ruth Clifford and Dorothy Ebersbach: Florida Fliers during World War II." *Tampa Bay History*: Vol. 20, Iss. 2, Article 6 (1998). Accessed June 11, 2023. https://digitalcommons.usf.edu/tampabayhistory/vol20/iss2/6.

Robinson, Arthur. "Miami Aviators Capture All but One of Orlando Prizes." *Miami Daily News*. May 6, 1946. Newspapers.com. https://www.newspapers.com/.

"Something New under Florida Sun." *Miami Herald*. February 5, 1947. Newspapers .com. https://www.newspapers.com/.

Story Cars. "1950 Aircoupe Autoplane." World's Largest Flying Car Archive (Part 2 of 3) (blog). November 15, 2021. https://www.story-cars.com/world-s-largest-flying -car-archive-part-2-of-3.

The Miami-Dade Parks, Recreation and Open Spaces Department. "Miami-Dade County Parks to Host 'A Walk Down Memory Lane with Carl Thompson' Celebrating the Life and Legacy of Larry and Penny Thompson and 35 Years of Larry and Penny Thompson Park and Campground." News release. November 15, 2012. The Miami-Dade Parks, Recreation and Open Spaces Department. https://www .miamidade.gov/parks/advisories/2012-11-15-larry-penny.asp.

The Ninety-Nines. (1966). 20th Anniversary Powder Puff Derby. Seattle, WA to Clearwater, FL. July 2–5, 1966 [Event program]. https://www.airraceclassic.org/pdf /programs/AWTARProgram_1966.pdf.

REFERENCES

The Ninety-Nines. All Woman Air Show. Amelia Earhart Field, Miami, FL. June 5–6, 1948 [Event program]. https://www.airraceclassic.org/pdf/programs /AWTARProgram_1948.pdf.

The Ninety-Nines. The First All Women's Air Show in the World. Peter O. Knight Airport, Tampa, FL. March 15–16, 1947 [Event program]. https://dotlewis.com /airshow47.htm.

The Ninety-Nines. "Women in Air Racing." Accessed June 19, 2023. https://www.ninety -nines.org/women-in-air-racing.htm.

"Two to Enter Women's Air Race." *Miami Herald.* July 31, 1951. Newspapers.com. https://www.newspapers.com/.

United Press. "Hurricane Again Gathering Strength for New Blow Now Aimed at Charleston Area." *Panama American.* September 17, 1945. https://ufdc.ufl.edu /aa00010883/05808.

United States Bureau of Labor Statistics. Washington, DC. CPI Inflation Calculator. Accessed June 17, 2023. https://data.bls.gov/cgi-bin/cpicalc.pl.

Vickers, Charlene. "Remains of Richmond Naval Air Station." Virtual Globetrotting (blog). Accessed June 11, 2023. https://virtualglobetrotting.com/map/remains -of-richmond-naval-air-station/view/google/.

Voltz, Luther. "City Vetoes $10,000 for Woman's Air Show." *Miami Herald.* January 31, 1948. Newspapers.com. https://www.newspapers.com/.

W, Dave. "Richmond Naval Air Station." The Historical Marker Database (blog). Last modified March 18, 2023. https://www.hmdb.org/m.asp?m=213649.

Whited Charles. "Columnists 'Good Wife,' Penny Thompson, Is Dead." *Miami Herald.* September 23, 1975. Newspapers.com. https://www.newspapers.com/.

Whited Charles. "Columnists 'Good Wife,' Penny Thompson, Is Dead." *Miami Herald.* September 24, 1975. Newspapers.com. https://www.newspapers.com/.

Wikipedia. "Gladys 'Penny' Thompson." Last modified March 29, 2023. https://en.wiki pedia.org/wiki/Penny_Thompson.

"Women Denied Beach Funds." *Miami Herald.* October 27, 1950. Newspapers.com. https://www.newspapers.com/.

"Women Fliers Arrive Here after Long Race." *Miami Herald.* June 3, 1949. Newspapers .com. https://www.newspapers.com/.

"Women Fliers on Radio Today." *Tampa Tribune.* March 19.1947. Newspapers.com. https://www.newspapers.com/.

"Woman Pilots Get Big Chance to Prove Their Place in Air." *Tampa Times.* March 14, 1947. Newspapers.com. https://www.newspapers.com/.

"Woman Pilots of 7 States to Meet Here." *Miami Herald.* May 2, 1948. Newspapers .com. https://www.newspapers.com/.

"Woman Pilots Rebel." *Orlando Morning Sentinel.* January 8, 1947. https://ufdc.ufl.edu /uf00079944/00186.

"Woman Sets New Air Speed Mark at 337 Miles an Hour." *Tampa Tribune.* March 17, 1947. Newspapers.com. https://www.newspapers.com/.

"Women Plan Air Events." *Miami Herald.* March 14, 1948. Newspapers.com. https:// www.newspapers.com/.

REFERENCES

"Women's Speed Record." *Kissimmee Gazette*. April 4, 1947. https://ufdc.ufl.edu/uf0007 9939/00779.

Wright, Lucille M. "Jamestown, N.Y., Chapter." *The Ninety-Nines Newsletter*. May 15, 1946. https://www.ninety-nines.org/pdf/newsmagazine/194605.pdf.

CHAPTER 8
Capt. Judith Neuffer Bruner (ret. Navy)

Associated Press. "2 Women Ready to Begin Flight Training in Navy." *Sarasota Herald Tribune*. March 2, 1973. NewspaperArchive.com. https://access.newspaperarchive .com/us/florida/sarasota/sarasota-herald-tribune/1973/03-02/page-12/.

Associated Press. "'Downgrade Carmen' May Regain Strength." *Sarasota Herald Tribune*. September 4, 1974. NewspaperArchive.com. https://newspaperarchive.com/sara sota-herald-tribune-sep-04-1974-p-1/.

Associated Press. "Female Pilot 1st to Thread Eye." *Orlando Sentinel*. September 3, 1974. Newspapers.com. https://www.newspapers.com/.

Associated Press. "First Woman Pilot Through Eye." *Tampa Tribune*. September 3, 1974. Newspapers.com. https://www.newspapers.com/.

Associated Press. "Hurricane Entered by First Woman Pilot." *Naples Daily News*. September 3, 1974. Newspapers.com. https://www.newspapers.com/.

Associated Press. "Navy Hurricane Hunter Laments End of an Era." *Miami Herald*. February 15, 1975. Newspapers.com. https://www.newspapers.com/.

Associated Press. "Navy Names First Girl Flight Cadet." *Sarasota Herald Tribune*. January 11, 1973. NewspaperArchive.com. https://access.newspaperarchive.com/us /florida/sarasota/sarasota-herald-tribune/1973/01-11/.

Associated Press. "Woman Navy Pilot Flies Through Hurricane's Eye." *Tallahassee Democrat*. September 3, 1974. Newspapers.com. https://www.newspapers.com/.

Associated Press. "Woman Pilot Set to Hunt Those Angry, Stormy Ladies." *Tampa Tribune*. June 14, 1974. Newspapers.com. https://www.newspapers.com/.

Associated Press. "Women Seeking Navy Wings Settled at NAS Pensacola." *Fort Walton Beach Playground Daily News*. March 7, 1973. NewspaperArchive.com. https:// access.newspaperarchive.com/us/florida/fort-walton-beach/fort-walton-beach -playground-daily-news/1973/03-07/page-5/.

Boatman, Julie. "Good FLYING Reads: Pinning on Wings of Gold." FLYING—View from Above (blog). March 29, 2022. https://www.flyingmag.com/pinning-on -wings-of-gold/.

Bureau of Naval Personnel. "Expanding the Role of Navy Women." *All Hands*. April 1973. https://media.defense.gov/2019/Apr/10/2002112485/-1/-1/1/AH197304.pdf.

Cokinos, Samara. "Carmen of 1974 Marked First Time Female Navy Pilot Flew Through Hurricane." WKMG ClickOrlando. September 2, 2021. https://www .clickorlando.com/weather/2021/09/02/carmen-of-1974-marked-first-time-fe male-navy-pilot-flew-through-hurricane/.

"Forming a More Perfect Union: Honoring Women in Naval Aviation." The Free Library (blog). March 22, 2016. https://www.thefreelibrary.com/Forming+a+more+perfect +union%3a+honoring+women+in+Naval+Aviation.-a0456276086.

REFERENCES

Genter, JT. "Storm Chasers: Take a Rare Look Inside 2 'Hurricane Hunter' Aircraft."
The Points Guy (blog). September 27, 2022. https://thepointsguy.com/news
/hurricane-hunter-aircraft-tour/.

Goddard Space Flight Center. "Judith N. Bruner—Serving Our Country in the Navy
and at NASA." People of Goddard (blog). August 26, 2014. https://www.nasa.
gov/content/goddard/judy-bruner-serving-our-country-in-the-navy-and-at-nasa/.

Goddard Space Flight Center. "Judith N. Bruner—Serving Our Country in the Navy
and at NASA—Part 2." People of Goddard (blog). September 16, 2014. https://
www.nasa.gov/content/goddard/judith-n-bruner-serving-our-country-in-the
-navy-and-at-nasa-part-2/.

"Hurricane Carmen." Forrest Gump Wiki (blog). Last modified May 11, 2022. https://
forrestgump.fandom.com/wiki/Hurricane_Carmen.

IronmanDaremo. "The Passing of a Pioneer . . . Judy Bruner, CAPT USN, Ret." Service
Academies Forums (blog). December 16, 2022. https://www.serviceacademy
forums.com/index.php?threads/the-passing-of-a-pioneer-judy-bruner-capt
-usn-ret.88705/.

"Judith Neuffer, Lt. j.g." US Navy Office of Information. Women in the Navy (blog).
Last modified March 29, 2023. https://www.navy.mil/Women-In-the-Navy/Past
/Display-Past-Woman-Bio/Article/2959039/lt-jg-judith-neuffer/.

Markowitz, Arnold. "Carmen Rips Yucatan, Skips Populous Areas." *Miami Herald*.
September 3, 1974. Newspapers.com. https://www.newspapers.com/.

National Aeronautic Association. "Judith Bruner to Receive Katharine Wright Trophy."
NAA press release. January 31, 2017. https://naa.aero/wp-content/uploads/2020
/03/Katharine-Wright-Trophy-Release-2014.pdf.

NASA. "Judith Bruner Women@NASA 2014." YouTube video, 5:05. December 2,
2014. https://youtu.be/htcmgkuxHnU.

NASA. "Judith Bruner." Women@NASA Series (blog). Last modified March 11, 2021.
https://women.nasa.gov/judith-bruner/.

NASA. "NASA's Earth Observing System Project Science Office." Last modified September 27, 2022. https://eospso.nasa.gov/content/nasas-earth-observing-system
-project-science-office.

"Obituary for Judith Neuffer Bruner." Wm. Reese & Sons Mortuary P.A. Accessed July
31, 2023. https://www.wmreeseandsons.com/obituary/judith-neuffer-bruner?lud
=4D16E9881069CE30DE9E6AD040677BDC.

Pace, Eric. "Navy Puts 1st Woman in Flight Training." *New York Times*. January 11,
1973. https://nyti.ms/447xbWq.

Petersen, Lt. Audrey "Pam." "Captain JoEllen Drag-Oslund: Female Naval Aviator
Trailblazer." US Navy Office of Information. January 11, 2023. https://www.navy
.mil/Press-Office/News-Stories/Article/3279358/captain-joellen-drag-oslund-fe
male-naval-aviator-trailblazer/.

Prentiss, Pat. "Judith Bruner Recipient of Katharine Wright Trophy." 99 News.
November/December 2014. https://www.ninety-nines.org/pdf/newsmaga
zine/20141112.pdf.

Proctor, Pam. "The Stormy Life of Navy Pilot Judy Neuffer." *Orlando Sentinel.* October 13, 1974. Newspapers.com. https://www.newspapers.com/.

UPI Telephoto. "Woman Hurricane Hunter Scores a First." *Sarasota Herald Tribune.* September 4, 1974. NewspaperArchive.com. https://newspaperarchive.com/sarasota-herald-tribune-sep-04-1974-p-1/.

US Congress. Senate. Commemorating 50 Years of Women Serving as Naval Aviators in the United States. Senate Resolution 212. 118th Congress. Introduced in Senate May 11, 2023. https://www.congress.gov/118/crec/2023/05/11/169/80/CREC-2023-05-11-pt1-PgS1632-4.pdf.

US Department of Defense. Celebrating Navy Women. U.S. Navy, 2021. Retrieved from https://media.defense.gov/2021/Mar/16/2002601542/-1/-1/1/2021_WIN%20EBOOK.PDF.

US Navy. "Significant Milestones for Women in Naval Aviation." Accessed August 3, 2023. https://www.navy.mil/50-Years-of-Women-Flying-in-the-Navy/.

US Navy Reserve. "Did You Know?" Facebook video, 1:37. May 12, 2015. https://www.facebook.com/watch/?v=10153239001642570.

Vujevich, Julie. "Women in Aviation—GW Reflects on Women's History Month." Defense Visual Information Distribution Service (blog). April 30, 2017. https://www.dvidshub.net/news/260995/women-aviation-gw-reflects-womens-history-month.

"VW-4 Has Navy's 2d Woman Pilot." *Jacksonville Jax Air News–Airwinger.* June 20, 1974. NewspaperArchive.com. https://access.newspaperarchive.com/us/florida/jacksonville/jacksonville-jax-air-news/1974/06-20/page-8/.

Wikipedia. "Judith Neuffer." Last modified June 10, 2023. https://en.wikipedia.org/wiki/Judith_Neuffer.

Wikipedia. "Lockheed P-3 Orion." Last modified July 31, 2023. https://en.wikipedia.org/wiki/Lockheed_P-3_Orion.

Women in Aviation International. "The First Class of Women Naval Aviators—Pioneer Hall of Fame." Accessed August 3, 2023. https://www.wai.org/phof-directory/the-first-class-of-women-naval-aviators.

Women in Aviation International. "The First Class of Women Naval Aviators—WAI 2017 Pioneer Hall of Fame." YouTube video, 2:26. June 21, 2019. https://www.youtube.com/watch?v=oP6bN0DeWto.

CHAPTER 9
Capt. Beverley Bass

"9/11 Pilot's Plane Was Diverted to a Tiny Town That Changed Her Life." *San Francisco Chronicle.* December 24, 2018. https://datebook.sfchronicle.com/theater/a-pilot-recalls-when-her-plane-was-diverted-to-gander-on-sept-11.

"A Famous Pilot, a Hit Musical and a Story of Resilience." American Airlines Newsroom (blog). July 8, 2017. https://news.aa.com/news/news-details/2017/A-famous-pilot-a-hit-musical-and-a-story-of-resilience/default.aspx.

Associated Press. "Pacesetting Captain." *Pensacola News Journal.* November 22, 1986. Newspapers.com. https://www.newspapers.com/.

REFERENCES

Clarke, Jay. "That Woman in Uniform May Be Your Airline Pilot." *Miami Herald.* December 18, 1977. Newspapers.com. https://www.newspapers.com/.

Davis, Pati. "I Thought It Was Neat . . . My Wife Kept Screaming 'Fly Baby Fly!'" *News-Press.* November 14, 1986. Newspapers.com. https://www.newspapers.com/.

Dolen, Christine. "'Come from Away' a Musical about Post-911 Healing, Arrives in Miami." *Miami Herald.* June 16, 2019. Newspapers.com. https://www.newspapers .com/.

Doris, Tony. "Career Course Turbulent for Female Pilot." *Tampa Bay Times.* October 9, 1986. Newspapers.com. https://www.newspapers.com/.

Fan, Katherine. "Capt. Beverley Bass: American Aviation Heroine." The Points Guy (blog). December 14, 2019. https://thepointsguy.com/news/beverley-bass-pilot -profile/.

Greater Miami Aviation Association. "Captain Beverley Bass." Accessed July 24, 2023. https://www.miamiaviation.org/speaker-captain-beverley-bass/.

Heithaus, Harriet Howard. "Come from Away." *Naples Daily News.* December 3, 2021. Newspapers.com. https://www.newspapers.com/.

International Society of Women Airline Pilots. "Our Story." Accessed July 27, 2023. https://isa21.org/our-mission/our-story/.

Jeknavorian, Mike. "Beverley Bass." 120 Seconds (blog). January 7, 2018. https://mike jeknavorian.com/beverley-bass/.

Johnson, Caroline. "Remembering Emily Howell Warner." National Air and Space Museum. July 17, 2020. https://airandspace.si.edu/stories/editorial/remembering -emily-howell-warner.

Martin, Lisa. "'Come from Away' Inspiration Beverley Bass Tells Her Story." *TCU Magazine.* Summer 2017. https://magazine.tcu.edu/summer-2017/come-away -inspiration-beverley-bass-tells-story/.

Oblander, Samantha. "Me & The Sky—Jenn Colella." YouTube video, 4:34. December 2, 2021. https://www.youtube.com/watch?v=5CxPdnHxh54.

O'Kane, Caitlin. "Female Pilot Honored: Beverley Bass, American Airlines' First Female Captain, Honored at TPG Awards." CBS News video, 1:46. December 10, 2019. https://www.cbsnews.com/news/female-pilot-honored-beverley-bass -american-airlines-captain-tpg-awards/3.

Patterson, Thom. "Pilots Share Their 9/11 Stories." *FLYING.* September 10, 2021. https://www.flyingmag.com/pilots-share-september-11th-stories/.

Paulson, Michael. "A Pioneering Pilot, a Broadway Show and a Life-Changing Bond." *New York Times.* April 16, 2017. https://www.nytimes.com/2017/04/16/theater /come-from-away-jenn-colella.html?searchResultPosition=1.

Pereira, Miriam. "Native Fort Myers Pilot Fulfills Dreams with Flying Colors." *News-Press.* July 19, 1999. Newspapers.com. https://www.newspapers.com/.

Powell, Kathleen. "They Saw Their Dreams and Are Living Them." *News-Press.* September 11, 1975. Newspapers.com. https://www.newspapers.com/.

Powell, Kathleen. "Winging Her Way to a Career with the Airlines." *News-Press.* November 9, 1976. Newspapers.com. https://www.newspapers.com/.

Runnells, Charles. "Fort Myers Pilot Gets Spotlight in Heartwarming 9/11 Musical." *News-Press.* December 10, 2021. Newspapers.com. https://www.newspapers.com/.

REFERENCES

Ryan, Michael. "Who's Driving This Plane?" *Parade Magazine.* July 19, 1987. Newspa
pers.com. https://www.newspapers.com/.

Smith, Paul Art. *"Come from Away* to Close on Broadway This Fall." Broadway Direct.
June 9, 2022. https://broadwaydirect.com/come-from-away-to-close-on-broad
way-this-fall/.

Stetson, Andrea. "Fort Myers Native Reminisces about Pioneering in Aviation, Making
Her Mark on Broadway." *Grandeur Magazine.* January 6, 2020. Reprinted *News-
Press.* February 21, 2020. https://www.news-press.com/story/news/2020/02/21/bev
erley-bass-reminisces-pioneering-aviation-making-mark-broadway/4787186002/.

United Press International. "All-Female Flight Crew Is Aviation First." UPI Archives.
December 30, 1986. https://www.upi.com/Archives/1986/12/30/All-female
-flight-crew-is-aviation-first/2054536302800/.

Wikipedia. "Beverley Bass." Last modified May 3, 2023. https://en.wikipedia.org/wiki
/Beverley_Bass.

Wikipedia. "Bonnie Tiburzi." Last modified November 18, 2022. https://en.wikipedia
.org/wiki/Bonnie_Tiburzi.

Wikipedia. "Helen Richey." Last modified April 20, 2023. https://en.wikipedia.org/wiki
/Helen_Richey.

Williams, Cynthia A. "Fort Myers Native Beverley Bass Made Aviation History."
News-Press. Modified July 7, 2017. https://www.news-press.com/story/entertain
ment/2016/03/19/fort-myers-beverley-bass-aviation-history-american-airlines
-broadway/81758696/.

"Women's History Month: A Timeline of Women in Aviation." Aerotech News &
Review (blog). Modified March 16, 2022. https://www.aerotechnews.com/blog
/2022/03/16/womens-history-month-a-timeline-of-women-in-aviation/.

CHAPTER 10
Capt. Patrice Clarke Washington

"Bessie Coleman's Aviation Community." The Official Website of Bessie Coleman.
Accessed August 16, 2023. http://www.bessiecoleman.org/community.php.

"Black History Month: Organization of Black Airline Pilots." Beautiful, Also, Are the
Souls of My Black Sisters (blog). February 18, 2008. https://kathmanduk2.word
press.com/2008/02/18/black-history-month-organization-of-black-airline-pilots/.

Black S.T.E.M. Heritage. "Patrice Clarke Washington: Bahamian Aviator." YouTube
video, 3:48. November 16, 2022. https://www.youtube.com/watch?v=WvuXG
GlobCE.

"Black Women Airline Pilots." *AvStop Online Magazine.* Accessed August 10, 2023.
http://avstop.com/History/BlackAirlines/womenairlinepilots.htm.

Boyd, Charles. "In Search of the Marine Corps' 1st African-American Female Pilot."
Black Collegian. February 1997. Gale General OneFile. https://link.gale.com/apps
/doc/A19263777/GPS?u=11947_gcpl&sid=bookmark-GPS&xid=c252d50a.

"Celebrating African Americans in Aviation—Women at the Forefront." San Diego Air
and Space Museum. Accessed August 10, 2023. http://sandiegoairandspace.org
/exhibits/online-exhibit-page/women-at-the-forefront.

REFERENCES

Culver, Virginia. "Pilot Marlon D. Green Fought Racial Discrimination." *Denver Post.* July 9, 2009. https://www.denverpost.com/2009/07/09/pilot-marlon-d-green -fought-racial-discrimination/.

Douglas, Deborah G. "American Women and Flight since 1940." *History of Science, Technology, and Medicine*: 1 (2004). https://uknowledge.uky.edu/upk_history _of_science_technology_and_medicine/1.

Fan, Katherine. "Flying High: The Living Legacy of Aviation Leader Capt. Patrice Clarke-Washington." The Points Guy (blog). February 8, 2022. https://thepoints guy.com/news/patrice-washington-aviation/.

Federal Aviation Administration, Department of Transportation. *Making History: People in Aviation Profile. FAA Aviation News: A DOT/FAA Flight Standards Safety Publication.* Washington, DC, 1996. https://books.google.com/books?id=3f05AQAA MAAJ&pg=RA8-PA21&lpg=RA8-PA21&dq=FAA+Aviation+News+January +1996+patrice+clarke+washington&source=bl&ots=Lz1dj1xAPq&sig=ACfU 3U0h3q-DBze5C8JqV9WEaLBbL1VYmg&hl=en&sa=X&ved=2ahUKEwigps Si1-aAAxWcQjABHcSoB8M4ChDoAXoECAQQAw#v=onepage&q=FAA%20 Aviation%20News%20January%201996%20patrice%20clarke%20washington&f =false.

Ho, Rodney. "Black Woman Pilot a Role Model." *Chicago Tribune.* February 12, 1995. http://articles.chicagotribune.com/1995-02-12/travel/9502120075_1_female -pilot-black-airline-pilots-aviation-history.

Hornblower, Margot. "The Still Unfriendly Skies." *Time.* August 28, 1995. https://con tent.time.com/time/subscriber/article/0,33009,983368-1,00.html.

Hughes, Zondra. "M'Lis Ward First Black Female Captain in Commercial Aviation." *Ebony.* January 2000. Gale General OneFile. https://link.gale.com/apps/doc /A58398518/GPS?u=11947_gcpl&sid=bookmark-GPS&xid=57caefce.

International Women Pilots Association. "Chapter News, Activities and Projects— Caribbean Section." *The Ninety-Nine Newsletter.* May 1985. https://www.ninety -nines.org/pdf/newsmagazine/198505.pdf.

"LaBelle, Jackson Win Trumpet Awards." Multichannel News. January 17, 2000. Gale OneFile: Business. https://link.gale.com/apps/doc/A59427402/GPS?u=11947 _gcpl&sid=bookmark-GPS&xid=5937488d.

"Letters to the Editor." *Ebony.* February 2000. Gale General OneFile. https://link .gale.com/apps/doc/A59110845/GPS?u=11947_gcpl&sid=bookmark-GPS &xid=a0c70f4a.

Lewis, Katelyn. "National Women in Aviation Week: Six Aviatrixes and Their Impact on Florida." *LAL Today.* March 9, 2021. https://laltoday.6amcity.com/national -women-aviation-week-fl#bessie-coleman.

Maksel, Rebecca. "Women Who Fly—Portraits of Female Pilots." *Smithsonian Air & Space Magazine.* December 19, 2008. https://www.smithsonianmag.com /air-space-magazine/women-who-fly-132844446/.

Moss, Shavaughn. "Flying High." *Nassau Guardian.* June 8, 2012. Archived December 23, 2016. https://web.archive.org/web/20161223195437/http://www.thenassauguardian .com/index.php?option=com_content&id=31534:flying-high&Itemid=58.

REFERENCES

Organization of Black Aerospace Professionals. Pioneers In Aerospace: OBAP Hall of Fame. https://obap.org/pioneers-in-aerospace/.

Our News. "Our People: Patrice Clarke Washington." Our News Video, 1:59. July 3, 2023. https://ournews.bs/patrice-clarke-washington/.

"Patrice Clarke Washington." Encyclopedia.com. Accessed August 14, 2023.https://www.encyclopedia.com/education/news-wires-white-papers-and-books/washington-patrice-clarke-1961.

Reichhardt, Tony. "Aviation's Jackie Robinson." *Smithsonian's Air & Space Magazine*. March 2007. https://www.smithsonianmag.com/air-space-magazine/aviations-jackie-robinson-16161631/.

Sawyer, Jerome. "Our People: Patrice Clarke Washington." *Our News*. July 3, 2023. https://ournews.bs/patrice-clarke-washington/.

"Soaring to New Heights." *Ebony*. July 1995. Gale General OneFile. https://link.gale.com/apps/doc/A17128528/GPS?u=11947_gcpl&sid=bookmark-GPS&xid=6d8e08eb.

"Social Changes in the Airline Industry—Patrice Clarke-Washington." Smithsonian National Air and Space Museum. Accessed August 14, 2023. https://airandspace.si.edu/explore/stories/social-change-airline-industry.

Sulton, James E. III. "African-American Women Pilots' Perceptions of Barriers to Success in Flight-Training and Strategies to Enhance Their Presence."Pepperdine University ProQuest Dissertations Publishing, 2008. 3311325. https://www.proquest.com/openview/74531045eb09fd33fe166fd9ed002c38/1?pq-origsite=gscholar&cbl=18750&diss=y#:~:text=The%20findings%20revealed%20that%20African,of%20role%20models%20and%20aviation.

Townsel, Lisa Jones. "Pilot: Theresa M. Claiborne." *Ebony*. March 1997, 96+. Gale General OneFile. https://link.gale.com/apps/doc/A19201551/GPS?u=11947_gcpl&sid=bookmark-GPS&xid=c7279aba.

United States Bureau of Labor Statistics. "Labor Force Statistics from the Current Population Survey." Last modified January 25, 2023. https://www.bls.gov/cps/cpsaat11.htm.

Urbinato, David. "Hard Work Pays Off for First Black Female Pilot." *Miami Herald*. December 16, 1994. Newspapers.com. https://www.newspapers.com.

Washington, Patrice Clarke, donor. Belt, Pilot, United Parcel Service (UPS). 1998. Inventory Number A20010058000. National Air and Space Museum, Washington, DC. https://airandspace.si.edu/collection-objects/belt-pilot-united-parcel-service-ups/nasm_A20010058000.

Washington, Patrice Clarke, donor. Blouse, Pilot, United Parcel Service (UPS). 1998. Inventory Number A20010056000. National Air and Space Museum, Washington, DC. https://airandspace.si.edu/collection-objects/blouse-pilot-united-parcel-service-ups/nasm_A20010056000.

Washington, Patrice Clarke, donor. Cap, Pilot, United Parcel Service (UPS). 1998. Inventory Number A20010053000. National Air and Space Museum, Washington, DC. https://airandspace.si.edu/collection-objects/cap-pilot-united-parcel-service-ups/nasm_A20010053000.

REFERENCES

Washington, Patrice Clarke, donor. Coat, Captain, United Parcel Service (UPS). 1998. Inventory Number A20010054000. National Air and Space Museum, Washington, DC. https://airandspace.si.edu/collection-objects/coat-captain-united-parcel -service-ups/nasm_A20010054000.

Washington, Patrice Clarke, donor. Trousers, Captain, United Parcel Service (UPS). 1998. Inventory Number A20010055000. National Air and Space Museum, Washington, DC. https://airandspace.si.edu/collection-objects/trousers-cap tain-united-parcel-service-ups/nasm_A20010055000.

Weslander, Eric. "Black Pilots' Group Gives Kids a Look at Careers in Aviation." *Courier-Journal.* July 26, 1997. Newspapers.com. https://www.newspapers.com.

Wikipedia. "Patrice Washington." Last modified December 3, 2021. https://en.wiki pedia.org/wiki/Patrice_Washington.

CHAPTER 11
Patty Wagstaff

"1st Annual Air Show of the Stars." Advertisement. *Orlando Sentinel.* April 15, 1998. Newspapers.com. https://www.newspapers.com.

"#2 The Aerobat: Patty Wagstaff." *Airport Journals.* June 1, 2005. http://airportjournals .com/2-the-aerobat-patty-wagstaff/.

Burnley, Samuel. "Patty Wagstaff Takes to the Skies Again at the Florida International Air Show." *Florida Weekly.* October 14, 2021. https://charlottecounty.floridaweekly .com/articles/patty-wagstaff-takes-to-the-skies-again-at-the-florida-international -air-show/.

Carter, Sharon. "On Your Own; Aerobats Explore Wild Blue Yonder." *New York Times.* December 18, 1989. https://www.nytimes.com/1989/12/18/sports/on-your-own -aerobats-explore-wild-blue-yonder.html?searchResultPosition=9.

Cooper, Ann L. "Patty Wagstaff: Fire and Air." The Ninety-Nines. Accessed August 24, 2023. https://www.ninety-nines.org/patty-wagstaff.htm.

DeYoung, Bill. "Get Set to Soar with the Best." *Stuart News.* November 10, 2004. Newspapers.com. https://www.newspapers.com.

Di Piazza, Karen. "There's More to Life Than Amelia Earhart." *Airport Journals.* April 1, 2003. http://airportjournals.com/theres-more-to-life-than-amelia-earhart/.

EAA AirVenture TakingOff Special. "Patty Wagstaff Legendary Aviator Interview." YouTube video, 10:23. August 18, 2021. https://www.youtube.com/watch?v=X7 fZdaMs5Jk&list=PLlLDlep63TSGt_DfrxQ-EEQPQCwQgR5eO&index=5.

Emblen, Mary L. "New Jersey Guide—Sussex Air Show." *New York Times.* August 21, 1994. https://www.nytimes.com/1994/08/21/nyregion/new-jersey-guide.html ?searchResultPosition=4.

Emmerich, Lisa. "Fliers Wow the Crowd at Orlando's Air Show." *Orlando Sentinel.* November 4, 2004. Newspapers.com. https://www.newspapers.com.

Faruqui, Mohhamad A. "Flier Earned Her Wings." *Panama City News Herald.* March 23, 2002. NewspaperArchive.com. https://access.newspaperarchive.com/us/florida /panama-city/panama-city-news-herald/2002/03-23/page-13/.

Freeze, Di and Holden, Henry. "Ron Kaplan: More Than Just a Job." *Airport Journals.* April 1, 2005. http://airportjournals.com/ron-kaplan-more-than-just-a-job/.

REFERENCES

Gary, Debbie. "Patty Wagstaff's Second Act." *Air and Space Magazine*. August 2011. https://www.smithsonianmag.com/air-space-magazine/patty-wagstaffs-second -act-27258964/.

"Heart of a Champion." Aircraft Owners and Pilots Association (blog). October 5, 2009. https://www.aopa.org/news-and-media/all-news/2009/october/05/heart -of-a-champion.

"'I Love the Feeling of Freedom.'" *Port Charlotte Sun*. October 8, 2019. Newspapers .com. https://www.newspapers.com.

International Aerobatic Club. "Getting Started." Accessed August 30, 2023. https:// iac24.org/getting-started/.

International Council of Air Shows (ICAS) Foundation Airshow Hall of Fame. "Jim and Ernie Moser, 2011." Accessed August 31, 2023. https://airshowfoundation .org/jim-and-ernie-moser/.

International Council of Air Shows (ICAS) Foundation Airshow Hall of Fame. "Patty Wagstaff, 2006." Accessed August 28, 2023. https://airshowfoundation.org/air -show-hall-of-fame/.

Lips, Jesse. "EAA Halls of Fame Induct Eight New Members." *Airport Journals*. December 1, 2005. http://airportjournals.com/eaa-halls-of-fame-induct-eight -new-members/.

Lips, Jesse. "Patty Wagstaff—Thrilling the Crowds." *Airport Journals*. April 1, 2008. http://airportjournals.com/patty-wagstaff-thrilling-the-crowds/.

"Meet Patty Wagstaff." The Official Patty Wagstaff Website. Accessed August 18, 2023. https://pattywagstaff.com/.

Moncada, Carlos. "'Have Helmet Will Travel,' Stunt Pilot Says." *Tampa Tribune*. October 5, 2003. Newspapers.com. https://www.newspapers.com.

National Aviation Hall of Fame. "Patricia 'Patty' Wagstaff." Accessed August 18, 2023. https://nationalaviation.org/enshrinee/patricia-patty-wagstaff/.

Patty Wagstaff Airshows, Inc. *Patty Wagstaff*. St. Augustine: Patty Wagstaff Airshows, Inc., 2022. https://pattywagstaff.com/wp-content/uploads/2023/01/Patty-Wag staff-2023-Autograph-Brochure.pdf.

Patty Wagstaff Aviation Foundation, Inc., State of Florida Division of Corporations. Accessed August 25, 2023. https://search.sunbiz.org/Inquiry/CorporationSearch /ConvertTiffToPDF?storagePath=COR%5C2023%5C0803%5C13056687 .Tif&documentNumber=N23000009272.

Patty Wagstaff Aviation Safety LLC. *Course Listing*. St. Augustine: Patty Wagstaff Airshows, Inc., 2023. https://pattywagstaff.com/wp-content/uploads/2023/08 /COURSE-LIST-V39-August-23-PDF.pdf.

Pima Air & Space Museum, Arizona Aviation Hall of Fame. "Patty R. Wagstaff." Accessed August 18, 2023. https://pimaair.org/hall-of-fame/patty-r-wagstaff/.

Price, Wayne T. "Female Pilot Stars in Air Show." *Florida Today*. February 20, 2011. Newspapers.com. https://www.newspapers.com.

Ryan, Michael. "I Want to Take It Higher." *Miami Herald*. August 20, 1995. News papers.com. https://www.newspapers.com.

St. Augustine Chronicles with Karen Zander. "Episode 7—St. Augustine Chronicles— Patty Wagstaff." YouTube video, 1:01:16. September 27, 2020. https://

www.youtube.com/watch?v=DHBOrsiJN-A&list=PLlLDlep63TSGt_DfrxQ
-EEQPQCwQgR5eO&index=8.

San Diego Air & Space Museum. "Living Legends of Flight—Patty Wagstaff." Hall of
Fame Induction video, 3:53. 2007. Accessed August 18, 2023. https://sandiegoair
andspace.org/hall-of-fame/honoree/patty-wagstaff.

San Diego Air & Space Museum Hall of Fame. "Patty Wagstaff." Accessed August 18,
2023. https://sandiegoairandspace.org/hall-of-fame/honoree/patty-wagstaff.

Smoke on Go. "Patty Wagstaff Interview Part 1." YouTube video, 14:14. July 2, 2020.
https://www.youtube.com/watch?v=TwBtNSllxKQ&list=PLlLDlep63TSGt
_DfrxQ-EEQPQCwQgR5eO&index=6.

Smoke on Go. "Patty Wagstaff Interview Part 2." YouTube video, 23:58. September 3,
2020. https://www.youtube.com/watch?v=qGpAyvzXXyU&list=PLlLDlep63
TSGt_DfrxQ-EEQPQCwQgR5eO&index=7.

"Veteran Flyer Is Stuart Air Show Star." *Indian River Press Journal*. September 26,
2016. Newspapers.com. https://www.newspapers.com.

Wagstaff, Katherine Hall, donor. Extra 260. 1993. Inventory Number A19930401000.
National Air and Space Museum, Washington, DC. https://airandspace.si.edu
/collection-objects/extra-260/nasm_A19930401000.

Wagstaff, Patty. "A Summer of Opportunity." *Plane & Pilot Magazine*. February 6, 2016.
https://www.planeandpilotmag.com/article/a-summer-of-opportunity/.

Wagstaff, Patty and Cooper, Ann Lewis. *Fire and Air: A Life on the Edge*. Chicago:
Chicago Review Press, 1997.

Weirauch, Chuck. "Patty Wagstaff—Still Thrilling the Crowds." *Airport Journals*. March
1, 2005. http://airportjournals.com/patty-wagstaff-still-thrilling-the-crowds/.

Wikipedia. "Patty Wagstaff." Last modified May 31, 2023. https://en.wikipedia.org/wiki
/Patty_Wagstaff.

Women in Aviation International (WAI) Pioneer Hall of Fame. "Patricia 'Patty' Wagstaff." Accessed September 1, 2023. https://www.wai.org/phof-directory/patty
-wagstaff.

"Women Pilots and Astronauts." *Panama City News Herald*. March 24, 2003. https://
access.newspaperarchive.com/us/florida/panama-city/panama-city-news-herald
/2003/03-24/page-14/.

Wright, John. "San Diego Air & Space Museum Inducts Five Pioneers of Aviation
Hall of Fame." *Airport Journals*. January 1, 2008. http://airportjournals.com/san
-diego-air-space-museum-inducts-five-pioneers-of-aviation/.

CHAPTER 12
Capt. Linda Pfeiffer Pauwels

"All Female Crew Makes Historic American Airlines Flight from Miami to Dallas on
International Women's Day." CBS Miami. March 9, 2021. https://www.cbsnews
.com/miami/news/all-female-crew-historic-american-airlines-flight-miami-dallas
-international-womens-day/.

"Alumni Going to MDC Hall of Fame." *Miami Herald*. May 19, 2005. Newspapers
.com. https://www.newspapers.com.

REFERENCES

"American Airlines Captain Publishes Poetry Book to Help Pilots during COVID." *Aerotime Hub.* August 12, 2021. https://www.aerotime.aero/articles/28569-cap tain-linda-covid-story.

"American Airlines Marks International Women's Day with All-Female Crew." American Airlines Newsroom (blog). March 8, 2021. https://news.aa.com/news /news-details/2021/American-Airlines-marks-International-Womens-Day-with -all-female-crew-ID-W-03/default.aspx.

"A Pioneering Pilot Who Writes Haiku, Too." *Miami Dade College Forum.* March 2021. https://mydigitalpublication.com/publication/?m=12704&i=699252&p=2&ver =html5.

Ceja, Jeannette. "Sky's the Limit." *palabra.* August 28, 2021. https://www.palabranahj .org/archive/skys-the-limit.

Hardiman, Jake. "What Happened to US Cargo Carrier Southern Air?" SimpleFlying (blog). April 1, 2022. https://simpleflying.com/what-happened-to-us-cargo-car rier-southern-air/.

Literary Aviatrix. "Pilot-Poet, Captain Linda Pauwels, on Beyond Haiku." YouTube video, 29:31. January 28, 2021. https://www.youtube.com/watch?v=9vkFT9YIEus.

Loretta Sanchez (CA). "In Honor of Linda Pawels for Her Achievements in the Field of Aviation." *Congressional Record—Extensions of Remarks* (November 14, 2002) p. E2023. Accessed September 6, 2023. https://www.congress.gov/crec/2002/11/14 /CREC-2002-11-14-extensions.pdf.

"MDC Honors 28 at Star-Studded Alumni Hall of Fame Dinner." *Miami Times.* June 8–14, 2005. https://ufdc.ufl.edu/UF00028321/00021/images/4.

Morris, Sammie L. "What Archives Reveal: The Hidden Poems of Amelia Earhart." *Libraries Research Publications,* 2006, Paper 28. http://docs.lib.purdue.edu /lib_research/28.

Negroni, Christine. "Amelia Earhart's Long-hidden Poems Reveal an Enigma's Inner Thoughts." *Washington Post.* October 17, 2021. https://www.washingtonpost.com /entertainment/books/amelia-earhart-poems/2021/10/14/7fc713fa-2cef-11ec -8ef6-3ca8fe943a92_story.html.

Ojito, Mirta. "Woman Lives Dream Flying707 Jets for Cargo Airline." *Miami Herald.* July 28, 1988. Newspapers.com. https://www.newspapers.com.

Pauwels, Capt. Linda. 2002. "Hispanic Americans: Strength in Unity, Faith and Diversity." Keynote Speech, Department of Transportation Hispanic Heritage Month Observance Opening Ceremony, Washington, DC, September 26, 2002 (on file with author).

Pauwels, Linda Pfeiffer. "From the Cockpit: Flying Is the Sweetest Part." *Orange County Register.* November 17, 2002. NewsLibrary.com. https://www.newslibrary.com/.

Pauwels, Linda. "Interview with Captain Linda Pauwels," by Bridges DelPonte. May 19, 2023 (on file with author).

Pauwels, Linda. "The Love of Learning Leads to a Trailblazing Career." American Airlines Newsroom (blog). March 10, 2017. https://news.aa.com/news/news-details /2017/The-love-of-learning-leads-to-a-trailblazing-career/default.aspx.

REFERENCES

Pettitt, Karlene. "Captain Linda Pauwels, Friday's Fabulous Flyer." *Flight to Success* (blog). January 22, 2021. https://karlenepetitt.blogspot.com/2021/01/captain -linda-pauwels.html.

Prince George's County Memorial Library System (PGCMLS). "Latinas in Aviation: Beyond Haiku with Linda Pauwels Co-Presented with College Park Aviation Museum." YouTube video, 46:08. September 23, 2021. https://www.youtube.com /watch?v=8Q-lOsc5RNk.

Ray, Laura. "First Latina American Airlines Captain Releases Book of Poems by Women Pilots." TravelAwaits (blog). October 31, 2021. https://www.travel awaits.com/2706214/women-pilots-write-poetry/.

Ruiz, Jacqueline S. *Latinas in Aviation*. Naperville, IL: Fig Factor Media, LLC, 2020.

Ruiz, Vicki L. and Sánchez Korrol, Virginia. *Latinas in the United States: A Historical Encyclopedia*. Bloomington: Indiana University Press, 2006.

The Betsy Hotel. "ESCRIBE AQUÍ/Write Here—The Betsy Hotel's 7th Annual Cele- bration of IberoAmerican Artists." Accessed May 21, 2023. https://www.thebetsy hotel.com/sites/default/files/2021-08/ESCRIBE%20AQUI%CC%81_Write%20 Here%20%20%E2%80%93%20The%20Betsy%20Hotel%E2%80%99s%207th%20 Annual%20Celebration%20of%20Iberoamerican%20Artists%20-%20August%20 3%2C%202021%20-%20Noon.pdf.

Totah, Jose. "Linda Pauwels, from San Pedro to the Cockpit of a Boeing 787." *For the Nation*. February 3, 2019. https://www.lanacion.com.ar/turismo/viajes/linda-pau wels-me-decian-que-era-imposible-nid2216255/.

Tulis, David. "Latinas in Aviation Festival Recognizes Pioneering Women." *Aircraft Owners and Pilots Association News & Media*. October 6, 2021. https://www.aopa .org/news-and-media/all-news/2021/october/06/latinas-in-aviation-festival-rec ognizes-pioneering-women.

Ubago, Maria. "Linda Pauwels: From the First Latina Pilot for American Airlines to Turning Her Peers into Poets." *El Español*. July 9, 2022. https://www.elespanol .com/mujer/protagonistas/20220709/linda-pauwels-primera-american-airlines -convertir-companeros/685181897_0.html.

Villa, Walter. "She Was American's First Latina to Captain a Flight. Now, She's a Pio- neer Poet, Too." *Miami Herald*. March 8, 2021. https://www.miamiherald.com /news/business/article249691033.html.

"WAI Members in the News." Women in Aviation International (blog). Accessed Sep- tember 5, 2023. https://lsc-pagepro.mydigitalpublication.com/publication/?i=6944 88&article_id=3916441&view=articleBrowser.

Wikipedia. "Linda Pauwels." Last modified August 14, 2022. https://en.wikipedia.org /wiki/Linda_Pauwels.

Chapter 13
Lt. Col. Christine Mau Kelley (ret. USAF)

AirForce Times. "Women's Groundbreaking Combat Flight Sparks Debate." *Visalia Times-Delta*. April 19, 2011. https://www.newspapers.com/article/126466057 /womensgroundbreakingcombatflightsparksd/.

REFERENCES

Aviatrix99. "All Female F-15 Fighter Pilot Crew Launches Historic Mission over Afghanistan: Dudette 07 Flight." YouTube video, 2:11. October 1, 2019. https://www.youtube.com/watch?v=gIq2Wj7p7A4.

Banglesdorf, René. "Fighter Pilot to Corporate Trailblazer: Christine Mau." The Leadership in Aviation Podcast. YouTube video, 27:03. August 4, 2023. https://www.youtube.com/watch?v=wI0b85PDv8g.

Callahan, Maureen. "Flight of the 'Dudettes.'" *New York Post.* April 10, 2011. https://nypost.com/2011/04/10/flight-of-the-dudettes/.

Castro, Ezzy. "First Woman to Pilot F-35 Fighter Jet Visits Seminole County Schools." *WKMG ClickOrlando.* January 24, 2020. https://www.clickorlando.com/news/local/2020/01/24/first-woman-to-pilot-f-35-fighter-jet-visits-seminole-county-schools/.

Collman, Ashley. "Trailblazing Female Air Force Pilot Makes History as First Woman to Fly New F-35 Fighter Jet." DailyMail.com. May 7, 2015. https://www.dailymail.co.uk/news/article-3072098/Trailblazing-female-Air-Force-pilot-makes-history-woman-fly-new-F-35-fighter-jet.html.

Cronin, 1st Lt. Hope. "Face of Defense: First Female F-35 Pilot Begins Training." US Department of Defense (blog). May 7, 2015. https://www.defense.gov/News/News-Stories/Article/Article/604590/.

Defense Visual Information Distribution Service. "Pioneering Female F-35 Pilot Reflects on Legacy of Women in Military Aviation." August 3, 2022. https://www.dvidshub.net/news/426441/pioneering-female-f-35-pilot-reflects-legacy-women-military-aviation.

Demerly, Tom. "For Nearly Two Years, Christine Mau Was the Only Woman F-35 Pilot." *Medium.* March 13, 2017. https://medium.com/war-is-boring/for-nearly-two-years-christine-mau-was-the-only-woman-f-35-pilot-c7a91152dfc8.

Demerly, Tom. "Meet the First Female F-35 Pilot." *The Aviationist.* March 8, 2017. https://theaviationist.com/2017/03/08/meet-the-first-female-f-35-pilot/.

"DEOMI Releases 2017 Women's History Month Poster." *Florida Today.* March 17, 2017. Newspapers.com. https://www.newspapers.com/.

Erdrich, Ron. "High-Flying Texan at Sweetwater WASP Reunion (with Video)." *Abilene Reporter-News.* May 29, 2016. https://www.reporternews.com/story/news/columnists/big-country-journal/2016/05/29/highflying-texan-at-sweetwater-wasp-reunion-with-video/92231332/.

Everstine, Brian W. "Air Force Removes Height Requirement for Pilot Applicants." *Air & Space Forces Magazine.* May 22, 2020. https://www.airandspaceforces.com/air-force-removes-minimum-height-requirement-for-pilot-applicants/.

Everstine, Brian. "First Female F-35 Pilot Completes Initial Flight." *AirForceTimes.* May 6, 2015. https://www.airforcetimes.com/news/your-air-force/2015/05/06/first-female-f-35-pilot-completes-initial-flight/.

Fox News Insider. "First All-Female Team Flies Historic Combat Mission in Afghanistan." YouTube video, 3:10. April 6, 2011. https://www.youtube.com/watch?v=LMv6LYursgQ.

REFERENCES

"Full Circle: Air Force F-35 Pilots Join F-35 Training Team." Website of Lockheed Martin Corporation. April 6, 2022. https://www.lockheedmartin.com/en-us/news /features/2017/full-circle—air-force-f-35-pilots-join-f-35-training-team.html.

Gaddie, Kevin. "First Female F-35 Pilot Closes Eglin Women's History Month." Eglin Air Force Base (blog). April 6, 2023. https://www.eglin.af.mil/News/Article-Dis play/Article/3354165/first-female-f-35-pilot-closes-eglin-womens-history-month/.

Harpley, Unshin Lee. "Trailblazer Maj. Gen. Jeannie Leavitt, First USAF Female Fighter Pilot, Retires." *Air & Space Forces Magazine*. September 25, 2023. https:// www.airandspaceforces.com/first-usaf-female-fighter-pilot-maj-gen-jeannie -leavitt-retires/#:~:text=She%20was%20the%20first%20woman,Nellis%20Air %20Force%20Base%2C%20Nev.

Hyatt, Jason. "Meet the First Female F-35 Pilot." Sofrep (blog). May 6, 2015. https:// sofrep.com/fightersweep/meet-first-female-f-35-pilot/.

Jagannathan, Meera. "This Mother of Two Is the First Woman to Pilot an F-35 Fighter Jet—She Talks Sexism and 'Killing Bad Guys.'" *MarketWatch*. May 12, 2019. https://www.marketwatch.com/story/the-first-woman-to-pilot-an-f-35-fighter -the-jet-doesnt-care-whether-youre-a-man-or-a-woman-2019-05-01.

Kelley, Christine Mau. "Interview with Lt. Col. Christine Mau Kelley (ret. USAF)," by Bridges DelPonte. August 10, 2023 (on file with author).

Kester, Marissa N. *There from the Beginning: Women in the U.S. Air Force*. Maxwell AFB, AL: Air University Press, 2021. https://www.airuniversity.af.edu/Portals/10/AU Press/Books/B_0172_THERE_FROM_THE_BEGINNING..pdf.

"Life as a Female Fighter Pilot." National Air and Space Museum (blog). October 3, 2016. https://airandspace.si.edu/stories/editorial/life-female-fighter-pilot.

LiveAirShowTV. "ViceCommander Christine Mau, Talks to Us about F-35." Joint Base Andrews Air Show 2016. YouTube video, 2:53. November 2, 2020. https://www .youtube.com/watch?v=kaXxapVrIQ8.

Marcin, Tim. "Who Is Christine Mau? First US Female Pilot to Fly Lightning II Fighter Jet." *International Business Times*. May 7, 2015. https://www.ibtimes.com /who-christine-mau-first-us-female-pilot-fly-lightning-ii-fighter-jet-1912257.

Mosbergen, Dominique. "Air Force Announces First Ever Female F-35 Fighter Jet Pilot, Lt. Col. Christine Mau." *HuffPost*. May 7, 2015. https://www.huffpost.com /entry/christine-mau-first-female-f35-pilot_n_7229768.

National Aeronautic Association. "Lt. Col. Christine Mau Selected as Recipient of 2016 Stinson Trophy." NAA press release. January 31, 2017. https://naa.aero /wp-content/uploads/2020/03/Stinson-Trophy-2016.pdf.

Reuters. "Meet Christine Mau, First Female F-35 Fighter Jet Pilot." *Express Tribune*. May 7, 2015. https://tribune.com.pk/story/882659/lockheed-f-35-gets-first-fe male-pilot-air-force.

Smith, Alexander. "Christine Mau Becomes First U.S. Female Pilot to Fly F-35 Lightning II Jet." NBC News. May 7, 2015. https://www.nbcnews.com/news/us-news /christine-mau-becomes-first-female-pilot-fly-f-35-lightning-n355101.

The Island Packet. "A Talk with Lt. Col. Christine Mau, the First Female F-35 Pilot." YouTube video, 2:06. May 13, 2015. https://www.youtube.com/watch?v=o1ZJX 8v0SPg.

Thompson, Staff Sgt. Peter. "So Others May Dream." 33rd Fighter Wing Public Affairs, Air Education and Training Command. March 9, 2017. https://www.aetc.af.mil /News/Article-Display/Article/1110795/so-others-may-dream/.

"Today in Military History: Senates Approves Female Combat Pilots." *We Are the Mighty* (blog). July 31, 2023. https://www.wearethemighty.com/articles/today -in-military-history-senates-approves-female-combat-pilots/.

US Military Power. "US Air Force F-35 First Female Fighter Pilot in Action." YouTube video, 9:18. November 26, 2021. https://www.youtube.com/watch?v=DfnPTeuB2ng.

Wong, Kristina. "Air Force Announces First Female F-35 Pilot." *The Hill*. May 6, 2015. https://thehill.com/policy/defense/air-force/241298-air-force-announces-first -female-f-35-pilot/.

CHAPTER 14
Col. Eileen Collins (ret. USAF)

Associated Press. "1st Woman Wins Command of Shuttle." *Orlando Sentinel*. March 5,1998. https://www.newspapers.com/newspage/234623911/.

Associated Press. "13 Women Triumphing Vicariously." *New York Times*. February 5, 1995. https://nyti.ms/3ShioGy.

Associated Press. "Another Test for Commander Lies on Earth." *New York Times*. July 27, 1999. https://nyti.ms/46S9dko.

Associated Press. "Class of '90 Optimistic about NASA." *Florida Today*. July 20, 1990. Newspapers.com. https://www.newspapers.com/.

Associated Press. "Columbia Lands First Female Commander at Controls." *Pensacola News Journal*. July 28, 1999. Newspapers.com. https://www.newspapers.com/.

Associated Press. "Crew Is Set for Rendezvous with Mir." *Orlando Sentinel*. September 10, 1993. Newspapers.com. https://www.newspapers.com/.

Associated Press. "First Female Shuttle Pilot Ready to Soar." *Press Journal*. January 30, 1995. Newspapers.com. https://www.newspapers.com/.

Associated Press. "NASA Readies for Shuttle Touchdown." *News-Press*. August 8, 2005. Newspapers.com. https://www.newspapers.com/.

Associated Press. "NASA Training First Female to Pilot Shuttle Mission." *Florida Today*. September 29, 1991. Newspapers.com. https://www.newspapers.com/.

"Astronauts Carry Mementos into Space." *Florida Today*. February 19, 1995. Newspapers.com. https://www.newspapers.com/.

Banke, Jim. "Y'all Did a Terrific Job Up There." *Florida Today*. February 12, 1995. Newspapers.com. https://www.newspapers.com/.

Biographical Data. Eileen Marie Collins (Colonel, USAF, Ret.) NASA Astronaut (Former). Lyndon B. Johnson Space Center. Accessed October 24, 2023. https://www.nasa.gov/wp-content/uploads/2016/01/collins_eileen.pdf.

Borenstein, Seth. "Discovery's Day Gets Off to Good Start." *Orlando Sentinel*. February 3, 1995. Newspapers.com. https://www.newspapers.com/.

Borenstein, Seth. Great Adventure Ends for Astronaut. *Orlando Sentinel*. May 22, 1997. Newspapers.com. https://www.newspapers.com/.

REFERENCES

Borenstein, Seth. "Sailing in Space above Earth Man's Work, Says Russian Official." *Tallahassee Democrat.* May 4, 1997. Newspapers.com. https://www.newspapers.com/.

Brainard, Jeffrey. "Shuttle Heading for Mir." *Tampa Bay Times.* May15, 1997. News papers.com. https://www.newspapers.com/.

Britannica, T. Editors of Encyclopaedia. "Eileen Collins." Encyclopedia Britannica. November 15, 2022. https://www.britannica.com/biography/Eileen-Collins.

Broad, William J. "Blasting Off on a Mission for Cosmic Science." *New York Times.* July 13, 1999. https://nyti.ms/3QgiSdl.

Cabbage, Michael. "Collins Guides Shuttle Home." *Orlando Sentinel.* July 28, 1999. Newspapers.com. https://www.newspapers.com/.

Cabbage, Michael. "'Good Luck, Godspeed.'" *Orlando Sentinel.* July 27, 2005. News papers.com. https://www.newspapers.com/.

Cabbage, Michael. "Shuttle Finally Roars to Life." *Orlando Sentinel.* July 23, 1999. Newspapers.com. https://www.newspapers.com/.

Cabbage, Michael and Shelton, Robyn. "Mission Accomplished." *Orlando Sentinel.* August 10, 2005. Newspapers.com. https://www.newspapers.com/.

Coledan, Stefano S. "Astronauts Express Confidence in Safety of Planned Mission." *New York Times.* January 8, 2005. https://www.nytimes.com/2005/01/08/us/astronauts-express-confidence-in-safety-of-planned-mission.html?searchResultPosition=9.

Collins, Eileen M. and Ward, Jonathan H. *Through the Glass Ceiling to the Stars.* New York: Arcade Publishing, 2021.

Connor, Holly J. "Dr. Sian Proctor, the First Black Woman to Pilot a Spacecraft, Makes History: 'A Phoenix Rising.'" *Ms. Magazine.* October 12, 2021. https://msmagazine.com/2021/10/12/sian-proctor-first-black-woman-pilot-spacecraft-spacex-stem/.

Dickey, Beth. "After Hiccup at Liftoff, Shuttle Puts Telescope into Space." *New York Times.* July 24, 1999. https://nyti.ms/49caT9A.

Dickey, Beth. "Woman's Work: Space Commander Eileen Marie Collins." *New York Times.* July 24, 1999. https://nyti.ms/46IAm9l.

"Diversity of Atlantis Crew Reflects Multinational Effort." *Florida Today.* May 14, 1997. Newspapers.com. https://www.newspapers.com/.

Dunn, Marcia. "Astronauts Wanted; Everyone Can Apply." *Tallahassee Democrat.* September 22, 1991. Newspapers.com. https://www.newspapers.com/.

Dunn, Marcia. "Collins Shows She's Got 'the RightStuff.'" *Florida Today.* August 22, 1999. Newspapers.com. https://www.newspapers.com/.

Duryea, Bill. "'Discovery' Mission Will Make History." *Tampa Bay Times.* February 3, 1995. Newspapers.com. https://www.newspapers.com/.

"First Female Space Pilot." *Tampa Bay Times.* March 18, 1996. Newspapers.com. https://www.newspapers.com/.

Foster, Amy. "The Gendered Anniversary: The Story of America's Women Astronauts." *Florida Historical Quarterly:* Vol. 87: No. 2, Article 5 (2020). https://stars.library.ucf.edu/fhq/vol87/iss2/5.

Hall, Elizabeth Wade. "Flying High: Eileen Collins Breaks Through Barriers." *Florida Today.* August 2, 1992. Newspapers.com. https://www.newspapers.com/.

Halvorson, Todd. "Crew Repeatedly Makes History." *Florida Today.* August 10, 2005. Newspapers.com. https://www.newspapers.com/.

REFERENCES

Halvorson, Todd. "Discovery Countdown Starts Today." *Florida Today*. January 29, 1995. Newspapers.com. https://www.newspapers.com/.

Halvorson, Todd. "Discovery Crew to Inspect Shuttle Cargo Today." *Florida Today*. December 10, 1994. Newspapers.com. https://www.newspapers.com/.

Halvorson, Todd. "Home, Safe." *Florida Today*. August 9, 2005. Newspapers.com. https://www.newspapers.com/.

Halvorson, Todd. "NASA Seeks Cause of Leaks." *Florida Today*. July 28, 1999. News papers.com. https://www.newspapers.com/.

Houston Chronicle. "Shuttle Crew, Cosmonaut to Fly around Mir Station." *Florida Today*. September 9, 1993. Newspapers.com. https://www.newspapers.com/.

Kennedy, Paul. "Flights of Fancy, We'll Never Fly without Some Help." *Florida Today*. July 7, 1991. Newspapers.com. https://www.newspapers.com/.

Kridler, Chris. "Astronaut Eileen Collins Retires." *Daily Spectrum*. May 2, 2006. News papers.com. https://www.newspapers.com/.

Kuta, Sarah. "Nicole Mann Becomes the First Native American Woman in Space." *Smithsonian Magazine*. October 6, 2022. https://www.smithsonianmag.com /smart-news/nicole-mann-becomes-the-first-native-american-woman-in -space-180980906/.

Leary, Warren E. "Joy Is Tinged with Sadness for Columbia." *New York Times*. August 10, 2005. https://www.nytimes.com/2005/08/10/science/space/joy-is-tinged -with-sadness-for-columbia.html?searchResultPosition=4.

Leary, Warren E. and Schwartz, John. "Shuttle Crew Seeks Assurance before Flight." *New York Times*. April 8, 2005. https://www.nytimes.com/2005/04/08/us/shuttle -crew-seeks-assurance-before-flight.html?searchResultPosition=8.

Long, Phil and Borenstein, Seth. "A Fantastic Mission." *Miami Herald*. August 10, 2005. Newspapers.com. https://www.newspapers.com/.

McCarthy, Molly. "Astronaut from Elmira to Hang Up Her Helmet." *Democrat and Chronicle*. May 2, 2006. Newspapers.com. https://www.newspapers.com/.

Merzer, Martin. "Just One Big Step." *Miami Herald*. July 27, 2005. Newspapers.com. https://www.newspapers.com/.

Moulton, Andrew. "A Day to Remember at New Memorial to Military Women." *Miami Herald*. October 19, 1997. Newspapers.com. https://www.newspapers.com/.

"NASA Grounds Two Astronauts." *Tampa Bay Times*. July 10, 1990. https://www.tampa bay.com/archive/1990/07/10/nasa-grounds-two-astronauts/.

Nesmith, Susannah A. "Discovery Blasts Off for Rendezvous." *Palm Beach Post*. February 3, 1995. Newspapers.com. https://www.newspapers.com/.

Reuters. "A Space-Age Taste Test of Coca-Cola." *Miami Herald*. December 18, 1994. Newspapers.com. https://www.newspapers.com/.

Speck, Emilee. "These Women Achieved Firsts of Spaceflight Leading the Way for Next Generation." Fox Weather. Accessed October 24, 2023. https://www.fox weather.com/earth-space/these-women-achieved-firsts-of-spaceflight-leading -the-way-for-next-generation.

Suriano, Robyn. "Atlantis Crew Heads Home after Farewell." *Florida Today*. May 22, 1997. Newspapers.com. https://www.newspapers.com/.

REFERENCES

Suriano, Robyn. "Collins Blazes New Trail." *Florida Today*. July 23, 1999. Newspapers .com. https://www.newspapers.com/.

Suriano, Robyn. "Pilot on Course to Land Another Milestone." *Florida Today*. May 12, 1997. Newspapers.com. https://www.newspapers.com/.

Thulin, Lila. "What It Was Like to Become the First Woman to Pilot and Command a Space Shuttle." *Smithsonian Magazine*. October 17, 2019. https://www.smithso nianmag.com/smithsonian-institution/what-it-was-become-first-woman-pilot -and-command-space-shuttle-180973343/.

United Press International. "NASA Selects 23 Astronaut Candidates." *Tampa Tribune*. January 18, 1990. Newspapers.com. https://www.newspapers.com/.

United Press International. "Woman Chosen as Pilot Trainee in NASA Group." *Miami Herald*. January 19, 1990. Newspapers.com. https://www.newspapers.com/.

Wikipedia. "Eileen Collins." Last modified October 11, 2023. Accessed June 15, 2023. https://en.wikipedia.org/wiki/Eileen_Collins.

York, Michelle. "A City Looks to the Skies, Proud of Its Own Astronaut." *New York Times*. March 29, 2005. https://www.nytimes.com/2005/03/29/nyregion/a-city -looks-to-the-skies-proud-of-its-own-astronaut.html?searchResultPosition=16.

PHOTO CREDITS*

---

*The appearance of US Department of Defense (DoD), Smithsonian Institution, National Air and Space Museum, or any third-party's photos/visual information does not imply nor constitute affiliation, endorsement, or approval of this book or its contents.

PHOTO CREDITS

Page

43   *Famous transatlantic flyer demonstrates new type plane to Navy officials. Clarence Chamberlain, famous Transatlantic flyer, and Ruth Nichols (in cabin) noted aviator, arrived in Washington today with the new Chamberlain cabin monoplane. In this photograph they are pointing out the many features of this new plane to Commander A. H. Douglas, Commandant of the Naval Air Station, and Commander J. H. Towers, Assistant Chief of the Naval Bureau of Aeronautics (right). Unusual visibility and special aerlons, which Chamberlain says practically makes it impossible for this ship to stall or go into a tailspin, are the new features.* 1930. Washington, DC. Harris and Ewing Photograph Collection, Library of Congress, Prints and Photographs Division, Photograph by Harris and Ewing, LC-DIG-hec-35819. Accessed May 24, 2023, https://www.loc.gov/pictures/item/2016878784/.

52   *Jacqueline Cochran—Internationally Known Woman Aviator.* 1940 (circa). Tallahassee, FL. State Archives of Florida, Florida Memory. Accessed June 2, 2023, http://www.floridamemory.com/items/show/34626.

62   *Women in test history. Jacqueline Cochran standing on the wing of an F-86. In 1953, Jacqueline Cochran made two supersonic dives in a Canadian-built F-86 Sabre, becoming the first woman to exceed the speed of sound. At her death in 1980, Cochran held more speed, distance, and altitude records than any other pilot, which remains true today.* 1953. Rogers Dry Lake, CA. Photo courtesy of Air Force Test Center History Office. Accessed June 2, 2023, https://www.aftc.af.mil/News/Photos/igphoto/2002600388/.

71   *Betty Skelton Frankman (later Erde)—Winter Haven, Florida.* 1950 (circa). Winter Haven, FL. State Archives of Florida, Florida Memory. Accessed June 4, 2023, https://www.floridamemory.com/items/show/152603.

73   *Pitts Special S-1C Little Stinker.* 2017. Chantilly, VA. Photo by Sanjay Acharya. (Revised from color to grayscale under Creative Commons Attribution-Share Alike 4.0 International License.) Accessed September 26, 2023, https://commons.wikimedia.org/w/index.php?curid=65147815.

76   *Penny Thompson in Civil Air Patrol Uniform.* 1964. Miami, FL. Photo by Bob East, *Miami Herald* (Creative Commons Attribution-Share Alike 4.0 International License). Accessed June 11, 2023, https://commons.wikimedia.org/wiki/File:Penny_Thompson_in_Civil_Air_Patrol_Uniform_1964.jpg.

77   *Devastation from Fire at Richmond Naval Air Station during Hurricane.* 1945. Miami, FL. State Archives of Florida, Florida Memory. Accessed June 11, 2023, https://www.floridamemory.com/items/show/38354.

87   *Lt. Judith Neuffer pre-flight check 1974.* 1974. Jacksonville, FL. Photo by US Navy. Accessed August 3, 2023, https://en.wikipedia.org/w/index.php?curid=13418444.

89   *USN 1147578 WP-3A Orion.* 1971. Jacksonville, FL. Naval History and Heritage Command Photo Archives/National Archives, photo # USN 1147578. Accessed August 11, 2023, https://www.history.navy.mil/our-collections/photography/numerical-list-of-images/nhhc-series/nh-series/USN-1147000/USN-1147578.html.

PHOTO CREDITS

Page

99   *Beverley Bass, American Airlines, First Female Captain.* 1986. (Courtesy of Beverley Bass)

103 *Beverley Bass Has Been Flying This Embraer Phenom 100 from 2017 to Present.* 2023. (Courtesy of Beverley Bass)

107 *Tuskegee Airmen in WWII.* Circa 1940s. Photo by US Air Force (VIRIN #10310-D-LN615-002). Accessed November 28, 2023, https://media.defense.gov/2011/Mar/10/2000278738/-1/-1/0/110310-D-LN615-002.JPG.

110 *Captain Patrice Clarke Washington.* Circa 1995–1996. Photo by Carolyn Russo, Smithsonian National Air & Space Museum (NASM A03353). Accessed October 2, 2023, https://airandspace.si.edu/multimedia-gallery/nasm-9a03353jpg.

119 *Patty Wagstaff.* 2006. Courtesy of Patty Wagstaff. Accessed August 22, 2023, https://pattywagstaff.com/galleryindex/.

122 *Patty Wagstaff Vertical in Extra 260.* n.d. Courtesy of Patty Wagstaff. Accessed November 28, 2023, https://pattywagstaff.com/galleryindex/.

131 *Cockpit Photo of Captain Linda Pauwels in a B787 Simulator.* 2021. Miami, FL. Photo by Stephen Gould—https://www.diariolasamericas.com/cultura/la-piloto-linda-pauwels-hace-poesia-las-alturas-n4233873 (Revised from color to grayscale under Creative Commons Attribution-Share Alike 4.0 International License). Accessed November 28, 2023, https://commons.wikimedia.org/w/index.php?curid=119971420.

136 *Amelia Earhart in Airplane.* 1936. Harris and Ewing Photograph Collection, Library of Congress, Prints and Photographs Division, Photograph by Harris and Ewing, LC-DIG-hec-40747. Accessed November 29, 2023, https://www.loc.gov/pictures/item/2016882728/.

142 *So Others May Dream.* 2017. Eglin Air Force Base, FL. US Air Force photo by Staff Sgt. Peter Thompson. Accessed November 29, 2023, https://www.aetc.af.mil/News/Photos/igphoto/2001709183/.

145 *Trailblazer Takes Flight.* 2017. Eglin Air Force Base, FL. US Air Force photo by Staff Sgt. Peter Thompson. Accessed November 29, 2023, https://www.aetc.af.mil/News/Photos/igphoto/2001709177/.

160 *STS-93 Commander Collins Demonstrates Her Weightlessness on the Middeck.* 1999. Space Shuttle *Columbia.* Courtesy of Lyndon B. Johnson Space Center/National Archives NAID: 23178677. Accessed October 5, 2023, https://catalog.archives.gov/id/23178677.

163 *STS-114—Collins on Forward Flight Deck.* 2005. Space Shuttle *Discovery.* Courtesy of Lyndon B. Johnson Space Center/National Archives NAID: 23398662. Accessed November 19, 2023, https://catalog.archives.gov/id/23398662.

ACKNOWLEDGMENTS

A NONFICTION BOOK REQUIRES A TEAM OF INDIVIDUALS AND ORGANIZA-tions to aid and support the author. I acknowledge and thank the diligent staff of the Charlotte County Library System and the Punta Gorda Charlotte Library for access to books, videos, interlibrary loans, and digital resources that are essential for independent researchers to explore often overlooked corners of Florida history. Without the public library system, this book would not be possible. I am also grateful to the State Archives of Florida, Florida Memory, for maintaining and offering a treasure trove of photos, documenting key figures and events in Florida history. With deep admiration and gratitude, I acknowledge and thank Capt. Beverley Bass, Lt. Col. Christine Kelley (ret. USAF), Capt. Linda Pauwels, and Patty Wagstaff for their time and effort in generously shar-ing their remarkable stories, insights, and photos with me. The courage, determination, and expertise of these trailblazing female pilots broke important aviation barriers and continue to inspire the next genera-tion in aviation. I acknowledge and thank Debra A. Murphy, Associate Acquisitions Editor, Pineapple Press, for her time, energy, and patience in answering my questions, editing my manuscript, working with her design team, and guiding this book to completion. I also acknowledge and thank Lauren Younker, former Acquisitions Editor, Pineapple Press, for reach-ing out to me about developing a Florida-based nonfiction proposal that got this ball rolling in February 2023. Last, but not least, I acknowledge and thank my husband, David Riddell, for being a wonderful beta reader of every chapter and for his love, support, and encouragement during the long process of researching, writing, editing, and launching this book.

INDEX

Page references for figures are italicized.

INDEX

INDEX

Cole, Duane US aerobatic champion: coach of Wagstaff, Patty, 116–17; Cole Brothers Air Show, 116

Coleman, Elizabeth "Bessie," 22–35, *28*; African American Eighth Infantry Regiment, Illinois National Guard, 33–34; African American Seminole Film Producing Company, 27–29; air shows, US, 26–27, 29–31; American Women Quarters Series, US Mint, 35; aviation firsts and major achievements, 25–26, 34–35; Black Heritage stamp series, US Postal Service, 35; Caudron Brothers Aviation School, 25; Chamber of Commerce, Orlando, FL, 31; Checkerboard Aerodrome, Chicago, IL, 27; childhood, 23–24; Coleman, George, father, 23–24; Coleman, John, brother, WWI veteran, 24–25, 34; Coleman, Susan, mother, 23–24, 34; Coleman, Walter, brother, Pullman Porter, 24; Curtiss JN-4 "jenny" biplane, 29–30, 32–33; death, Paxon Field, 32–33; Dornier seaplane, 26; early careers, 24–25; France, 25–26; funeral service, burial, Chicago, IL, 33–34; funeral service, Orlando, FL, 33; funeral services, Jacksonville, FL, 33; German Benz plane, 26; Germany training, 26, *27*; Glenn Curtiss Field, Long Island, NY, 26; International Air and Space Hall of Fame, 2014, 35; Jacksonville, Florida, 30–33; Lawton L. Pratt Funeral Home, 33; lectures, 30; National Aviation Hall of Fame, 2006, 35; National Women's Hall of Fame, 2001, 35; Negro Tri-State Fair, Memphis, TN, 27; Negro Welfare League show, Jacksonville, FL, 30, 32; Netherlands training, 26; Orlando, Florida, 23, 30–33; Palomar Park, Los Angeles, CA, 29; parachute jumping, 30–32; St. Petersburg, Florida, 30; Tampa, Florida, 30–31; Texas Aviation

Hall of Fame, 2000, 35; wing-walking, 30

Collins, Col. Eileen, 148–64; Air Force career, 150–55, 163; Air Force ROTC, 151–52; Air Force Test Pilot School (TPS), 153–55, 163; aviation firsts and major achievements, 149–52, 154–55, 157–58, *160*, 162, 164; birth, Elmira, NY, 150; *Buck Rogers* television series, 150; Cape Crusader, 156; Chandra X-ray Observatory telescope, 159; Collins, James, father, city surveyor, 150; Collins, Rose Marie (O'Hara), mother, 150; Corning Community College, 151, 164; educational credentials, 150–51, 153; Edwards Air Force Base, CA, 154–55, 163; Elmira, NY, "Soaring Capital of America," 150; First Lady Astronaut Trainees (FLATs), 149; Gargarin Cosmonaut Training Center, Star City, Russia, 157; Gemini astronauts, 150; International Air and Space Hall of Fame, 164; Johnson Space Center (JSC), Houston, TX, 154–55; Kennedy Space Center (KSC), Cape Canaveral, FL, 149, 156–59, 161–63; Lockheed C-141 Starlifter cargo-transport plane, 153; Mercury 13 program, 149, 159; NASA career, 154–64; National Aviation Hall of Fame, 164; National Women's Hall of Fame, 1995, 164; Operation Urgent Fury, Grenada, 153; retirement, 163–64; Smithsonian's National Air and Space Museum, 164; space shuttle *Columbia*, tragedy, 2003, 161–62; space shuttle program, 156–63; STS-63, Space Shuttle *Discovery*, 1995, 156–58; STS-84, Space Shuttle *Atlantis*, 1997, 158; STS-93, Space Shuttle *Columbia*, 1999, 158–59, *160*, 160–61; STS-114, Space Shuttle *Discovery*, 2005, 161–63, *163*; T-38 supersonic jet training, 152, 154–56, 158, 162; Texas Aviation Hall

INDEX

"Jorge," father, 127; Pfeiffer, Mabel Gaspard, mother, 127–8; Pfeiffer, Walter, brother, 127, 130; Rodriguez, Francisca, maternal grandmother, 128; September 11, terrorist attacks, 132; Smithsonian's National Air and Space Museum, 136; Stylinska, Tamara, paternal grandmother, Auschwitz survivor, 128; UN humanitarian missions, 129–30; Wardair, Canadian airline, teenaged job, 128; writing career, 133–37

Powell, William J., pilot: founding the Bessie Coleman Aero Club, 34

Proctor, Dr. Sian: and SpaceX commercial flights, 164

Quimby, Harriet, pilot, 3

Ride, Dr. Sally, first American woman in space, 49, 152, 158

Rogers, Capt, Harry Wright, WW I Navy pilot: death, 45; instructor to Nichols, Ruth Rowland, 38–39

Roosevelt, First Lady Eleanor: and Cochran, Jackie, 58; support for women in war effort, 59

Roosevelt, President Franklin: and Cochran, Jackie, 58

Skelton (Frankman Erde), Betty, 64–73, 79; All-Woman Air Show, 1947 and 1948, 68–69; aerobatics planes, 66–69; automotive firsts and major achievements, 70–73; aviation firsts and major achievements, 66–69, 73; barefoot flying, 65, 69; birth, Pensacola, FL, 65; The Blue Angels, 67; Campbell-Ewald, marketing agency, 70, 72; Civil Air Patrol (CAP), major, 66; commercial pilot's license and ratings, 66, 68; Erde, Dr. Alan, second spouse, 72; Feminine Aerobatics Championships, 68; "First

Lady of Firsts," nickname, 70, 71; first solo flight, age 12, 65; Florida air shows, 66–67, 69; Florida Sports Hall of Fame, 1977, 73; Florida Women's Hall of Fame, 1993, 73; Frankman, Donald, first spouse, 72; General Motors, Corvette marketing, 70, 72; Great Lakes 2T1A biplane, 66; International Aerobatic Club Hall of Fame, 1988, 73; mascot, chihuahua, Little Tinker, 67–68; Mercury 7, same space testing as males, 70–71; Miss Florida Aviation, 1947, 67; Motorsports Hall of Fame of America, 2008, 73; National Association for Stock Car Auto Racing (NASCAR), 70; National Aviation Hall of Fame, 2005, 73; Naval Air Station Pensacola, FL, 65; Navy Flight Exhibition Team, 67; Pitts Special S-1C, *Little Stinker*, 67–69, 73, *73*; Southeastern Air Exposition, Jacksonville, 67; "The Sweetheart of the Blue Angels," 67; Taylorcraft planes, 65, 72; Winter Haven, FL life, 72; Women's Airforce Service Pilots (WASPs), age limit rejection, 65–66

Smith Prescott, Dessie, 14–21; Air Commerce Act of 1926, 16–17; aviation firsts and major achievements, 16–17, 21; backcountry living, 15–16, 18–21; birth, Island Grove, Alachua County, 15; Booth, Candace, caregiver, 21; childhood, 15; Curtiss JN-4 "Jenny" biplane, 16, *17*; Davis Island, Tampa, flights, 17–18; Daytona Beach, flights, 17; death, Crystal River, FL, 21; early careers, 16; first female licensed fishing, hunting guide, 20; Florida land boom, 1926, 16; Florida Women's Hall of Fame, 1968, 20, *21*; flying lessons, 16; Kinnan Rawlings, Marjorie, friendship, 18–20; log cabin, Sparr, FL, 16; Marjorie

ABOUT THE AUTHOR

Bridges DelPonte is an award-winning author of fiction and nonfiction works. Bridges has published extensively on women breaking legal barriers in military service branches and at military academies, including articles in *New England Law Review*, *Hastings Women's Law Journal*, the *Roanoke Times*, and *Richmond Times-Dispatch*. Her legal nonfiction articles earned numerous writing awards, including two National Hoeber Memorial Awards. Her legal mystery, *Deadly Sacrifices: A Marguerite Montez Mystery*, featuring a Portuguese-American prosecutor on her first homicide case, won a Royal Palm Literary Award (silver/second place) from the Florida Writers Association (FWA). She has also published an underwater fantasy novel, *Bridles of Poseidon*, a children's book, *The Little Dusties: The Roar of the Silver Dragon* (with illustrator Michelle Bakay), numerous short stories in anthologies, and content for educational video games. She is a member of the Women's Fiction Writers Association (FWA), Sisters in Crime, Inc., and Citrus Crime Writers. After decades as a legal educator, Bridges writes and lives full-time in southwest Florida with her husband, Dave, where they enjoy harbor walks, kayaking, bocce, pickleball, and taking really terrible golf swings. To learn more about her writing, please visit her author website, https://bridgesdelponte.wordpress.com/, or friend her on Facebook, https://www.facebook.com/bridges.delponte/.